University Centre at
Blackburn
College

Telephone: 01254 292165

Please return this book on or before the last date shown

SHORT LOAN	
7 DAY LOAN ONLY	
NO RENEWAL	

The Work-based Learning Student Handbook

Second edition

Edited by

Ruth Helyer

 palgrave

First edition published 2010
Second edition published 2015 by
PALGRAVE

Palgrave in the UK is an imprint of Macmillan Publishers Limited,
registered in England, company number 785998, of 4 Crinan Street,
London N1 9XW

Palgrave Macmillan in the US is a division of St Martin's Press LLC,
175 Fifth Avenue, New York, NY 10010.

Palgrave is a global imprint of the above companies
and is represented throughout the world.

Palgrave® and Macmillan® are registered trademarks in the United States,
the United Kingdom, Europe and other countries

ISBN 978–1–137–41383–3

This book is printed on paper suitable for recycling and made from fully
managed and sustained forest sources. Logging, pulping and manufacturing
processes are expected to conform to the environmental regulations of the
country of origin.

A catalogue record for this book is available from the British Library.

Typeset by MPS Limited, Chennai, India.

Printed in China.

I want to dedicate this book to James Marlborough Allen who inspired me so much with his wisdom and gentle intellect

Contents

List of figures and tables

Figures

Tables

Preface to the second edition

In spite of countering recommendations from classic educational thinkers like John Dewey, we have taken a wrong turn in higher education when we view knowledge as something that is permanent. I make this claim because if knowledge is indeed permanent, it means that it is something that can be passed from one person to another; namely, from the person who knows (the teacher) to the person who doesn't (the student). But what if knowledge can be considered fluid; what if knowledge can be acquired fresh from the improvisations that we make while working in practice? In this case, our reflection, usually with others, can expand and even create new knowledge at the same time that we are engaged in improving the respective practice. In this case, knowledge would arise not from a transfer from one mind to another, but as a contested inquiry among learners as they contribute their own interpretations and suggestions for addressing the problem at hand.

Welcome to the world of work-based learning. Compared to the traditional provision of higher education, students learn by doing real work that is designed to support and integrate with classroom-based knowledge acquisition. Students make sense out of their workplace experiences and construct knowledge through a process of negotiation between these experiences and their own cognitive frameworks.

In this second edition of the already invaluable *Work-Based Learning Student Handbook*, Ruth Helyer and her team have brought the philosophy of work-based learning down to earth to explain its principles and practices not only for students but for anyone who wants to know how work-based learning really works. There are many interconnecting features in work-based learning, but among my nominations for the most critical would be: the deployment of action projects with reflection; reliance on social learning through the assistance of peer learning teams and coaches; learning contracts and assessment; accreditation of prior learning, and the deployment of virtual tools to facilitate learning across space and time. All of these features are covered extensively in this book, providing its users with a pathway to mobilise their own work-based study along with a learning-to-learn perspective that reinforces an underlying work-based learning principle that promotes the search for contemporaneous questions over stale knowledge.

In the space remaining, I want to add my own voice to the efforts of the contributors to this volume by suggesting some of the unique pedagogical advantages offered to students through work-based learning.

1. **It is integrative**. When I indicate that learning need not be separated by space and time, I am suggesting that learning may be always occurring. Theory, in this case, may be introduced as much during or after experience as before in order to question the assumptions of practice. Indeed, the connection between a tutor's intentions and the students' understanding is often achieved through contemporaneous action.

2. **It is spiral**. Theory makes sense only through practice, and practice makes sense only through reflection as enhanced by theory. So, any theory, no matter how developed, requires application in practice. In this way, knowledge undergoes construction and transformation.

3. **It is reflective**. Reflective practice, conducted in real time, can facilitate the rethinking necessary to discover how what we did contributes to an unexpected or expected outcome. Reflective practitioners are critical thinkers who in questioning the underlying assumptions of their actions and of those of others consider not just what has been explained but what *needs* to be explained.

4. **It is rich**. Conventional education often suffers the risk of leaving inexperienced students with the impression that field problems can be nestled into neat technical packages. Work-based learning, on the other hand, helps students think independently, function without sufficient data or extrapolate beyond given data, change their approach in mid-stream, and continually reflect and inquire.

5. **It is social**. Students benefit from active dialogue with one another within the workplace and within the classroom. As workers, students learn as much by collective action and skills as by rational private thought. As they become comfortable sharing their experiences, their private and public reflections intersect so as to contribute to the spiral of learning.

6. **It is reciprocal**. The practices within work-based learning are not wedded to a specific location. It does not matter whether we start in the classroom or in the workplace. As long as each informs the other, work-based learning can occur. The process is thus reciprocal, with the student learning from exposure to work and the worker learning from exposure to classroom theory.

Good luck to all who are undertaking a new adventure in work-based learning. Bring along this book to help light the fire.

Joe Raelin
Boston, USA
1 July 2014

Acknowledgements

Acknowledgements and thanks are due to the chapter authors who make this book interesting, accessible, relevant and innovative, but also to the many friends, students and colleagues who have contributed on many levels and often invisibly, to the ideas represented here.

I am also very grateful to Teesside University for providing an environment where creating such a book is supported and encouraged.

Thanks also to the Palgrave team, especially Bryony Ross, for making this an enjoyable and manageable experience, and Manavalan BhuvanaRaj at MPS for his meticulous professionalism.

The manuscript would never have been finished without the amazing support I get from my family – so massive thanks to them, Neil, Max, Megan, Frankie and David.

But the biggest debt is to Dionne Lee – whose intelligence, dedication, organisational skills and sense of humour have been invaluable – thank you!

In addition, the authors, editor and publishers wish to thank Pearson Education for permission to reproduce copyright material from:

Kolb, David, *Experiential Learning: Experience as a Source of Learning & Development*, 1st, ©1984. Printed and Electronically reproduced by permission of Pearson Education, Inc., Upper Saddle River, New Jersey.

Ruth Helyer
2015

Notes on contributors

Matt Bromley started in academia as a lecturer and has since held roles as a subject manager and senior workforce development fellow, responsible for the development of innovative higher education programmes for employers and their employees. Matt is currently working as Academic Manager for Professional Executive Education at the University of Derby Online with a focus on engaging and inspiring learners within the workplace through social and online pedagogies.

Jenny Fleming is Senior Lecturer at the Auckland University of Technology, New Zealand. She leads the cooperative education programme in the Bachelor of Sport and Recreation. She has a PhD from Deakin University, Australia and a Masters of Science from the University of Auckland. Her recent research interests, including her PhD, have focussed on work-integrated learning.

Sue Graham joined Northumbria University's work-based learning team in 2001 with interests in pedagogy, learning styles and curriculum development. She helped develop Northumbria's flexible work-based learning framework and has supported other universities to design work-based programmes. More recently Sue has been involved in related policy developments, such as Higher Apprenticeships in Universities.

Ruth Helyer is Head of Workforce Development (Research & Policy) at Teesside University and National Teaching Fellow of the Higher Education Academy. Actively developing the work-based learning agenda since the early 2000s, she has become a nationally acknowledged expert in this area, involved in the development of numerous working students and their companies. As Programme Leader for the innovative Negotiated Learning Scheme at Teesside University, she championed work-based learning, resulting in the University becoming one of the forerunners in the UK sector in business engagement activities. Ruth is also the editor *Facilitating Work-Based Learning: a Handbook for Tutors* (Palgrave, 2015) *and* editor in chief of the Emerald peer-reviewed journal *Higher Education Skills and Work-Based Learning* (HESWBL – the official journal of UVAC).

Elaine Hooker is Head of Employer Partnerships at Teesside University where she works with both internal and external clients, to manage, coordinate and develop work-based learning initiatives. Elaine is also responsible for quality assuring the process and practice of collaborative partnerships between business and the University.

Kevin Ions is Programme Leader for Work-Based Studies at Teesside University. He has considerable experience of involvement in higher education workforce development initiatives including the development of bespoke programmes for industry. His research interests include organisational learning, reflective practice and motivation of work-based learners.

Judie Kay is Associate Director, Careers and Employability, RMIT University, Melbourne, Australia, responsible for implementation of university-wide employability services and projects; these include the implementation of mentoring and graduate employment programs across six key regions in Asia. Judie is also President of the Australian Collaborative Education Network (ACEN) and a Board member of WACE, representing Australia.

Ann Minton is Senior Work Force Development Fellow for the University of Derby Corporate, working with organisations and individuals, to identify personal and professional education requirements and develop solutions. Ann holds external examiner and consultant positions at a number of UK Higher Education Institutions and was the academic lead for a JISC funded project that developed an innovative online tool for the assessment of prior learning, together with publishing many book chapters and journal articles.

Conor Moss has worked in higher education for many years and is currently Business Engagement Fellow and Principal Lecturer at Sheffield Hallam University, responsible for the development and implementation of innovative, flexible and employer focused learning solutions to a range of public and private sector organisations to aid them in the development and engagement of their staff.

Jenny Naish is National Teaching Fellow and expert in Work-Based Learning (WBL) having contributed to the growth and acceptance of WBL at home and internationally through her roles at Middlesex and Teesside Universities. Most recently she held the post of Dean of the Business School at York St John University, UK.

Paula Nottingham is Programme Leader for BA (Hons) Professional Practice in Arts and works with the Masters and Doctorate in Professional Studies programmes at the Institute for Work Based Learning at Middlesex University. Her background is in the creative arts and lifelong learning with a focus on higher education.

David Perrin is Head of the Centre for Work Related Studies (CWRS) at the University of Chester. This is one of the largest providers of negotiated work-based learning in Europe with around 1,000 undergraduate and postgraduate students. His academic background is in political and economic theory and today he specialises in the recognition of prior learning (RPL) in higher education.

Garth Rhodes has worked in the field of Vocational Education and Training for over 35 years. In his earlier career he developed and co-ordinated the youth and adult education training programmes for Northumberland County Council. In 1993, he moved to Northumbria University where he was in the forefront of developments in work-based learning. He retired from his position as Head of Flexible Learning at Northumbria in 2013 but continues to maintain an active interest in work-based learning.

Susan Smith is Assistant Dean for Business Engagement in the School of Social Science, Business and Law at Teesside University. She has an extensive track record of university business engagement and is passionate about how people learn to lead and manage, having designed and taught on many leadership development and entrepreneurship programmes. Her current research focuses on social theories of learning in relation to leadership development.

Laurie Smith is Visiting Teaching Fellow at Lancaster University Management School and independent trainer and facilitator. He works with small and large businesses on organisational and leadership development. In addition, Laurie trains people on action learning and coaching techniques in order to empower peer-to-peer and lifelong learning.

Norma Sutcliffe is Senior Lecturer in Work-Based Studies at Teesside University. Her research interests include investigating links between preferred learning styles, reflective practice and the ability to articulate prior experiential learning with an aim to provide flexible and innovative approaches to the Accreditation of Prior Learning (APL).

Ly Tran is Senior Lecturer in curriculum and pedagogy at Deakin University, Australia. Her research focuses on teaching and learning in international education. Her book *Teaching International Students in Vocational Education: New Pedagogical Approaches* won the 2014 International Education Association of Australia Excellence Award for Best Practice/Innovation in International Education.

Tony Wall is a specialist in personal and organisational transformation and is Senior Lecturer at the University of Chester's Centre for Work Related Studies, UK. He facilitates learning with professionals around the globe and was nominated for four outstanding teaching awards in 2014.

Tracey White is Principal Lecturer and Work Based Distance Learning Programmes Manager at the University of Lincoln. She works with external partners and internal stakeholders to manage, co-ordinate and develop work-based learning initiatives. Her specific area of expertise is employer responsive provision where she has forged successful partnerships between higher education and employer organisations, designing tailored work-based learning programmes.

Barbara Workman has a background of nursing and teaching with expertise in accreditation and facilitation of work-based learning across all higher education levels and a range of subject disciplines and organisations; after 20 years as an academic she is now working as an HE consultant. As National Teaching Fellow and Principal Fellow of the HEA, she is committed to sharing and facilitating good practice in work-based learning in higher education.

Introduction

Ruth Helyer

What is this book about?

Undertaking Higher Education (HE) is a challenge for everyone, but it becomes more complex if you spend the majority of your time at work, with little time for study and limited experience of formal education. Work-based learning (WBL) appears in HE in various formats – you might be studying for an honours degree via a Work-Based Studies programme, or undertaking a much shorter award; your course might be delivered on a campus, at your place of work, online, or by some combination of these; it may or may not include gaining credit for learning you have already undertaken. Whatever the details, this handbook covers the key areas you need to know about and offers you invaluable advice to ensure that you maximise your WBL experience; so dip in and out of it, finding what you need when you need it. You don't have to read everything at once, or in a definitive order.

Because the book's chapters have been put together by WBL experts from a variety of universities and organisations they are filled with diverse examples of leading practice, presented as case studies and scenarios in which real people benefit from engaging with HE-level work-based learning. The students cited show how to thrive in a learning environment, while employed and juggling personal commitments – despite mostly not having attended university at 18 or undertaken 'A' levels. There are also numerous activities and exercises for you to try, tick-lists for you to use and 'hints and tips' designed to make the learning process easier for you.

What is Work-based Learning (WBL)?

The information provided about WBL is designed to help you place your own experience in context; it will also help you to describe your learning journey to your line manager, colleagues, family and friends. Boud and Solomon (2001) summarise the major characteristics of HE work-based learning as follows. Not all of these will apply to your circumstances, but they give a flavour of the potential of work-based learning as a powerful development tool:

1. A partnership between an external organisation and an educational institution is established (contractual agreements).
2. The learners involved are employees (negotiate learning plans).
3. The learning programme followed derives from the needs of the workplace and the learner, and not from a pre-defined academic curriculum.
4. The learning programme will be individually adapted to each learner according to their previous educational experience, work experience and training.
5. Learning is taking place as an integrated part of projects/tasks in the workplace.
6. The learning outcomes are assessed by the educational institution (Boud and Solomon, 2001).

Work-based learning is what is 'learned' by working – not reading about work, or observing work, but actually undertaking work activities. Interactions with others are often crucial to your learning (see Chapter 9 for a discussion of social learning). Reading and research will still be involved, especially if you're aiming for a formal qualification; this is learning from *real* work and *real* life and accepting how inextricably linked those activities are. As the sophistication and level of your job increases, so does the likelihood that you will also be undertaking research and studying theory.

Your 'work' may not be full-time paid employment. Perhaps you are learning in a work placement, or as a volunteer. WBL involves many diverse students who are actively *doing* the things they're learning about (and actively learning from this doing). You learn in your workplace and/or the classroom, further supported by electronic and mobile technologies. Increasingly communication between you, your tutors and your peers will be carried out online, and your university or college will offer you introductory support and skills sessions to make sure you get the most out of these new and developing technologies (see Chapter 1 for HE skills and Chapter 8 for social media learning tools).

WBL commonly uses the Recognition of Prior Learning (RPL) to recognise, acknowledge and accredit learning from previous experience and qualifications. This reduces the amount of time taken to obtain an award (and potentially also the cost if this means that you undertake fewer modules) (see Chapter 5). As a WBL student gaining credit towards your award through

RPL is especially empowering if you initially felt out of place and in a hurry at university; there need be no such thing as 'missing your chance'. You may also find that you are able to include, in your programme, Continuing Professional Development (CPD) activities that you undertake anyway (see Chapter 6).

As well as the unusual aspects of being a WBL student you will also benefit from the traditional outcomes of HE – the development of intellectual, personal, critical and analytical skills, which will support and complement your practical skills and knowledge. You are likely to have much more life experience than an 18-year-old student; furthermore you will probably find that your student peers in your class or study group differ widely in age, background and aspirations (this can even be the case when you are all from the same company). However, as motivated, employed people prepared to work hard in order to successfully fit studying into already busy lives you will also have much in common. Because HE-level WBL programmes take account of your existing knowledge and expertise they are the best, and certainly most time-effective, HE study route for you. Some of WBL's best features are that it:

- Acknowledges skills and knowledge gained at work.
- Maximises your time (a) – via RPL (Recognition of Prior Learning) and APL (Accreditation of Prior Learning) (Chapter 5).
- Maximises your time (b) – by integrating existing and ongoing workplace CPD and projects (Chapters 6 and 12).
- Combines education and development – for the 'real' world (Chapter 2).
- Offers networking opportunities – your peers will all be employed too (Chapters 8 and 9).
- Links you into routes to various HE awards (Chapter 4).

And the key characteristics of WBL programmes?

- Use your work role to provide/inform the curriculum (Chapter 6).
- Focus on your individual learning plan/contract/agreement (Chapter 6).
- Facilitate cross-disciplinary working, spanning subjects and sectors (Chapters 4 and 12).
- Actively recognise and accredit prior learning, both experiential (learning gained first hand through doing) and certificated (from previous relevant qualifications) (Chapter 5).
- Acknowledge that learning is taking place in diverse locations (Chapters 3, 8 and 10).
- Offer flexibility re: time, place and style of study, for example, there may be off-campus, out of hours and electronic options (Chapter 8).
- Allow longer (and looser) timeframes in which to complete awards (Chapters 4, 5 and 6).
- Encourage negotiation of title, and content, of award (Chapters 4 and 6).
- Keep compulsory modules and campus attendance to a minimum, while still offering plenty of support (Chapter 7).

- Offer generic skills modules – invaluable whatever your job role or career stage (Chapters 1 and 2).
- Operate beyond the academic calendar – for example, many recruit and run modules more than once a year.
- Support reflective practice and self-analysis (Chapters 2 and 6).
- Offer innovative methods of learning, teaching and assessment (Chapter 11).
- Utilise technology, e-learning, distance learning, peer-learning and social learning (Chapters 8 and 9).

Graduates of work-based studies programmes frequently state that they could never have undertaken HE-level study without such a route:

> 'I could never have obtained my degree without a scheme like this. I left school with no qualifications and never felt like I could belong at university. The work-based studies programme proved me wrong! It is so flexible, it meant I could attend sessions and tutorials after work. I also completed a lot of the assignments at home, at work and in the library, and based all of my major submissions on work tasks that I would have had to complete as part of my job, even if I wasn't studying.' (Student A)

They also offer an ideal progression route, if you already hold a smaller award (see Chapters 4, 5 and 6); or some kind of professional qualification that you can, potentially, accelerate to full honours degree status. The multiple step-on and step-off points characteristic of WBL programmes make this possible. Schemes often use a skeleton structure (see Chapter 4 for more information on this as well as the example below), which can be 'fleshed out' in ways flexible enough to meet your individual requirements.

Example   A typical programme framework: undergraduate

Level	Core modules	Optional modules	Credit awarded via APL	Credit	Total credit
Level 4	*Study Skills* *Programme Planning*			*10* *20*	*10* *20*
Level 4		*Subject-specific module*		*30* *20*	*30* *20*
		RPL module	*RPL credit awarded for prior experiential learning*	*40*	*40*

Level	Core modules	Optional modules	Credit awarded via APL	Credit	Total credit
Require 120 at each level					*120/120*
Level 5	*Research Methods/ Practitioner Inquiry*			*20*	*20*
Level 5			*Credit awarded for prior experiential learning*	*40*	*40*
Require 120 at each level					*60/120*
Level 6 (honours)	*CPD module Project/ Dissertation*			*20* *40*	*20* *40*
Level 6					
Require 120 at each level					*60/120*
Graduation					*240/360*

The remaining credits needed will come from a combination of RPL/ APL claims; taught modules; skills modules; WB projects; and open and independent learning.

(See Chapter 4 for further information on frameworks, including masters and doctoral levels.)

Example   Student B

Student B is an employed process engineer with a Higher National Diploma (HND) in Mechanical and Electrical Engineering. She obtained this within five years of enrolling (there are usually regulations around the age of qualifications). She joined the Work-based Studies programme at her local university when she found out that her HND could count towards a BSc in Engineering Studies. The table below shows how she completed her programme of study. She obtained 120 credits at Level 4 and a further 50 credits at Level 5 by matching the precise learning gained from her HND against the learning outcomes of her new course. She then gained further credits at Level 5 for undertaking a core module about the process of recognising, and claiming for, prior learning (this module carries 20 credits, but through its assessment process – a portfolio of evidence – she was able to claim a further 50 credits at Level 5 for her experiential learning). This completed the equivalent of the first and second year of traditional undergraduate full-time study. At Level 6 she studied a taught module about continuing professional development (20 credits, evening attendance), undertook 'Research Methods' (20 credits, evening attendance), an engineering module (20 credits, day release) and two work-based projects, one carrying 20 credits and one 40. The large project, equivalent to a dissertation, involved developing a completely new process for her employer. This student was awarded a 2:1 classification for her BSc in just two years.

Example   BSc in Engineering Studies: Student B (see above)

Level	Core modules	Optional modules	Credit awarded via APL	Credit	Total credit
Level 4			*HND Mechanical & Electrical Engineering*	*120*	120
Require 120 at each level					120/120
Level 5		*RPL module*	*HND APL claim*	*50* *20* *50*	
Require 120 at each level					120/120
Level 6 Honours	*Research Methods* *CPD module* *Work-based projects*	*Engineering module*		*20* *20* *20* *1 × 20 & 1 × 40*	
Require 120 at each level					120/120
Graduation					360/360

Who studies this way?

Insufficient time to study full-time?

'[WBL] is an ideal solution if you can't commit to full-time study but have the right experience. I'd tell anyone to go for it.' (IT Trainer to Primary School Teacher)

Thinking of your next career move?

'[T]he opportunity to obtain credits for prior learning and professional work-based experience means that my Business Management degree not only reflected my experience and career path as a professional police officer but will benefit me in being considered for other managerial roles outside policing.' (Police Inspector)

Want to accelerate your career in a limited time frame?

'I was a teaching assistant, but always wanted to teach; the Work-based Studies programme acknowledges my teaching experience and existing qualifications. I've been able to fast track myself; what should technically have been eight years of study has been reduced to three years. I've also personalised my programme to suit my areas of interest, Special Educational Needs.' (Teaching Assistant to Teacher)

Would benefit from presenting existing workplace projects in an academic format? (Chapter 12)

'I wanted to do an Engineering degree, but also choose my own relevant modules. The [WBL route] allowed me to do this and also claim credit for areas of major experience and learning, as well as transfer my previous qualifications into university credits, in effect, reducing my study time and fees. Choosing specific modules to suit my employment needs has been ideal. I'm a process engineer, responsible for the productivity and optimisation of manufacturing equipment. On this degree pathway I can learn more about managing engineering projects and process improvements, as well as taking standard technical modules.' (Engineer)

The comments from these students show how varied the backgrounds and expertise of work-based learners are; the networking opportunities and shared practices you will gain from being part of a HE WBL community will really enrich your learning experience (Chapter 9).

You are probably older than the traditional HE student, but this is *not* the hindrance new WBL students often presume it will be. You have a head start on the wisdom and skills front, and the experience of practical applications. This is your chance to build on all of this by connecting your new educational goals to your professional and personal experience. You might feel that you need to make an extra effort to catch up on the theory and abstraction side of things, but this is worth the effort; there is always more to learn, and it really enhances your workplace practice. WBL students tend to have a goal-orientated and structured approach, an attitude that ensures the achievement of great things through engagement with HE, not least because of your professional approach to being assessed (Chapter 11).

What's so good about Higher Education anyway?

HE-level learning carries credit; this makes it possible to offer you awards and qualifications. There is a system in place to track and quantify what you have learned and to compare this learning to other learning of a similar level of difficulty and complexity. Credit is used in the HE sector as a portable, international 'currency'. Because HE-level learning carries credit, your study pathway is flexible, adaptable, valued, tailor-made and tied into a recognised quality system. The HE credit system recognises successful completion of modules, courses and programmes.

Why are you engaging with Work-based learning?

WBL is:

- *Bespoke* – designed around your needs.
- *Relevant* – connects to your real workplace activities.
- *Student focused* – the emphasis is on what you want/need to learn.
- *Credit-bearing* – has a discernible worth attached, recognisable globally.
- *Added value* – encompasses your work and life needs and interests – the qualification can feel like a bonus.
- *Realistic* – in terms of flexible timescales and feasible expectations.
- *Supported* – your employer will see the benefit and may support with mentorship, time off, assistance with fees (ask your line manager).
- *High status* – HE award could bring promotion, pay rise, new job.
- *Ongoing* – ties into progression and your continuous development.
- *Enjoyable* – it really can be! You have such an influence on the content.
- *Cutting edge* – you learn, develop and use innovative, new practice.
- *Different* – this is not 'run of the mill' – it is largely what you make it.

Key subjects and activities across chapters of this book

Headline chapter content	
Academic credit	Chapters 4 & 5
Academic qualifications	Chapters 4 & 5
Accreditation	Chapters 4 & 5

Headline chapter content	
Action learning	Chapters 3 & 9
Accreditation of Prior Learning (APL) claims	Chapter 5
Assessment	Chapter 11
Autonomous Learning	Chapters 2 & 6
Building blocks	Chapter 4
Certificated learning	Chapters 4 & 5
Collaboration	Chapter 9
Communities of Practice (CoP)	Chapters 8 & 9
Continuing Professional Development (CPD)	Chapter 6
Cross-cultural WBL	Chapter 10
CV and job description	Chapters 5 & 6
Developing whole person	Chapter 2
Digital identity	Chapter 8
Employability skills	Chapter 2
English as a second language	Chapter 10
Enterprise	Chapter 2
Experiential Learning Theory (ELT)	Chapter 9
Feedback	Chapters 7, 11 & 12
Flipped Learning	Chapter 2
Foundation degrees	Chapter 4
Frameworks	Chapter 4
Generic/transferable skills	Chapter 2
Group learning	Chapter 9
Growth Mindset	Chapter 3
HE context	Intro and Chapter 1

Headline chapter content	
HE skills	Chapter 1
Higher Level Apprenticeships	Chapter 4
Identity	Chapter 9
Industry relevance	Chapters 3 & 12
International WBL	Chapter 10
Internet	Chapter 8
Interns	Chapter 2
Learning contract/agreement	Chapter 6
Learning opportunities	Chapter 4
Learning Outcomes	Chapter 11
Learning styles	Chapters 2 & 6
Learning to Learn	Chapter 2
Levels and Level descriptors	Chapter 1, 4, 5 &11
Lifelong learning	Chapter 2
Mentors	Chapter 7
Mobile technology	Chapter 8
Modules	Chapter 4
MOOCs	Chapter 8
Multicultural WBL	Chapter 10
Negotiation	Chapter 6
Networking	Chapter 9
Online learning	Chapter 8
Organisational development	Chapter 3
Personal Development Planning (PDP)	Chapter 6

Headline chapter content	
Peer Supported Learning	Chapter 9
Personal Learning Network (PLN)	Chapter 8
Practitioner Inquiry	Chapters 11 & 12
Professionalism	Chapter 3
Professional qualifications	Chapter 4
Programme Planning	Chapter 6
Progression	Chapter 4
Projects (WB)	Chapter 12
Recognition of Prior Learning (RPL)	Chapter 5
Reflection/Reflective skills	Chapters 2
Reflecting forwards	Chapter 9
Research methods	Chapters 11 & 12
Salient learning	Chapter 9
Self-development	Chapters 2 & 3
Skills for learning	Chapters 2 & 8
Social context	Chapter 9
Social learning	Chapters 8 & 9
Social media	Chapter 8
Sparkling Moments	Chapter 9
Support networks	Chapters 7, 8 & 9
SWOT analysis	Chapters 3 & 6
Teaching approaches	Chapter 4
Technological learning tools	Chapter 8
Terminologies	See separate section

Headline chapter content	
Transcultural WBL	Chapter 10
Tutors	Chapter 7
University options	Chapter 4
Virtual communities of practice (VCoP)	Chapter 8
Work placements and live briefs	Chapters 11 & 12
World Wide Web (WWW)	Chapter 8

Reference

Boud, D. and Solomon, N. (eds) (2001) *Work-based Learning: A New Higher Education* (Buckingham: Society for Research in Higher Education/Open University Press).

Adapting to higher education: Academic skills

Ruth Helyer

In this chapter you will learn:

▶ how far you have already come in your learning journey;
▶ what higher education (HE) is, how it works and how it changes over time;
▶ about different styles of academic writing;
▶ what the different levels of study are;
▶ how to manage your time better.

Where am I now?

University programmes that include work-based learning (WBL) usually commence by asking 'where are you now?' and combining exercises, discussions and self-audit procedures to help form a clearer picture of what you have already learned at HE level, be it from different kinds of study in your past or from your experiential learning (learning, by doing). Studying for a higher education (HE)-level work-based learning (WBL) qualification will enhance your professional profile and advance your career, as well as bringing personal enjoyment and satisfaction.

Personal development plans (PDPs) are designed to help with this by focusing precisely on *your* learning (Chapter 6). Exercise 1.1 helps to analyse your thoughts before you write your plan; populate the lists with what is important to you personally.

Exercise 1.1   Achievements and ambitions

1. What have I achieved already? (be specific)	3. What do I want from my job?
Personally	
Work-related	
2. What skills and qualities enabled these achievements?	4. What would facilitate (F) and prevent (P) me getting what I want? (for example, required qualifications [F] or lack of relevant experience [P])

Work-based programmes usually allow what you have learned already to 'count' towards your new award, therefore it is important to give time and effort to this introspective part of your study. By recognising, and claiming credit for, prior learning, from study and/or experience (Chapter 5), you find the starting point for your new programme of learning. WBL students comment on the empowerment this gives them; gathering strategic evidence of what you have learned already focuses on your key strengths, often taken for granted. Measuring what you know against your Higher Education Institution's (HEI's) level descriptors (see later in this chapter, and Chapters 4 and 11) proves that you are learning in the workplace, often with work colleagues, and operating there at a level comparable with HE. This will improve your confidence and instil feelings of belonging as you embark upon your HE adventure. WBL students come from a wide variety of occupations, but certain character traits frequently recur and may come to the fore as you begin your personal development plan (PDP) and begin to ask questions of yourself:

- *New to HE?* Have not been in any educational setting for some years? You will require generic and academic skills alongside subject-specific skills.
- You bring *professional knowledge* – perhaps working at levels far higher than your formal qualifications suggest. Your incidental and opportunistic learning applied in an academic setting creates an empowering synergy (Chapter 12).
- WBL programmes attract, and welcome, learners from *all sectors* and backgrounds.

- You are probably *older than traditional students* at the same level; it is almost a prerequisite, and certainly a benefit, that you are old enough to have gained learning through experience (Chapter 5).
- You have certain *motivations* for entering HE: to expand qualifications; improve career prospects; justify job position; fulfil long-held personal wishes; respond to a turning point in life – all normal.
- You are a *part-time student* but you are also *employed.* This may be part or full-time work, paid or unpaid (voluntary or family business), self-employment and/or business owner, seasonal or contract work – again, all normal.
- You can only attend the campus *outside 'office hours'* (perhaps you have 'day release' to attend certain modules). The flexibility of WBL awards, and the RPL/APL process (as described in Chapter 5), facilitate the completion of awards in a comparatively short period of time.
- You will be *paying your own fees*, self-supported and financially independent. If your employer pays your fees they may expect some input into your choices. Recent increases in course fees may make this more of an issue.
- You will have a *complex* life, and commitments (family, work, community). Coping with this complexity proves you are capable, motivated and prepared to juggle the demands of time, finances, energy, intellect and emotions.
- The *study route* is non-regular; it is individualised and also offers varying methods of attendance and assessment. You will need to be a flexible, adaptable individual to survive.
- As well as intellectual challenges there are *logistical* ones; the impact of evening attendance on tutor and facility availability – cafes, car parks and so on.
- You will rely on *virtual learning environments* for some sessions and for pastoral support (you will need access to a computer for this and a certain level of ability) (Chapter 8).
- You will be relying on family, friends and work colleagues for *support* and understanding. Line managers might need to give permission to access work-related information needed for assignments (Chapter 7).
- You will need to negotiate and manipulate the *HE credit system* to understand how many credits at each level you require to obtain your award (see Chapter 4 for a table of these).

These traits are widespread and recurring; you are part of a wide community of learners who have a lot in common. Many students now choose to also work; your peers will, like you, be asking themselves: 'Where am I now?' as well as relating to at least one of the categories below:

- *At a crossroads* – there are several options open to you. You feel that work-related study will focus your mind as well as giving you extra HE qualifications.

- *At a dead end* – you have gone as far as your current job role will allow and you need a new, higher-level qualification to move on.
- *On a plateau* – you are unable to progress any further in your career/sector without a degree.
- *Confused* – the discipline of study will help you to clarify your profile/ thoughts/aims into a format for progression and development.
- *Bored* – it is time to do something new with your working life.
- *Frustrated* – passed over for promotion by younger, less-experienced colleagues, because they have HE-level qualifications.
- *Time on your hands* – responsibilities towards dependants have altered.
- *Slightly envious* – partner/friends have achieved academic success.
- *Inspired* – your own offspring are doing well at university or college.
- *Underpaid* – there is pressure on you at work to take on extra responsibility, yet rewards for this are tied to level of qualification.

There are numerous reasons for taking stock of your own learning and development, and embracing WBL will certainly help you with this, but like all worthwhile activities, the results will be directly related to what you put in. WBL programmes usually commence with exercises and activities designed to get you thinking, part of which will probably be creating a new CV and job description. These won't be like the ones you use for job applications but will instead be specifically designed to get to the heart of how much you have learned from actively 'doing' (Chapters 5 and 6). This self-audit encompasses looking back to gather evidence of your skills, expertise and learning. This evidence proves where you are 'now', and acts as a catalyst for where you go next. Self-audit activities are sometimes part of a module, with a name like 'Make Your Learning Count' or 'Recognition of Prior Learning' in Chapter 5. These modules guide you, step-by-step on a journey unpicking, evidencing and claiming for what you have previously learned.

If you have decided that you would like to obtain an HE-level award in relation to your occupation and that a WBL route is the best way for you to do this, then the next question you need to ask yourself is how much involvement will your employer have? Do you need to ask if it is OK for you to enrol on a course? As WBL courses are often held outside office hours you might not need your employer's permission, but your university assignments (Chapter 11) will almost certainly need information and real-life activity from your workplace, and this will be enhanced by your employer's involvement; indeed, you may not be allowed to quote details about the company without this involvement.

Your employer may also offer to pay your fees and perhaps allow you some-time away from the workplace within office hours. The more positive the impact of your studies on the organisation (Chapter 3) the better it is, as this will make your employer feel more inclined to offer you support (Chapter 7). You might want to keep your university attendance from your employer because you are planning to change your career or job? This closes down options for certain means of study and development, but is sometimes unavoidable. Alternatively, your employer might be the driving force behind your university attendance. If this is the case, are you part of a group of students all from the same company? This changes the focus of your studying by placing a stronger emphasis upon your employer's expectations. Or you may be part of a mixed group or class, made up from students from across the same sector but from diverse companies? Or even, differing sectors, if your chosen course of study is suitable for many sectors (for example, Leadership and Management).

To get the most out of your learning experience you need to think about how you personally learn best (Chapters 2 and 6). Be honest about how much of an independent learner you can be; if you need the constant input of a tutor or teacher then WBL is probably not going to work for you, because you need to be capable of self-direction (even if this doesn't come naturally to you). You will not be left totally alone and told to 'get on with it', especially not at first, but you will be expected to be a motivated, self-starter who is capable of using their initiative, and probably somebody who is intellectually curious. This means taking responsibility for your own learning and your own time management (see below), as nobody is going to hand you the answers or write the syllabus on the board. Your study will be about *your* work and how *you* learn, and therefore is far too personalised for a didactic style of teaching to be useful.

WBL programmes are usually negotiated programmes framed by a personal learning contract (Chapter 6); this increases individuality and appropriateness but reduces commonality. It can also reduce interaction with your peers; you might find yourself, on the odd occasions when classroom attendance is necessary, among other students with whom you feel you have little in common. However, although these other students come from different work disciplines they are embarking on a similar journey to yourself – one that involves time and effort on top of holding down employment – and this similarity is enough to spark friendships over coffee. Traditional undergraduates on the campus for three years full-time doing the same course cannot escape each other – for you and your peers interaction may require a bit more conscious effort! Your individually planned programme will differ in content and pace from that of other students but the ethos of your learning journey is the same, and hopefully you might spend enough time with them, in generic core modules, for example, to form supportive relationships and networks.

TIP Challenges for (WBL) students

- Academic expectations, policies and procedures.
- Academic skills (writing, presentation, note-taking, literature reviews and so on).
- How does the HE credit system operate?
- Learning agreements or contracts – planning your own study route.
- Being part of a group of diverse students.
- Unfamiliar HE setting.

You could well need extra support and feedback, and your tutors will provide this (Chapter 7). *But* your increased professional profile, when compared to the average 18-year-old student, means that you are far more likely to have the confidence and experience to ask for help and guidance – please do.

What is HE?

In the UK HE follows secondary education and college (sixth form and further education colleges, FECs). HE is offered through universities and some FECs and specialist institutions (Higher Education Institutions, HEIs). Originally HE was aimed at 18-year-olds, but its culture of developing the whole person – something very attractive to employed students – means that it attracts students of all ages and backgrounds wishing to undertake HE-level qualifications (HA, FdA, BA, BA Hons, MA, PhD and so on). Because HE awards are widely recognisable, well-reputed and of high profile they are rigorously quality assured by the Quality Assurance Agency (QAA), www.qaa. ac.uk/en

WBL HE-level qualifications undergo exactly the same processes and are of an equally high standard to the more traditional qualifications and use the same terminology; if you study for a BA it will still be called that. HE quality processes are externally monitored and strictly adhered to in order to keep the qualifications that UK HEIs award at a recognised level. WBL programmes have differing kinds of demands but utilise the same levels of academic rigour as comparable taught courses. It is a different, but not easier or lesser, way of obtaining a qualification; indeed, it could be argued that it is often a more demanding route due to the high levels of self-motivation required.

Exercise 1.2   Different courses

List what you perceive to be the *similarities* and *differences* between traditional HE and an HE-level WBL programme; even if you haven't attended an HEI yet, you will have ideas about what happens there.

Traditional university course	University-level WBL programme
Similarities	**Similarities**
challenging high level demands critical thinking leads to university qualification	challenging high level demands critical thinking leads to university qualification
Traditional HE course	**HE-level WBL programme**
Differences	**Differences**
Focus on one or two subject areas Taught in lectures on campus Have to leave work Mostly 18	Focus on my work and work activities – Applied learning Tutorial and other support at a distance Can opt for part-time All ages

You will enjoy the flexibility of undertaking some of your university-level learning off campus; this helps you to fit your learning around the demands of your work or family and to study at your own pace, at times and in locations that suit you. Your programme will be designed around the interests and concerns of your workplace and professional practice, to combine academic and theoretical knowledge with work-based skills.

Historically universities have been viewed as seats of knowledge where specialist lecturers transmit information to pupils through timetabled tutorials and lectures, using set texts from a pre-decided syllabus. This content-heavy position has shifted considerably in recent years, and you will find that interaction between you and your tutors is far more negotiated and personalised. Rather than a set curriculum, designed around material that must be covered (with the suggestions of 'correct' answers and 'cramming' that go with that), you should view it as a personal vehicle that you can use to get you to where you want to be. This new kind of learning/teaching relationship enhances learning opportunities, while retaining the established strengths of HE.

TIP How to tell it's HE

- Awards credit that values and measures all learning (at level).
- Develops intellectual and personal skills, together with specific knowledge in key areas.
- Improves the many facets of every individual student with holistic programmes, courses and modules.
- Acknowledges and validates skills, knowledge, experience and work-practice.
- Facilitates learning that transforms and improves lives.
- It is innovative – which inevitably includes rethinking, changing and some disruption!
- It offers all of this to everyone who stands to benefit from it.

The changing culture of HE

HE has changed considerably in recent years, and will continuing to evolve. The largest component of this changing landscape is the growing number of non-traditional students, like you. This shifting HE population can be attributed to many factors, but they include: equalisation of opportunity; an ageing population and workforce; increased demand for up-skilling and re-skilling in response to skills gaps and shortages; changes in the economic and employment markets; globalisation; rapidly developing technologies, and so on. HEIs have had to be innovative about how they acknowledge non-traditional educational experience, and this innovation has led to a marked increase in the use of articulation of achievement, and accreditation of company in-house training, both practices with the potential to offer you advanced standing. Working with you, and perhaps your employer, makes HE more responsive and more likely to develop and deliver relevant learning opportunities – programmes of a bespoke, negotiated, adaptable and often multi-disciplinary nature.

HE qualifications hold a parity of esteem across the learning sector and beyond. Some career pathways demand graduate status, but having a degree is not the same as having a professional licence to practice; you will still need to undertake the requisite training for these careers in order to also obtain the professional qualifications, usually strictly overseen by the appropriate professional body. Your HE-level WBL study adds a further dimension to your very job-specific qualification, and it includes the rounded qualities that the majority of employers state they are looking for, namely, a mix of cognitive and non-cognitive skills and achievements that help you to become a fully developed person – useful at work, at home and in your community (see Chapter 2 for a fuller discussion around employability). This is why many employers are now looking for 'graduate status', rather than the specific subject of the degree.

As with the majority of degrees, on your work-based programmes you will undertake a large project or dissertation (40 or 60 credits at Level 6, equivalent of the third year) to achieve honours. Your project will investigate a work-based issue and, like all learning, will result in changes (Chapter 12). The impact this has on your workplace will depend on your work role, and the size and scope of your employer; however, there is the potential for you to make a real difference to the workplace practices of you and your colleagues. Many WBL students increase the profitability of their workplace by applying the results of their work-based projects, which has ensured that WBL has become positively associated with not just personal change but also organisational change (Chapter 3).

If it is in keeping with your profile and areas of expertise, while allowing you to still cover any compulsory modules, most work-based programmes permit, and indeed encourage, you to largely populate your programme with work-based projects (Chapter 12). You and your employer stand to gain from combining a piece of work activity (which needs to be carried out anyway) with an academic assessment (Chapter 11). For you, a busy employed student, this reduces campus attendance; for your employer it offers unrivalled research resources and a high-quality written report.

While much of your learning takes place at work, you will need to fit reading and writing about WBL into your own time, and develop the requisite timetabling skills for this. Also, you will find that all university courses now widely utilise web technologies, both for learning strategies but also for communication, so it is important that you hone your skills in this area to get the very best out of the internet and your HEI's virtual learning environment (VLE), but also the plethora of other social media and mobile technologies so widely available to you now. The potential offered by technology is crucial to you as a WBL student, who is, typically, always employed and often spending time working around the world. Online technologies and social media innovations mean that if you have access to a laptop/tablet and the internet you can progress your studies wherever you are. Some WBL programmes are totally online, and to get the best from these you must develop your web technology skills to your fullest capacity (Chapter 8).

So WBL pushes boundaries on many levels: by acknowledging previous learning and encouraging you to evidence and build upon your knowledge and expertise; by utilising different ways of learning, such as extensive use of mobile technologies; and by encouraging change and growth in the HE sector itself as WBL can enhance and progress what the academy knows already, as well as bringing different kinds of students.

Exercise 1.3   The good and the bad

List the advantages and disadvantages of undertaking a WBL programme in HE. For example: time needed to study; balancing other commitments; cost implications; travel; self-confidence and so on.

Advantages	Disadvantages
The only route?	*I will be busier*
Promotion	*I feel unsure/nervous*
Validation	*I worry about the cost*
Ammunition	

You and your employer bring expertise and knowledge with you, and are more like partners with the potential to facilitate truly cutting-edge work, very different from the old model of HE where subject-based knowledge trickles downwards towards an empty recipient (you!), usually in a classroom setting, on a full-time basis, over a set period of weeks and years, culminating in being 'tested' with essays and examinations. Methods of learning, teaching and assessment need to go way beyond this if they are to fulfil the needs of the 21st-century varied body of learners, and to capitalise on the learning that occurs where the workplace and academia intersect (Chapter 11).

Usually the way in which you study a subject is part of the subject's formation and integrity; there are well-established expectations around what the curriculum contains (sometimes called 'the canon') and how it is accessed. However, as Gibbons et al. suggest, 'The bounds of the intellectual world and its environment have become blurred' (Gibbons et al., 1994: 37).

When knowledge is produced outside of the university a more active style of learning is involved, and it is impossible to separate the learning from the activity. This is not learning something then applying it, but learning while you work (Gibbons et al., 1994 describe these distinctly different styles as Mode 1 and Mode 2 knowledge). Similarly Biggs (constructivist debate, 2003) claims that you construct something personal from your activity that makes you learn, and that *what* you construct depends upon your motives, your intentions, your previous learning, your previous knowledge and probably also other factors like learning outcomes and assessment criteria.

So while formerly HEIs' strengths were summarised as research and theory there is now growing evidence to suggest that learning and doing cannot be separated. Therefore to use knowledge to its fullest potential it must be implemented, performed and enhanced as part of a synergy. Ideally, as a learner, you will not only 'do', you will focus on *why* you are doing what you are doing, *how* you are doing it and the theory behind it. It is worth you doing some research for yourself into the interesting debates around the nature of knowledge. Many cultural theories have considerably weakened the position of strength HEIs held over deciding what could be legitimately classed as knowledge (see, for example, the work of Jean-François Lyotard). Elda Nikolou-Walker describes this learning revolution as, '"marrying" academic skills within "real life" circumstances', a process that 'brings theory out of the classroom, right onto the desk in the office, onto the shop floor, or wherever individuals seek to *build* and *use* knowledge' (Nikolou-Walker, 2007: 539, italics in original).

Writing for academic purposes

As with knowledge within HE there are also traditions around how academic work looks and sounds; you might be worried that you will be expected to write, read and respond in a narrowly defined way and subsequently be judged against others who have more recent experience of studying than yourself. This is not the case; you will be offered help and advice about academic practices, including modules that have been specifically devised to bring you 'up to speed' with academic writing conventions (presentation and format) in a limited timeframe (claiming credit for your previous learning through RPL is great but it does shorten the timeframe of your overall study). Due to the negotiated and personalised nature of your programme, and the specifics of your working environment and sector, it may be that your assessments will not involve writing essays – not all HE assignments do (Chapter 11). For work-based learners it is more usual to undertake an assessment tailored to your work activities; for example, your tutors may observe you giving a presentation to your managers about a workplace initiative, and then mark a copy of the report you produce.

As previously suggested, the advanced standing your previous learning can offer is fantastic as it means you can complete your study in a shorter (and often more affordable) timeframe. However, the obvious downside to this is that less time overall means you need to be both quick and effective in all of your study plans; you do not have the luxury of extended periods of time to ponder. A good RPL claim could propel you into the equivalent of the second, or even third, year of undergraduate study (or the corresponding stage of your postgraduate route). This is a deserved recognition of your previous learning, and the level of the experiences, skills and responsibilities of your job, but it also stops you having the time and space of multiple years' full-time study and campus attendance in which to experience academic conventions, reading, writing, taking notes, researching effectively, understand marking systems and so on, which those students opting for more traditional routes get. You have to learn fast! But, realistically, some of what a typical full-time student is learning is not appropriate for you, and many of your other skills are far in excess of theirs. They are being taught about learning; your job (and life) has already taught you how to learn. What you need now are some methods of translating that learning into formats that can be ratified by HE. Make the most of the self-audits and exercises your university utilises to highlight your areas in need of development and try your best to address these areas. Most universities, as well as having specific modules to polish up these skills also have web pages and drop-in centres, typically in the library. There are also excellent study skills books and websites available on the market; make the most of your HEI's library catalogue but also Google, Amazon and more (Chapter 8). Your university will provide module and programme handbooks, which are another resource for getting up to speed with the skills a particular module needs. Many universities also have websites designed to help you with study skills – for example, see dissc.tees.ac.uk. Sites like this are dedicated to improving your writing and sharpening your learning skills, and provide invaluable, down-to-earth tips and useful links to other sources of support.

Level descriptors

To help you to be sure that you are attaining HE-level academic standards your institution uses level descriptors, published standards that state the institution's expectations of student achievement at each level of study. 'Level' refers to the difficulty of study; Year One for a full-time undergraduate is Level 4. HE levels, then, are not referring to individual marks or grades, but the level your *course* is at. Your HE work-based learning will also be measured against your institution's level descriptors; these differ between institutions, but all are based around those suggested by the Quality Assurance Agency (QAA) (see Chapter 4).

TIP **Typical words you will find in level descriptors**

Level 4 (first-year undergraduate)
- *Demonstrate* you can use a systematic approach in *acquiring knowledge* and the *underpinning concepts* and *principles* associated with this *knowledge.*
- *Use* a range of *subject-specific, cognitive* and *transferable skills.*
- *Evaluate* the appropriateness of *differing approaches* to *solving problems.*
- *Communicate* outcomes in a *structured* and *clear* manner.
- *Discuss* your findings from texts, journals and other data.

Level 5 (second-year undergraduate – expectations increase)
- *Demonstrate* your ability.
- *Apply* and *evaluate* key *concepts* and *theories.*
- *Select* and *use* a range of *cognitive and transferable skills* and *problem-solving strategies.*
- Effectively *communicate information* and *debates.*
- *Accept responsibility* for personal outcomes.
- *Reflect* on, for example, workplace experience.

Level 6 (Honours level, final-year students – levels of difficulty and sophistication increase)
- *Demonstrate* that you have certain abilities.
- *Critically review,* consolidate and extend a body of knowledge.
- *Critically evaluate* ideas and material from a range of sources.
- *Transfer* and *apply* subject-specific, cognitive and transferable skills to complex situations.
- Your skills of *communication* and *argument* should be considerably honed by this stage.
- *Demonstrate your acceptance* of your accountability for determining and *achieving* both your own outcomes and team outcomes.
- *Evidence* your *critical* and *analytical reflection.*
- You will be expected to give *evidence* in a variety of formats.

Level 7 (Master's level)
- Operate in *complex, changeable* and/or *expert* environments.
- Are *enterprising, resourceful* and *accountable.*
- Have a *profound* and *methodical* understanding of your area of *expertise,* but also the *interfaces* with other areas of expertise.
- Understand relevant theory.
- Are using *personal critical responses.*
- Have *designed* and then *carried out significant research/practitioner inquiry.*
- *Practise autonomously.*

TIP **Level 8 (Doctoral level)**

- Provide evidence of *your work* at the *cutting edge of knowledge*.
- Prove your *autonomy, initiative* and *professionalism*.
- *Demonstrate groundbreaking theoretical research knowledge*.
- *Evidence* your *wide-ranging cognisance* of practices.
- *Confirm an enhanced level* of abstract thinking and technical ability.
- *Progress theory* and research methods through independent thought and original work.
- *Communicate highly* effectively.

These lists give a flavour of the expectations of those assessing HE-level learning and begin to show the stages in your journey from novice through competence and proficiency to autonomous expert. Make sure that you refer to the level descriptors specifically used by your own institution. SEEC also provide some useful guidelines – www.seec.org.uk/seec-credit-level-descriptors-2010/.

You will also need to interpret them through your own sector's legal requirements and governing bodies. They are not devised to catch you out, but rather as helpful guidelines for you to aim at. Having something clearly defined is better than not knowing what success might look like.

Time management

WBL students are without exception busy working people; to make a success of your HE study you will need to master time management. Many things occur during the day that waste our time: the telephone interrupts; visitors surprise; feelings of stress and tiredness, even illness, catch up. Sometimes we avoid what needs doing for no very good reason, allowing ourselves to be distracted by less important, even less interesting matters. Why does this happen? Procrastination doesn't have to be a sign of laziness; maybe you are avoiding facing up to what you should be doing because it is difficult to work effectively without all of the necessary information? Or because your line manager hasn't made it clear what is expected of you? Having all of the necessary information and planning your time appropriately, and realistically, makes it easier to carry out your tasks in an organised, efficient manner. Trying to work in an unplanned (even shambolic!) way may initially feel like 'getting straight on', but in the long run unplanned activity is a proven time waster. This is not to suggest that there is no place for spontaneity in the workplace – there is – but when trying to achieve certain outcomes, within a set timescale, a plan is necessary. If you think about what kind of events or issues regularly disturb your working environment you will be well on the way to developing a plan to check against this and help you cope with the extra demands of study.

Exercise 1.4   'What disrupts you?' (and what you can do about it)

Interruptions?	Poor planning?	Things out of your control? (or seem to be?)			
Meetings	Working without necessary tools and/or information	Tiredness			
Phone calls	Lack of/poor communication	Illness			
Emails	Unclear objectives	Procrastination			
Uninvited visitors (even invited ones sometimes!)		Personal responsibilities			

What else have you added to the list? Disruptions are sometimes out of your hands, but at other times they are self-inflicted, and occasionally they fall into both of these categories; they are out of your hands, yet your response is making the situation worse not better. You may not have been given the necessary information, but perhaps you have not sought it out either? Or perhaps you have chosen to ignore it, thinking you know better? Some disruptions are the knock-on results of an earlier disruption, in a vicious circle of insufficient time – for example, the stress you are feeling that is significantly compromising your performance may well be a direct result of you attempting to achieve something that was *never* possible. Unclear or wildly ambitious objectives can often create this situation, especially when these objectives are linked to an overall lack of good communication. Modern life is complex, so don't add to your own stress by being unrealistic about what you can fit in.

TIP **Good time management skills**

- Be *realistic* – don't set yourself up to fail.
- *Record* your activities, and how long they take on a *log* – you might be surprised.
- Set *boundaries, clear goals* and *time limits.*
- Use a *calendar* – something like *Outlook diary* on your PC can send you reminders and really help you to plan your time, as well as letting (chosen) others see when you are busy and when you are free.
- *Contacts* – keep well-ordered records, which saves time looking them up – use your mobile devices to the best of their (and your!) ability.
- *Delegate* – pass things on – nobody can do things just like you, but it often doesn't matter.
- Similarly, *accept help* – welcome the involvement of appropriate others.
- *Minimise distractions* and deflections – create a working environment for yourself that suits you.
- *Overall schedule* – keep perspective of the bigger picture.
- *Plan/prioritise/balance* – what is really important? (urgent isn't the same thing).
- Say *'no'*, *'not now'* and *'later'!*
- Use a clear *task list* and subsidiary *'to do lists'* – breaking tasks down helps.
- *What else would you add to this list of tips? You know yourself better than anyone*
- _____
- _____

Try to utilise, monitor and adapt a number of key suggestions from the Tips above; keep track of your activities in a system that produces the best results for you. WBL does not rely on a pre-set curriculum, but encourages and facilitates a negotiation of the programme content, pace and location, between you and your tutor(s), so focus on what works for you. There is minimal pre-decided content – you bring the bulk of the content with you – and this requires enhanced levels of responsibility from you as a learner. The flexibility of WBL means that you are largely responsible for using your time wisely. Your programme will be bespoke to you, but you will have many interested stakeholders (Chapter 7). It is your responsibility to satisfy them all: your employer, colleagues, fellow learners, tutors, mentors, customers, partners, family, friends and of course, yourself. This demands a high level of commitment to your course of study; tailoring your programme brings enhanced freedom and self-direction but also requires that you take ownership of your own learning. Don't be daunted, you are already operating as a professional, as Burns and Costley suggest: 'These learners already have intellectual capital, what they seek from HEIs is not so much factual knowledge as ways to research and develop knowledge, reflect and evaluate situations and think autonomously' (Burns and Costley, 2003: 45).

Summary

1 WBL is facilitated learning; it is not a teacher writing on the board, but relies heavily on you, the learner.

2 You are required to behave differently to how you might expect a 'typical student' to behave.

3 You personalise your study and focus on what is of interest to you and appropriate to your job.

4 You will be pushed beyond your comfort zone (that is where the opportunities are).

5 The speed and route of learning is under your control; it is a bit unnerving at first.

6 You will get to know and understand your own learning styles, strengths and weaknesses – leading to greater autonomy as a learner.

7 You will develop a critical distance and ability to reflect, which will allow you to monitor your own progress – the following chapters will assist you with this.

References

Biggs, J. (2003) *Teaching for Quality Learning at University: What the Student Does*, 2nd edn (Maidenhead: Society for Research into Higher Education and Open University Press).

Burns, G. and Costley, C. (2003) Non-Traditional Students and 21st Century Higher Education. In: *Knowledge, Work and Learning: Conference Proceedings of the Work-Based Learning Network of the Universities Association for Lifelong Learning*, compiled by D. Hollifield and issued on CD.

Gibbons, M., Limoges, C., Nowotny, H., Schwartzman, S., Scott, P. and Trow, M. (1994) *The New Production of Knowledge: The Dynamics of Science and Research in Contemporary Societies* (London: Sage).

Nikolou-Walker, E. (2007) 'Critical reflections on an evaluative comparative analysis of work-based learning through organizational change mechanisms', *Reflective Practice*, 8 (4), 525–43.

Suggested further reading

Billett, S. (2001) *Learning in the Workplace: Strategies for Effective Practice* (London: Allen & Unwin).

Cunningham, I., Dawes, G. and Bennett, B. (2004) *The Handbook of Work Based Learning* (Aldershot: Gower Publishing).

Durant, A., Rhodes, G. and Young, D. (eds) (2009) *Getting Started with University-Level Work Based Learning* (Middlesex: Middlesex University Press).

Helyer, R. (2011) 'Aligning higher education with the world of work', *Higher Education, Skills and Work-based Learning*, 1 (2), 95–105.

Helyer, R. and Lee, D. (2012) 'The 21st century multiple generation workforce: overlaps and differences but also challenges and benefits', *Education + Training*, 54 (7), 545–578.

Raelin, J. A. (2008) *Work-Based Learning: Bridging Knowledge and Action in the Workplace*, rev. edn (San Francisco, CA: Jossey-Bass).

Chapter 2

Building capabilities for your future

Ruth Helyer and Judie Kay

In this chapter you will learn:

- ▶ what employability skills are and how to develop them;
- ▶ that learning in the workplace and learning as a student overlap;
- ▶ about reflective skills and their crucial nature;
- ▶ differences between subject and generic/transferable skills;
- ▶ how to track, evidence and articulate your skills;
- ▶ strategies and mechanisms to continue learning;
- ▶ about international perspectives on employability.

What do we mean by employability skills?

It is easy to think that employability skills are about gaining employment, and that if you have a job already, as many of you reading this do, you no longer need to worry about them. The truth is that we all need to constantly hone and polish our skills due to the rapidly changing nature of the world, and as a consequence the workplace. It is highly unlikely that you will have the same job, or work in the same industry, for your entire working life; not only are we all living longer but sectors and job roles are constantly changing and evolving to keep pace with ongoing changes in society and the environment. So, having a job is great, but if you wish to stay employed, get promoted, maybe change companies, or profession, then you really need to update your skills regularly, in fact so regularly that it becomes second nature to you to want to learn and develop, and to therefore constantly look for opportunities to do so. Sometimes 'skills' are viewed as being within the domain of vocational courses, and not part of HE. But this is not the case; being skilful crosses many developmental boundaries and levels, and we all need skills, of different kinds and at different levels, if we hope to thrive in the 21st-century workplace.

In order to develop yourself effectively you also need some information about which sets of skills are most valued by employers, most useful in life and most relevant to your future career development. Sometimes when employability skills are referred to what is actually meant is *job-seeking skills*, such as writing an impressive and relevant CV; honing your interview techniques; and knowing where to look for job opportunities. While these are all very important, within this chapter what we are referring to are the skills that make you useful and successful in a workplace. Again, this definition can be unravelled a little further as these could be very job-specific, operational skills. What this chapter hopes to demonstrate is that in addition to these job-specific skills, it is the transferable and life skills that have the potential to really offer you benefits, as they are required in *all* jobs and sectors, as well as being useful in your life outside work; skills like adaptability, communication and resilience.

Higher education (HE) graduates have always been sought after as employees because as well as proving their expertise in a named area – such as engineering, law or medicine – they also, due to the nature of HE study, have well-developed skills of, for example, analysis, operating autonomously, problem-solving and creativity, skills that are uniformly valued by employers of all kinds and across all industry sectors. However, following a global recession and in a highly competitive jobs market many graduates are finding it very difficult to secure employment in the sectors they were aiming at. A consequence of this is an increased emphasis on skills that transcend sectors, such as: working with others; the ability to work in a global environment; networking; being innovative; making connections and synthesising information; distinguishing yourself from the competition. The world is rapidly evolving, therefore workers need to also be open to change; and one of the best ways to do this is to resolve to become a lifelong learner, whatever your connection with HE – be it as a full-time student or a part-time student, perhaps with a full-time job.

We refer you to the Australian Qualifications Framework, which is useful as it outlines generic skills in four broad categories: fundamental skills; people skills; thinking skills; and personal skills. In HE these are generally known as graduate attributes, defined by each higher education provider, and embedded into their programmes. These are in addition to the professional accreditation standards defined by professional bodies. *The Australian Blueprint for Career Development* Ministerial Council on Education Employment Training and Youth Affairs (2009) identifies the skills, attitudes and knowledge that individuals need to develop and manage their careers; equally important to both students and those already employed, it applies in particular to work readiness and can be contextualised:

Personal management
- build and maintain a positive self-concept;
- interact positively and effectively with others;
- change and grow throughout life.

Learning and work exploration
- participate in lifelong learning supportive of career goals;
- locate and effectively use career information;
- understand the relationship between work, society and the economy.

Career building
- secure/create and maintain work;
- make career-enhancing decisions;
- maintain balanced life and work roles;
- understand the changing nature of life and work roles;
- understand, engage in and manage the career-building process.
  education.gov.au/australian-blueprint-career-development

Workplaces are becoming ever more multicultural as a reflection of changes in society; in addition, companies are increasingly global, with connections across a range of countries through customer or supplier relationships. The skills and experience in these multicultural contexts, and for engaging globally, are ever more sought after by employers. With increased global mobility, many graduates (and other employees) can expect to either undertake international assignments or work in other countries, with this trend expected to rise. Indeed, there is now much more global mobility of students during their studies, with many universities actively supporting students to undertake placements or study in other countries. Building the skills to be successful in this global environment is now more important than ever. The capacity to understand, be sensitive to and tolerant of different cultural beliefs, values and styles, together with an awareness of their impact on behaviour and a capacity to adapt behaviour to be effective, is central to working globally (more in Chapter 10 on this). In addition, recognising the many benefits that flow from diversity in workplaces, and through links globally, as well being aware of and effective at working to remove barriers is required to be effective and use diversity to full affect.

Case Study 2.1   Gaining global experience and cross-cultural skills

Experiences at Western Digital, Thailand
WD, a Western Digital company, is a long-time innovator and storage industry leader known for producing reliable, high-performance hard disk drives. Headquartered in the USA, WD has branches all over the world, with its largest manufacturing base in Thailand, where the company employs over 26,000 workers. WD Thailand partners with over 60 universities worldwide, providing a range of work placements to students annually.

Case Study 2.1 (continued)

Alex, a Mechanical Engineering student from the University of Victoria, Canada, participated in a cooperative education programme with WD Thailand for four months in 2012.

I expected this experience would be rewarding and fun, but I did not imagine it would be life-changing. I had never before contemplated working outside of Canada, but this experience opened my eyes and led me to fall in love with both WD and Thailand, and it has opened up a range of possibilities for me.

After returning to Canada, Alex applied for and was successful in obtaining a graduate engineering position at WD in Thailand.

Although Alex found the company to be very welcoming, friendly and supportive, there were some differences from a typical Canadian company. These differences were not so much in terms of the technical skills required but the personal skills, particularly cultural and communication skills. Here are some of Alex's tips for succeeding in a different cultural context:

- Empathy: be aware of others around you and look for any signs of discomfort;
- Sensitivity: be alert to cultural differences around personal space, religion, tone of voice and jokes to avoid offending others;
- Communication: adjust your speaking to suit the varying levels of English comprehension of your listeners and avoid idioms and cultural references;
- Willingness to learn: try to learn the culture and language as this shows respect and enhances both your understanding and acceptance by others;
- Attitude: smile – smiles are very powerful – and be approachable.

Alex found that the other strategies for success are similar to other contexts. These include working hard; having a positive, helpful attitude; being curious and sincere; and networking wherever possible with top executives and leaders in the organisation to build your knowledge of industry and company.

Now having benefited from the diverse professional experience available at WD and the additional self-confidence and enhanced personal and communication skills that the experience helped him develop, Alex feels well equipped and confident to build on his career whether it be in Canada, Thailand or elsewhere.

Building these crucial skills if you are not employed

As you will see from Case Study 2.1, there is much to be gained from experience of the real workplace. Generic skills are key to gaining, and being successful in, employment and shaping a career; but how do you build those skills if you are not employed? If, like Alex, you are able to participate in either a placement or industry-based project during your HE studies, you should grasp the opportunity as it will provide you with: valuable knowledge about workplace contexts; evidence to inform your career path choices; real-world industry networking, in addition to the opportunity to extend your employability skills. Being proactive and prepared when approaching these opportunities will enable you to get the most from them. Ensure you have researched the organisation and reflected on what experiences and learning you are aiming to achieve, as well as what experiences and learning you take with you.

If there are not placement options open to you volunteering can also open up a wealth of possibilities, whether it is with community groups, not-for-profit organisations, on or off campus, or volunteering in another country. You not only can make a valuable contribution to society but also extend your personal, and sometimes your professional skills, dependent on the volunteering you undertake. Volunteering can also be a good option if you are already employed but would like a change of direction in your career pathway. By volunteering in a different kind of organisation (third sector) you can grow and test new skills and make sure that you are suited to a different environment or role. As with industry placements and projects, being clear about what skills you want to gain through volunteering, and being prepared and proactive, will ensure you not only make a valuable contribution but also maximise your personal skills development, and the professional and community networks you gain. Taking the time to reflect on the experience (more on this later in the chapter) and being able to articulate the skills developed will be valued by future employers.

Mentors are a valuable resource, so consider locating one, either through a formal mentoring programme such as a university-run scheme, or informally by approaching alumni from your university or someone in the areas you are interested in. LinkedIn is a great resource to use to make these connections (Chapter 8). Mentors can provide invaluable industry knowledge and assist you in setting career goals, help your career management and prompt you to critically reflect on your personal and professional skills. The key here is to be proactive and very clear; communicate to your mentor what you are hoping to achieve from their input in the mentoring arrangement. The onus really is on you to make the most of the mentoring opportunity; be mindful of your mentor's time and work commitments, and focus discussion on areas where your mentor can provide input. Always ensure that you are punctual and prepared for each mentoring meeting whether it be face-to-face or conducted virtually.

Case Study 2.2   RMIT University Global Mentoring Program

RMIT University (Melbourne, Australia) runs a range of mentoring programmes for students across its campuses in Australia and Vietnam, aimed at enhancing student employability and graduate outcomes. The Global Mentoring Program links RMIT alumni with international students (individually or in small groups). Mentors are sourced through RMIT's global alumni network from China, Vietnam, Singapore, Indonesia, Hong Kong and Malaysia. The mentoring pairs are provided with an induction and resources to guide and support the mentoring process, which occurs by phone, email or Skype. Topics that are discussed include:

- local workplace and recruitment practices;
- industry-specific knowledge;
- interpersonal skills, including professional networking and confidence-building;
- potential career paths;
- sourcing internships and placements.

The programme evaluation demonstrates the value of mentoring, with 82% of mentors and 92% of student respondents indicating that they had benefited greatly. Students indicate that they would recommend mentoring to other students, with comments including:

'I have learnt how to sell myself in an interview.'
'I gained country-specific knowledge and some tips for my CV.'
'I developed overall knowledge of how the industry runs and the skills required in order secure a job in the current competitive market.'
'I learnt industry insight in my country of interest.'
'It assisted me to think more carefully on the options of taking up internships at that location.'

Mentors too were very positive about how the programme:

- connects them to future employees;
- develops their understanding of the new generation of graduates;
- allows them to improve their own skills, such as communication and technology skills;
- enables them to give back to their profession by assisting students;
- enables them to share their industry knowledge.

The majority of mentors were keen to continue mentoring in the next cycle of the programme.

Reflection

Employability is clearly a complex mixture of elements – elements that differ from job to job but with the same basic outcome of making you a desirable employee. In a rapidly developing society you need to be adaptable and multi-faceted to cope with changing circumstances; this need for reinvention requires a receptive and self-aware person, and your employability skills need to be honed and enhanced (Helyer and Lee, 2014). The skills that will help you include: analysis and critical debate; being able to make connections and read widely; also broader multi-faceted skills including creativity, imagination and entrepreneurship. Among the most useful and powerful skills you can develop are the skills of reflection – working towards becoming a reflective practitioner is one of the best attributes you can bring to your job role, and it will enhance the development of your future career immeasurably (Schön, 1983).

If you are undertaking a work-based studies style programme you will probably be hoping to claim some academic credit for relevant learning you have already accumulated (see Chapter 5 for RPL/APL). In order to be successful in this claim you are encouraged to look back and critically reflect on past learning (more on this also in Chapter 6). To get the most from your studies you must actively reflect on your work activities, as part of continuously evaluating, reviewing and improving performance, satisfaction and results. Combined with your new academic skills this reflection will encourage you to change your practices within the workplace, hence enhancing your personal performance, but also the overall performance of your organisation (see Chapter 3). You will almost certainly already be utilising critical reflection, even if this has been intuitively up until this point.

Humans reflect in order to understand events in their lives, and as a consequence hopefully add and enhance meaning. 'Looking back' and examining the past in order to learn from what happened, and perhaps not repeat mistakes, makes sense. This is what Schön terms 'reflecting on action', but reflection does not stop with looking back, although it is very useful to learn from what we have experienced. It is also about reflecting on what you are doing right now, together with your thoughts and feelings about that. Schön called this 'reflection in action': 'reflection in action is where we may reflect in the midst of action without interrupting it. Our thinking serves to reshape what we are doing while we are doing it' (Schön, 1987: 26). There are some overlaps here with the principles of mindfulness. One of the main reasons for you to sharpen your reflective skills is that it is these skills that enable you to analyse how your other skills are doing. Without some honest reflection, how would we know that we need to polish our time management skills (Chapter 1) or organisational skills (Chapter 3)? Other than things frequently going wrong for us!

David Gray cites reflecting actively and usefully as a process that generates the development of 'a dynamic synergy and dialectic between academic learning and work-based practice' (Gray, 2001: 24).

TIP **Reflect to get the most from combining learning and working**

- Reflect strategically on your learning through past experiences.
- Remember, the activity and the learning process are entwined – not separate entities.
- Reflect not just on your programme of study but also more generally along your life path.
- Make the most of your programme's guided self-audit (Chapters 5 and 6).
- Establish where exactly you are – in terms of career, personal development and learning.
- Acknowledge what you can already do – for example, 'write reports' – this feeds into academic writing, an area you might be convincing yourself you know little about.
- Reflection makes you realise that you already have a good base on which to build your next stage of development.
- Don't worry, reflective skills can be 'taught' and measured.
- Become a reflective practitioner – strive to continually improve your practice' active reflection is key to this.

You will be reflecting on your actions, automatically, to a certain extent, but focusing this activity into a structured response maximises its usefulness and encourages you to become a reflective and self-aware person. This means that you will be looking both backwards and forwards (and sometimes sideways!) to make connections with what you are currently undertaking. This kind of evaluation can feel fragmented and disjointed – don't worry, that is normal – it utilises the knowledge that lies deep within you (tacit knowledge). This is so deep you probably take it for granted and don't explicitly acknowledge it, but it is the data you use to make instinctive decisions based upon your accumulated knowledge from past actions and experience. Michael Eraut (1994) discusses the subtle nuances between the tacit, that which is implicitly acknowledged and referred to, rather than that which is explicitly pointed out. You might choose to use formalised reflection as a method for offering feedback to your employer or tutor; it is a good way to share outcomes. Because reflection is a vital part of personal development HE work-based learning programmes encourage you to become actively and analytically reflective.

Reflection begins almost as soon as we are born and has always, even if subliminally, affected how you view yourself and define your identity and profile. Lacan's theories about, what he calls, 'the mirror stage' centre on the idea that once humans have seen their reflection (as an infant) they develop an enhanced self-awareness and begin to view themselves differently, indeed as a complete entity rather than the disjointed arms and legs they have looked down upon as a small baby. This suggests that reflection is closely tied to how we view ourselves both physically and mentally (Lacan, 1977). By actively considering our thoughts and actions we become aware of the power of reflective thinking as a tool for continuous improvement, and this obviously has implications beyond the personal. If used effectively and purposefully, reflection facilitates ongoing personal *and* professional learning; this develops and creates practitioners capable of demonstrating their progression towards learning outcomes and required standards, while also providing a structure in which to make sense of their learning, so that concepts and theories become embedded in practice, while constant thought and innovation are simultaneously fostered.

Reflection as a development tool

Try this exercise: think of a time when an experience and its outcomes have had an effect on your actions. This will happen all of the time but we do not always acknowledge the process. Complete the grid below with what happened – it might be from work, study or your personal life. What was the outcome? Was it deemed a success? Did you learn anything? Did you change your methods and thoughts because of your evaluation of your experience? Questioning and considering our learning experiences is an extremely powerful way to develop future strategies, approaches and tactics in order to build skills to tackle future similar situations, as well as further enhancing the skills that made you successful on this occasion.

Exercise 2.1   Scrutinise your successes (or your failures if you're feeling brave!)

What happened? Event Activity Incident Experience	*Attended jewellery workshop*		
Consequence? Result Outcome Product	*Made earrings*		

Exercise 2.1 (continued)

Thoughts Feelings Reactions Impressions	*I enjoyed it but it was harder than anticipated*		
Be proactive Contemplate Think Deliberate	*Research and planning would have helped*		
Interrogate Analyse Question Consider the thoughts/feelings of other parties Evaluate	*Class too large for space, time and amount of equipment* *Didn't enjoy lunch session – took own food as advised but area overcrowded*		
The details What, Why, When, How, Where and Who?	*For my birthday at a small arts centre close to home with daughter and about 15 strangers*		
Which skills helped you **succeed**?	*Confidence Friendliness*		
Which skills areas felt **lacking**?	*Drawing Using a saw and other small tools Patience*		
Did you 'think on your feet' (**'In action'**) and amend things as you went along? Or did all your analysis come at the end? (**'On action'**)	*Yes, altered design and changed coloured stone*		

Exercise 2.1 (continued)

Looking to the future – Develop: Strategies Approaches Tactics	*Would do it again but would plan product in advance* *Would look for same teacher as she was very good* *Would look for smaller classes/private session*		
Would you do exactly the same next time?	*No* *Ask for more information in advance* *Think about ideas before the class* *Go out for lunch*		

(Any skills that are highlighted by Exercise 2.1 as needing further development can be carried forward to the 'Skills Grid' – see Table 2.1).

Exercise 2.1 requires you to 'look back' and analyse past events and experiences; the aim of this is to place past experience within the context of what is happening in the present, and what may happen in the future. Within your WBL study you will encounter HE sessions that include learning theories and styles, meta-cognition, self-analysis of strengths and weaknesses, and personal statements (see Chapters 3, 6 and 9), and you will be encouraged to reflect on what has worked well for you in the past when you have undertaken tasks and tackled situations in certain ways. This kind of reflection will also be usefully formalised into reports, essays, journals, logs or diaries. Your reflective writing can take a more personal style than that which you might have at first expected to be producing for university assignments, but it still needs to be structured and purposeful. Writing about your active reflection embeds within you good practice for your future continuous professional and personal development activities.

Developing an ongoing ethos of reflection means you challenge and question *why* tasks were undertaken in a certain way rather than *how* they were carried out, and furthermore become accomplished at recognising that you are learning and building your skills continuously; it is not a standalone process. Tutor interaction will be built into this process, with debriefing, support and the possibility of observational visits to your workplace (or alternatively pre-arranged work placements if you are not employed). Employers have much to gain from encouraging staff to actively reflect on their work practices, as Cox claims: '"learning through work" is integral to the whole reflective practice process and can provide valuable opportunities for individual action research in the work context' (Cox, 2005: 471). It is crucial to remember that you are not separate to that context, but an intrinsic part of it. Reflective practice has the potential to impact positively upon you and your workplace/job-role; feedback from former WBL students refers to its transformative effect.

Active reflection is usually included in the core modules of a WBL programme. You may find that you are required to compile a series of short narrative statements (500–1000 words) in which you purposefully reflect upon your learning processes during different modules and activities. These statements are often transformed into a 'Portfolio of Active Reflection', which includes your experience of various modules, your current and past activities and your future plans – all situated within a framework of personal and professional development. The ideal scenario is that as a reflective practitioner you share your ability to critically reflect and analyse, together with your higher-level ideas, with your company colleagues. You will become a practitioner for whom it is the 'norm' to continuously reflect, plan and develop; you will routinely revisit the manner in which activities are conducted, rather than assuming that the 'old way is the best'.

This is often illustrated in a circular format (see Figure 2.1), which can be slightly misleading as the process of reflection is more iterative and messy than a neat circle suggests. There *is* a certain circularity to moving through the stages of Review, Research and Reflect but it is a forward-moving loop of enquiry – rather than a 'closed off' or 'fenced in' circle. To prevent an emphasis on looking back (despite this being needed) some prefer the term 'reflecting forwards', which foregrounds the developmental nature of the process.

In HE-level work-based learning the acknowledging of what *has* been, *is* being and *will be* learned is at the core of your interaction with your tutors and your peers. This questions the 'correct' order of things, as you repeatedly look back, forth and across, via your experiential learning. This postmodern approach to learning can be seen as simultaneously liberating, because of the opportunities it offers, and frightening, as it removes boundaries and the purported 'safety' they bring (Helyer, 2007). Teaching innovations such as MOOCs (see Chapter 8), and flipping the classroom (Bergman and Sams, 2012) equally play with the order of learning and prove that it is flexible and changeable.

WBL programmes inevitably involve a personal and professional 'stock-take' (Chapters 3 and 6). An important element of this is 'looking back' to analyse your past learning experiences. This might feel uncomfortable. Many WBL students are older than the average traditional student, and feel the need to 'catch up'; you want or need that qualification (perhaps others in your workplace are graduates, or your career has changed into a graduate profession since you joined it) and you feel aware that you are not 18 and

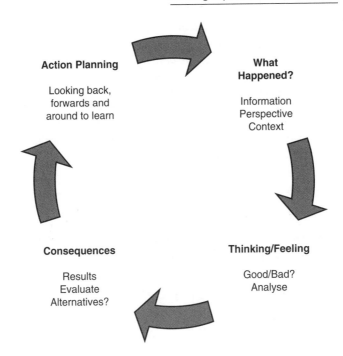

Figure 2.1   Review, research, reflect and learn

do not have A levels. No doubt you did not enrol with a university in order to look back; you want to move forwards towards a qualification, like every other student. Being genuinely reflective takes time; it can be painful and is invariably more difficult than you anticipate; some facets of your practice may need to be 'unlearned' or at least amended. As Elaine Cox (2005) states, 'encouraging reflective practice at all levels is beneficial for students undertaking any kind of work-based activity, even though … there is often resistance to the process and difficulty in initial development of the reflective and analytical skills required' (Cox, 2005: 461). You will be guided through the process; this is an issue in itself as you must learn to trust your tutor (who will be adept at reflective processes) in order to be open and honest with them: 'To engage in reflective practice, people need a sense of security' (Osterman and Kottkamp, 2004: 68).

Where do skills come from?

It is something of a 'Catch-22' that to be employed you need to both 'learn' and to 'experience' the workplace – if you are a full-time university student it is difficult to find time in which to adequately experience 'real' work, which has a usefulness and relevance to your future career aspirations. Similarly, those who are in full-time employment must juggle to find the time for any serious professional learning and development, especially if that is to be away from their workplace and at HE level. While the growing place of work-based learning in HE is becoming an established part of the answer to the second of these conundrums, the former is still taxing both students and education institutions. There follows a case study of one UK University's Internship Programme, part of their strategy to address the very real challenge of developing and enhancing graduate skills for the workplace.

Case Study 2.3   Experiencing the workplace

Teesside University's (UK) Internship Programme
     This programme supports graduates to:

- gain real-life work experience (12-week paid placement);
- develop their employability and job-seeking skills;
- inform their career choices and progression;
- benefit from personal development workshops at the University.

Since 2012 the programme has attracted increasing numbers of graduates, from 46 (2012) to 122 (2014), and employers from 46 (2012) to 79 (2014). The graduates' subject backgrounds, and the organisations' sectors are diverse; a wide variety of roles are offered, mostly in the voluntary; public; culture and heritage; manufacturing; marketing and branding; creative and digital sectors.
     Research findings from all three cohorts have shown a significant impact on the interns' confidence and employability skills:

> *'I know what the industry pace is now.'*
> *'I've developed industry knowledge.'*
> *'I've gained time management and project management skills.'*

In the 2014 cohort 89% stated that the experience critically offered them an understanding of a real-life working environment. A questionnaire, designed to track improvements, clearly demonstrated the programme's positive impact, and the individual's increasing awareness of their own skills. The biggest improvement was in communication skills, followed by ability to work independently, problem-solving and innovative/creative skills:

> *It's taught me that employers are looking for graduates who not only have the subject-skills from their degree but also ... character, drive and*

Case Study 2.3 (continued)

ambition ... I didn't really consider it much before, but it's a lot about the person and having the right attitude. It's taught me to develop my skills for talking to different kinds of people.

The majority of employers felt that the graduates' skills exceeded their expectations, and were pleased with the skills demonstrated, including: creativity; a can-do approach and an ability to undertake key work tasks. Employers suggested that during placement significant improvements had been made in: ability to work independently; self-organisation; communication skills; problem-solving skills, and skills of negotiation. These skills can begin at university but need to be continued in working life:

'It has made me realise that you can never be perfect and need to constantly keep up your skills and adapt to change. This will only happen with practice.'

Dionne Lee
Teesside University
D.lee@tees.ac.uk

One of the findings of the research mentioned in Case study 2.3 was a repeated request from graduates that work placements be made available earlier in their studies rather than at the end when they have graduated. Integrating work experience into HE programmes would also help to embed an ethos of lifelong learning and continuous professional and personal development in learners.

The Skills Grid – evidence your skills acquisition

You may be aware of how important it is to develop your skills, but are you taking the time to record your development, together with evidence? Sitting in front of an employer at an interview, applying for a new job or negotiating a promotion, when the panel asks you to *prove* you are good at what you claim, can be tricky and uncomfortable. Take the time to record your learning activities, and their outcomes, and you will have all the facts at your fingertips, enabling you to articulate your skills and experience. One good way to do this is to develop a Skills Grid – see Table 2.1. Try to complete the details now for a skill you think you have, or want to actively develop. The grid works equally

Table 2.1 The Skills Grid

Skill	What I learned?	Where & when I learned?	How I learned?	Evidence	Location of evidence	Progression What next?
Communication	How to speak to large group **Think of the other skills elements within this – like using technology and working with your fellow presenters**	Group Work assessment Chem Eng class May 2015 **Where you learn can be diverse and may be ongoing?**	By preparing & giving a presentation & responding to questions and feedback Discussed with tutor and rest of group first Thought about what I did and didn't enjoy myself in presentations Thought about the presentations I give in my part-time job **What activities did you do? Did you undertake research? Or write reports?**	1) Copy of presentation – PP slides 2) Copy of hand-out I created 3) Video of presentation 4) Blog that began due to discussion **Quality is better than quantity here The key things that prove you have learned? (they usually include change)**	On USB stick disc Printed examples in file On mobile phone Online – link is – xxx **Be precise Focus on keeping records that are meaningful to YOU**	Currently undertaking advanced PP course Have written up the presentation, taking feedback into account – will give report to fellow students and the tutor Signed up for 'Communicating Effectively' course at Summer University Aware that I need to develop techniques to make sure audience understand **Learning never ends – take responsibility, keep planning and recording**

Skill	What?	Where & when?	How?	Evidence	Location	What next?

well for planning and/or recording. There is an example on there to get you started.

Use the grid to also make connections between activities – for example, something that worked well at work could equally help you in your studies, and vice versa. Skills development can feel very much about your job and career, but it is also deeply personal, and is about you taking responsibility for what you are going to be good at; for the construction of your career identity; for your own career self-management and the meaningfulness of your learning experiences. You will be interpreting and contextualising events and situations in transition from study to workplace/life, as well as back in the other direction; above all, this is about making and maximising upon connections and overlaps, between subject study and specific skills study, between work or work-placements and career counselling. In order to take responsibility for your own development you need to be able to carry out a self-audit of yourself, to help you to pinpoint your self-identified needs. In Chapter 6 there is a personal training needs analysis (TNA) exercise, and undertaking this will help you to start articulating where you need to learn and develop.

Summary

1   View developing your skills as an ongoing project.

2   Keep records, with evidence of how when and where you developed your skills.

3   Keep up to date with what is happening in sectors and areas you are interested in.

4   Look out for suitable mentors (and try to find time to mentor others).

5   Take opportunities to be actively reflective.

6   If you hold relevant workplace knowledge, share it with others.

7   Make connections across areas of your life – many skills are very transferable.

References

Australian Qualifications Framework Council, Australian Qualifications Framework, 2nd edn, January 2013.

Bergman, J. and Sams, A. (2012) *Flip Your Classroom: Reach Every Student in Every Class Every Day* (Washington, DC: ISTE ASCD).

Cox, E. (2005) 'Adult learners learning from experience: using a reflective practice model to support Work-based Learning', *Reflective Practice*, 6 (4), 459–472.

Eraut, M. (1994) *Developing Professional Knowledge and Competence* (London: Falmer).

Gray, D. (2001) *A Briefing on Work-based Learning*, LTSN Generic Centre Assessment Series No. 11 (York: Learning and Teaching Support Network).

Helyer, R. (2007) 'What is employability? Reflecting on the postmodern challenges of Work-based Learning', *Journal of Employability and the Humanities* (Lancashire: University of Central Lancashire).

Helyer, R. and Lee, D. (2014) 'The role of work experience in the future employability of Higher Education graduates', *Higher Education Quarterly*, 68 (3). 348–372.

Lacan, J. (1977) *The Mirror-Stage as Formative of the I as Revealed in Psychoanalytic Experience,* translated by Alan Sheridan in *Écrits: A Selection* (New York: W.W. Norton).

Ministerial Council on Education Employment Training and Youth Affairs (2009) *Australian Blueprint for Career Development.* Available at http://www.blueprint.edu.au.

Osterman, K. and Kottkamp, B. (2004) *Reflective Practice for Educators: Professional Development to Improve Student Learning*, 2nd edn (Thousand Oaks, CA: Corwin Press).

Schön, D. A. (1983) *The Reflective Practitioner: How Professionals Think in Action* (New York: Basic Books).

Schön, D. A. (1987) *Educating the Reflective Practitioner* (San Francisco, CA: Jossey-Bass).

Suggested further reading

Andrews, G. and Russell, M. (2012) 'Employability skills development: strategy, evaluation and impact', *Higher Education Skills and Work-Based Learning*, 2 (1), 33–44.

Boud, D., Keoghr, R. and Walker, D. (eds) (1985) *Reflection: Turning Experience into Learning* (London: Kogan Page).

Bridgstock, R. (2009) 'The attributes we've overlooked: enhancing employability through career management skills', *Higher Education Research & Development*, 28 (1), 33–44.

Helyer, R. (2011) 'Aligning Higher Education with the world of work', *Higher Education, Skills and Work-Based Learning*, 1 (2), 95–105.

Helyer, R. and Lee, D. (2012) 'The 21st century multiple generation workforce: overlaps and differences but also challenges and benefits', *Education + Training*, 54 (7), 545–578.

Helyer, R. and Lee, D. (2014) 'The Role of Work Experience in the Future Employability of Higher Education graduates', *Higher Education Quarterly*, 68 (3), 348–372.

McMahon, M., Patton, W. and Tatham, P. (2003) *Managing Life Learning & Work in the 21st century* (Subiaco: Miles Morgan Australia).

Moon, J. (2004) *A Handbook of Reflective and Experiential Learning: Theory and Practice* (London: Routledge).

Nikolou-Walker, E. and Garnett, J. (2004) 'Work-based LEARNING. A new imperative: developing reflective practice in professional life', *Reflective Practice*, 5 (3), 297–312.

Russell, T. (2005) 'Can reflective practice be taught?', *Reflective Practice*, 6 (2), 199–204.

Siebert, S. and Costley, C. (2013) 'Conflicting values in reflection on professional practice', *Higher Education Skills and Work-Based Learning*, 3 (3), 156–167.

Chapter 3

Developing yourself, developing your organisation

Kevin Ions and Norma Sutcliffe

In this chapter you will learn:

► how to develop your professional qualities/characteristics;
► what the advantages and disadvantages are of being a learner-worker;
► how to develop a growth mindset;
► how to recognise the type of organisation you work in;
► how to carry out an organisational SWOT analysis;
► how to enhance organisational learning through work-based learning initiatives.

Developing yourself

Are you a professional?

Increasingly, within Higher Education (HE) work-based learning (WBL) qualifications take the title of Professional Studies, thereby highlighting the personal and professional development and practice features of a WBL qualification. The reason for this is that Professional Studies courses normally take theory and combine this with work-based practice, while also enhancing professional expertise through research in the form of a work-based project.

However, while the focus is on the professional, and while we may refer to ourselves as professionals, do we ever stop to think what defines a professional and why such esteem is attached to the concept? For example, professional bodies have a powerful role to play in assuring quality of expertise, generally by promoting codes of practice and conduct that set standards of approach; these must be adhered to in order to be identified as a professional. Such standards are designed to give the public confidence that services will be delivered by a qualified expert. Furthermore, the professional gains a sense of pride through belonging to a community of shared practice. This highlights the influential role professional bodies have on their members and the public in general. When looking to purchase goods and services we are more likely to do so from a professional, and especially one who belongs to a recognised body or organisation, as we assume that it means the practitioner holds professional knowledge and skills that enable them to be experts in the field. However, have you ever questioned anybody who uses the term professional? For instance by asking:

- What makes you a professional?
- How much knowledge do you have to acquire before you can claim to be a professional?
- What kinds of behaviour should be expected from a professional?

And of yourself:

- In my present role, can I legitimately use the term?

The term professional pre-dates industrialisation and is derived from the Latin word '*profiteor*', which means to declare yourself as a craftsman possessing a specific body of knowledge. However, if you research 'professional' as it is used today, the concept can be confusing because of the range of meanings associated with the word, depending on the occupation of the individual involved. Furthermore, public perception is a powerful force, and 'meaning' can be externally imposed through observation and interpretation. If professionalism means that to be a professional, you are expected to engage in a code of practice in relation to how service and the delivery of it is performed, either written or unwritten, then arguably 'meaning' in a modern, ever-changing workplace and interpretive context must, and will, evolve. Nevertheless, current definitions fall into two distinct themes: (a) *competence*-based and context-specific (task and performance) (Sockett, 1996) and; (b) *mindset*-based, considering aspirational values and specific behaviours, while remaining context-specific (Evans, 2008).

Considering these two themes, it would appear that being a professional carries a number of characteristics that can be divided accordingly:

- expertise, proficiency and excellence;
- character, attitude and conduct.

Exercise 3.1   Being a professional

Each of the definitions of professionalism below highlights the arguments mentioned above and may give you some indication of the reasons you might refer to yourself as a professional. Do you recognise yourself?

Exercise 3.1 (continued)

Of, relating to, engaged in, or suitable for a profession: lawyers, doctors, and other professional people.	Yes/No
Conforming to the standards of a profession: professional behaviour.	Yes/No
Engaging in a given activity as a source of livelihood or as a career: a professional writer.	Yes/No
Performed by persons receiving pay: professional football.	Yes/No
Having or showing great skill; expert: a professional repair job.	Yes/No
A person following a profession, especially a learned profession.	Yes/No
One who earns a living in a given or implied occupation: hired a professional to decorate the house.	Yes/No
A skilled practitioner; an expert.	Yes/No

However, professionalism as far as a work-based learner is concerned should focus on practitioner control and proactivity in order to *develop* and *enhance* professional practice. The first step to you taking control is to reflect upon what it means to you to be a professional; without this you cannot effectively develop yourself as one.

Exercise 3.2   Identifying and enhancing your professional characteristics

Using the table below draw up a list of at least six personal qualities/characteristics that demonstrate you are a professional. For each characteristic you have identified, provide some evidence to back up your claim.

Personal quality/characteristic	Evidence
Example – *Expertise*	*Member of a professional body*
1.	
2.	
3.	
4.	
5.	
6.	

Exercise 3.2 (continued)

Now, reflecting on your list, provide a list of aims/actions to further improve your professionalism.

Aim	Action
1.	
2.	
3.	

What is a learner-worker?

Learning at, and through, work lies at the very heart of a work-based learning programme, whether encouraging future learning and development or reflecting back to recognise learning already achieved. However, when it comes to Performance Development Reviews or annual appraisals, why do we struggle to recognise the learning that has allowed us to contribute effectively as employees of an organisation? Is it that we don't think of ourselves as *learner-workers*?

Theoretical standpoints on workplace learning appear to fall into two distinct categories – those that favour the individual and their responsibility for learning at and through work, and those that favour the organisation and their responsibility to provide learning opportunities for the employee (Hager, 2001). Nevertheless, what is distinct about both arguments is the concept of workplace learning – meaning that we are all *learner-workers*. Our lack of skill in recognising this comes from a cultural background of learning that prepares us for work, through what we see as formal learning in schools, colleges and universities. However, the changing world of work now means that we need to acknowledge the fact that in order to remain in employment we must constantly learn, update skills and improve our effectiveness: indeed, be a learner-worker.

Boud and Soloman (2003) consider the variety of understandings that workers bring to the term 'learner-worker' and the problems and opportunities that this brings. Their research focused on interviewing people on their views of workplace learning and exactly what they believed it was. For some it meant personal development, while for others it meant only learning about the job or role they were engaged in, giving no real focus on personal development or goals that would initiate change. For many the recognition that we learn at work is only apparent when we consider what is termed as formal learning experiences (discussed later in this chapter); when we undertake training courses in-house or externally, where somebody else is in charge of the learning experience. We recognise this learning because it matches the pattern of learning we were used to in a classroom scenario. However, for Boud the workplace provides numerous and varied learning opportunities in a social setting where knowledge is constructed and transferred daily through the practice of work: through trial and error, discussion or even observation. As Solomon (2005: 101) argues: 'There is a relationship between work experience and learning, and therefore that being a worker also means being a learner.'

Nevertheless, Boud and Solomon (2003), while arguing and acknowledging that we are all '*learner-workers*' consider the strengths and weaknesses posed by using such a term, not only for the individual but also for the organisation. While being identified as a learner-worker demonstrates a willingness on the part of the individual to acquire knowledge, to those who are unfamiliar with the term there is an assumption that you are a novice lacking skills and competences. For example: would you feel comfortable visiting a dentist who openly stated that he or she was a learner-worker? Your natural instinct would mean that you would probably avoid such a practitioner. Conversely, if you think logically about medical advancement and technology, the dentistry profession is constantly evolving and changing with new procedures, meaning that learning is constantly taking place. You would hardly visit a dentist who did not improve their effectiveness by keeping up with advancements in their chosen career, in which case you may accept the term applied to this profession. However, if you employed a firm of builders to construct an extension to a house who, if asked, declared themselves to be '*learner-workers*', would your approach to them be the same? This is the dilemma that the term brings. Furthermore, workshop discussions with students have revealed that for some their experiential knowledge is undermined when they are repositioned as learner-workers, for example, when new processes and procedures are developed without consultation and the learner/expert sees no value in learning to develop new practices.

Exercise 3.3   Being a learner-worker

Draw up a list of the advantages and disadvantages to you and to your organisation of being a learner-worker.

	Advantages	Disadvantages
You		

Exercise 3.3 (continued)

Your organisation		

Being a *learner-worker*, as long as that learning brings value to you, your personal and professional development and the organisation that you work for will only be recognised as a strength once you and your peers acknowledge that everyone engaged in an occupation is continually learning in the day-to-day activities of work.

Developing a growth mindset

You must be reading this and wondering what is meant by a 'growth mindset'? To help explore what this means, ask yourself the question: *why don't we ever see an unmotivated baby?* Babies and young children tend to be inquisitive, not afraid to 'have a go'. They appear to realise that the more effort they put into something the better they will be at it. They persist despite setbacks, capitalising on mistakes and confronting their deficiencies headlong. They display the human traits of what Dweck (2006) calls a growth mindset.

A growth mindset is an orientation to learning that is characteristic of those who tend to believe that learning is incremental, that intelligence can be increased through effort and that mistakes are opportunities for improving and learning new things. However, many of us, because of the way we may have been taught in school and because we tend to engage in learning that is all about passing exams, may come to believe that we may only be able to reach a certain academic standard or achieve rather limited goals in our careers. This belief may begin with streaming you into a particular class, entering you for a particular level of exam or might even be the result of the type of feedback that you received from teachers or parents about your academic ability. Once you complete your formal education this belief may have limited you in terms of your ambition and career choices. You may even have come to the conclusion that: *some people are born intelligent, it comes easy for them, I can learn new things but my intelligence is limited* ... or that it is better to stick with what you are good at and not take risks that may highlight your weaknesses. Believing that you have only a finite amount of intelligence and/or ability that cannot be altered is indicative of a fixed mindset (Dweck, 2006).

From reading the above you may already have identified whether you have a growth or a fixed mindset – but why does it matter to you as a work-based learner what mindset you have? According to Dweck (2006), research has shown that people who have a fixed mindset tend to be superficial learners who give up when faced with obstacles, whereas those with a growth mindset tend to be deep learners who persist in the face of difficulty leading to ever-greater achievement and success. What is important as a work-based learner is that it is possible to change your mindset from a predominantly fixed mindset to a predominantly growth mindset so that you can achieve your full potential. Dweck's research suggests that to develop a growth mindset you need to:

- Believe that the brain can develop like a muscle – you can get smarter by exercising it.
- Push yourself out of your comfort zone by choosing difficult tasks that offer opportunities for learning something new or improving your knowledge and skills.
- Confront your weaknesses and think of strategies for dealing with them.
- Don't compare yourself to others either favourably or unfavourably – only be interested in improving your own learning.
- Focus on and recognise the *effort* you have made despite setbacks.
- Persist in the face of difficulty.

As a work-based learner recognising the value of your own experiential learning, you are probably already motivated to learn at work. To improve your ability to learn and achieve you should seek out new and challenging learning opportunities in order to develop both professionally and personally. It has always been the consensus that a job that is perceived to be challenging and therefore interesting will bring professional fulfilment and satisfaction; this can be achieved by developing a growth mindset.

Exercise 3.4   Developing a growth mindset

Identify and complete at least two work-related tasks that you know you will find difficult (for example, developing and giving a presentation to work colleagues) but which will offer considerable opportunities for learning new things and/or improving your knowledge and skills.

Keep a reflective diary of the barriers you face while undertaking the tasks and the strategies you use to overcome them.

When you have completed the tasks, draw up a list of learning points, what went well, what went less well and what you would have done differently.

Developing your organisation

What type of organisation do you work for?

Before examining how you might help to develop your organisation through your work-based learning programme it is useful to have some understanding of the type of organisation you work for. Your organisation can be categorised as either public sector, private sector or voluntary (third) sector.

Public sector organisations

These are financed through taxation and provide public services that are often free at the point of delivery. Such organisations are owned and controlled by central or local government and include Prisons, the National Health Service (NHS), the Civil Service, Schools and Libraries. The disadvantages of public sector organisations include that they can be too bureaucratic, which consequently may lead to inefficiency and high cost, with any losses made being met by the taxpayer. Such organisations may also be subject to political interference, which can result in excessive change and consequently change fatigue among employees. Macintosh et al. (2007), for example, highlight the difficulties of overcoming change fatigue when managing change in the NHS. However, public sector organisations do provide essential services to the public, are subject to central planning to meet identified needs and any profits can be reinvested in improving services.

Private sector organisations

These are owned, controlled and financed by private individuals or groups and are run as enterprises with the aim of making a profit for their owners. There are four main categories of private sector organisations: *Sole Trader, Partnerships, Limited Liability Partnership (LLP)* and *Limited Liability Company (LLC)*.

Setting up as a *Sole Trader* is the simplest way to run a business as it is self-managed and financed by an individual through assets and/or loans, with all decisions and risks taken by the sole trader. There are no registration fees, but accounts must be kept and audited for tax purposes via self-assessment tax returns. While an advantage for the sole trader is that all profit is theirs, a disadvantage is that all risk remains firmly with them and they are therefore personally liable for all debts incurred by the business.

Partnerships of two or more people can be set up and financed with money raised from the partners' own assets. A legal partnership agreement (although not a legal requirement) is often drawn up to ensure that each partner understands his or her individual obligations and roles and responsibilities, and partners share in the decision-making process and the risks, costs and responsibilities associated with the business. As each partner is classed as being self-employed, they must each submit an annual tax return. In addition, a partnership tax return must also be submitted. Partnerships are a simple and flexible type of business in which risk is shared among partners, but problems can arise if there are disagreements.

Limited Liability Partnerships (LLPs) are the same as ordinary partnerships except that liability is limited to the amount of money invested in the business and any personal guarantees the partners have given to raise finance. LLPs in the UK must be registered at Companies House and have at least two designated members. Designated members are accountable in law for failing to carry out legal responsibilities.

Limited Liability Companies (LLCs) exist in their own right, with company finances being distinct from the personal finances of their owners. Financed from shareholders, loans and/or retained profits, a Director or Board of Directors are responsible for management decisions. Shareholders may be individuals or companies and although they share profits in the form of dividends, they are not responsible for the company's debt. However, should the company fail, shareholders may lose some or all of their investment. As with an LLP, LLCs must be registered with Companies House, and in this instance all accounts must also be filed with them.

There are two types of Limited Liability Company: a *Private Limited Company*, which can have one or more shareholders but cannot offer shares to the public; or a *Public Limited Company*, which can offer shares to the public and must have issued shares to a value of at least £50,000 before it can trade.

Voluntary sector organisations

These are often referred to as 'not-for-profit' or 'the third sector' organisations. Such organisations exist for a wide range of purposes including (but not limited to) providing help to those in poverty, the advancement of education, environmental protection, animal welfare and advancement of the arts, culture heritage and science. They are managed as businesses, and targets and budgets need to be set in order to ensure that they break even to guarantee their survival. They raise money through a wide range of activities including fundraising events, grants, donations and through retail stores.

Exercise 3.5   Identifying the type of organisation you work for

As a work-based learner you may be expected to implement changes to your own practice and/or to your organisation. Find out what type of organisation you work for and draw up a list of things that may help or hinder the changes you might wish to implement.

Changes to implement	Assistance	Barriers

Organisational SWOT analysis

In order for any business or organisation to be successful, it must understand the competitive environment that it is a part of; in other words, it needs to be sure of the market and also be fully aware of competitors. Being aware of the business environment means ensuring that customer demands and expectations are met; defining the market accurately is the key to success.

Private sector organisations have traditionally operated in a competitive environment, and as such have had to ensure that they maintain an awareness of the competition. However, public sector organisations, since they were funded through government taxes, traditionally had few, if any competitors. This has now altered, and public and 'not-for-profit' organisations increasingly find themselves part of the competitive environment. For example, the university where you are probably studying for your work-based degree, while remaining in the public sector has increasing competition from Further Education establishments offering degree programmes, other universities, private educational providers and online distance programmes. In order to attract students to programmes of study a full understanding of the competition's offer is essential. This means that regardless of your place of work, your organisation serves *customers* by satisfying a need or a problem; however, you are not alone, as your competitors currently work in the same or similar marketplace and offer solutions to the same needs and problems. The need to retain existing customers and encourage potential new customers is a key principle of organisational development. This requires strategic planning, and a SWOT analysis is often used as part of the business planning process – it is useful in understanding an organisation's current position or situation, which when analysed can lead to decision-making in different contexts.

You have probably heard the term SWOT analysis – SWOT is the acronym for Strengths, Weaknesses, Opportunities and Threats. You may have even been asked to produce an individual analysis of your own when considering your professional development, as part of a Work-Based Studies module. However, you have probably completed a personal SWOT analysis without knowing anything about this developmental tool. The framework was first developed by Albert Humphrey, of the Stanford Research Institute (SRI), Stanford University, California, from research undertaken during 1960–70. The research was funded by the Fortune 500 companies (the list of the top 500 public and private companies ranked by gross revenue in the USA), to consider the problems of corporate planning and to seek a new system for planning change. The SWOT analysis was developed through interviewing 1,100 organisations and through the completion of a 250-item questionnaire completed by 5,000 executives (Stanford Research Institute, 2005).

Analysing the findings, it was discovered that a business or organisation can be divided into two distinct parts: the *base business* and the *development business.* The Stanford research showed that every 5–7 years the *development business* had to bring about change in order to remain successful. In order to ensure effective change there was a need for careful planning; hence the first prototype of the SWOT framework was published and tested in 1966. Furthermore, the SRI recommended that development should not only be left to managers to determine, but that employees should also be involved in submitting their own opinions about what was positive and negative about the business; this highlighted that positive involvement of employees in the decision-making processes leads to support for change and development.

A SWOT analysis tool is now commonly used as an initial step in the business planning process. It allows organisations to review their strategy, position themselves in the market place and determine the direction in which they want to take the organisation.

TIP Ways to use an organisational SWOT analysis

Discuss with others in your organisation whether you could use an organisational SWOT analysis to:

- assess the company's position in the market;
- examine methods of sales distribution;
- review a product or brand;
- assess a new business idea or strategic option, such as entering a new market or launching a new product;
- consider and evaluate an opportunity to make an acquisition;
- evaluate a potential partnership or change of supplier;
- evaluate potential for outsourcing a service, activity or resource;
- analyse an investment opportunity.

As highlighted, the original SWOT analysis recommended the inclusion of employees. This is where you come in, as many forward-thinking businesses and organisations use SWOT sessions, where employees are placed into teams of 2–4 people and are asked to brainstorm ideas for organisational development. At these sessions ideas are consolidated and reviewed before a list of solid objectives are achieved that will facilitate a successful strategy for change.

So how does the SWOT work and how can you gain a clear picture of your organisation's Strengths, Weaknesses, Opportunities and Threats? Let's take a look at a typical framework using a traditional template (Figure 3.1).

You will see that the SWOT matrix is divided into four elements according to the acronym, the first two letters of the acronym referring to internal

	Positive	Negative
Internal	**Strengths**	**Weaknesses**
External	**Opportunities**	**Threats**

Figure 3.1 Organisational SWOT analysis template

factors. This means that you need to consider the Strengths and Weaknesses of the organisation by evaluating the resources and experience available. As an example it is usual to consider:

- Human Resources – employees, target audience and any volunteers;
- Physical Resources – buildings, location, facilities and equipment;
- Financial Resources – funding, investment and other sources of income;
- Current organisational processes – hierarchical departments, employee programmes, manufacturing processes and so on.

When considering the above the key to success is to be honest, critical and evaluative, meaning that you need to identify where the organisation performs well and where it may be failing. Without objectively taking control of the internal factors, the external factors cannot be assessed.

The final two elements of the matrix, Opportunities and Threats, refer to the external influences on the organisation. As an example you may consider:

- Economic trends – local, regional, international, global;
- Market trends – technological, new products, change in customer/ consumer needs and desires;
- Demographics – customer/consumer age range, gender, culture;
- Monetary – costs of materials, exchange rates and so on;
- Government legislature/restrictions.

When drawing up a SWOT analysis you may find that there is an overlap, so, for example, what could be considered to be Strength could also be viewed by some as Weakness. Say investment is running high: it is a strength, but if you rely on external investment, you must keep investors satisfied so that they do not invest elsewhere, making it also a weakness. Furthermore, where strengths and weaknesses are listed they won't necessarily match the external Opportunities and Threats, although there should be some correlation between the two. This correlation should help you to identify an area of need. The SWOT analysis aids the organisation in strategically planning for change to satisfy that need. It highlights the opportunities that are open to an organisation for developmental purposes.

Exercise 3.6   Carry out an organisational SWOT analysis

Carry out an organisational SWOT analysis for a proposed organisational change (for example, introducing a new product or service, a new marketing strategy, outsourcing a service and so on).

Organisational learning

One of the main reasons why you decided to undertake a work-based learning programme may be that you have gained considerable learning through your work and life experiences but have no academic qualification that recognises such learning; perhaps you want to strengthen and develop your skills and knowledge in a particular discipline such as management, leadership or teaching. It is clear that the global pace of change is so rapid that people must continuously learn new work-related skills rather than rely purely on the skills they already have (Johnson, 2002). However, many people, some of whom are sponsored by their employer, may also wish to develop new and innovative approaches to work-based problems that will not only develop them professionally but will also develop the organisation in which they learn and work. Work-based learning programmes, therefore, not only provide professionals with the opportunity to make a constructive contribution to the vigour and health of the organisations in which they work, but also keep their own skills and knowledge up to date. This suggests that it is useful for work-based learners to understand something about the relationship between individual learning and organisational learning so that opportunities for developing both self and the organisation can be maximised.

So what is organisational learning? Organisational learning focuses on the naturally occurring processes of learning that take place in all organisations (Ortenblad, 2001). It refers to how knowledge is created, captured and disseminated throughout organisations, and is especially important because knowledge is a key source of competitive advantage and innovation in organisations. However, organisational learning may or may not have a positive impact on organisational development. While some organisations focus learning proactively to meet business objectives, others do so without effort and therefore may develop bad habits that harm the organisation (Kim, 1993). Bad habits may arise from the fact that individuals are not always rational beings who act logically – they use information they acquire in selective ways to support their own agendas (Easterby-Smith et al., 1999). As a work-based learner it is therefore important to have some understanding of how individuals learn at work and how individual learning is transferred between individuals and the organisation.

The first step is to acknowledge that you are a *learner-worker*, and that every day within the workplace you learn through formal, informal and incidental learning opportunities (Marsick and Watkins, 1990). What you need to be aware of are the differences between them.

Most of you will recognise *formal learning*, which generally refers to any intentionally constructed learning activity often available through an organisation's Human Resources Department and facilitated by a trainer/tutor.

Informal learning refers to any learning that is unplanned: it depends upon learning as a social practice. This occurs through the everyday activities of listening, observing, mentors who informally discuss a problem, and through reflective practice (see Chapter 2), which might happen through staff meetings, debriefs or communities of practice (see Chapter 9). It is important that you recognise the value of informal learning as a source of new knowledge that can be captured and transferred throughout the organisation. Many work-based learning students who have been taught reflective practice models recognise the value of such informal learning, as it focuses on the active engagement of the individual in seeking new knowledge rather than the organisation always taking the lead role.

Finally, *incidental learning* is seen as a sub-set of informal learning, as this is the learning and new knowledge that you gain through your own practice of trial and error. Such integrated development practices (Marsick and Watkins, 1990) are learning opportunities that are ongoing and arise within our daily work routines and take place within the domains of informal and incidental learning, often triggered by an internal or external stimulus.

In addition to understanding the different types of learning opportunities that are available to you, it is also important to understand what constitutes good organisational learning practices so that your learning will contribute to organisational development. This is especially important when considering work-based projects that can have tangible organisational benefits (see Chapter 12). An organisational learning checklist, which can be used to assess learning initiatives such as work-based projects, was developed by Ions (2012). The checklist (Table 3.1) was developed based on a review of the literature on organisational learning, and is a simple but useful tool that can be applied to a range of learning initiatives to ensure that organisational learning is considered as an integral part of the initiative. The checklist is based on organisational learning principles such as promoting continuous

Table 3.1   Organisational learning checklist

Checklist item	Completed (yes, no, working towards)
Specify objectives of learning initiative	
Link learning initiative objectives explicitly to organisational goals/objectives	
Identify and justify whether learning is (a) single (simple problem-solving) or (b) double loop (Transformative)	
State the proposed organisational impact of the initiative	
Create a detailed action plan including skills and knowledge necessary to achieve objectives and the learning resources required	
Identify the type of organisational culture in which the learning initiative will occur	
Identify how organisational culture might impact on the success or failure of the initiative	
Provide evidence of organisational impact on completion of initiative	
Provide evidence of dialogue with colleagues (own team and across organisational boundaries) in developing/undertaking the initiative	
Identify further opportunities for learning on completion of learning initiative	
Provide evidence of learning that occurred to meet objectives	
Provide evidence that individual learning was captured and transferred throughout the organisation	

Source: Adapted from Ions and Minton (2012).

learning opportunities, linking individual performance to organisational performance, promoting reflection, inquiry and dialogue, transferring learning from individual to organisation and consideration of organisational culture.

By using the checklist as a means of assessing learning initiatives in the workplace it is possible to develop work-based innovations that have tangible and measureable outcomes for both the organisation and the learner. Case Study 3.1 presented below provides an illustration of this.

Case Study 3.1   Organisational learning in practice

Alex works in business performance for a large manufacturing company. As part of her Work-based Learning Leadership and Management degree she undertook a work-based project to improve processes for decontaminating and re-using certain pieces of expensive equipment. Her company already delivered best practice but she felt that this could be further improved. The project enabled the process to be future-proofed. In order to successfully deliver the project Alex worked with her workplace colleagues to put in place a new system that improved the current overall process. Alex's project resulted in a new centralised cleansing unit, costing £1.5m, with a dedicated team of staff recycling the equipment. The unit has been very successful, as it offers a more efficient way of working.

Within the project Alex blended theory with practice in order to enhance her work operations, while also improving her project management skills and strengthening her leadership and management skills. Alex was collaborative, working with a diverse range of colleagues from right across the company; she successfully brought together academic research and knowledge gained through professional experience to make a positive contribution to the manufacturing processes.

By centralising the system, economies of scale and timing have been made. The organisational learning captured from Alex's project is now being applied throughout different branches of her company, and could be used by other companies also across the UK and globally.

Exercise 3.7   Improving organisational learning

Complete the organisational learning checklist below (explanation given in Table 3.1, Ions and Minton (2012)) to assess a work-based learning initiative related to your programme of study. The initiative may be a work-based project, a negotiated learning module or any other initiative that involves individual and organisational innovation.

Exercise 3.7 (continued)

Checklist item	Completed (yes, no, working towards)
Specify objectives of learning initiative	
Link learning initiative objectives explicitly to organisational goals/ objectives	
Identify and justify whether learning is (a) single (simple problem-solving) or (b) double loop (Transformative)	
State the proposed organisational impact of the initiative	
Create a detailed action plan including skills and knowledge necessary to achieve objectives and the learning resources required	
Identify the type of organisational culture in which the learning initiative will occur	
Identify how organisational culture might impact on the success or failure of the initiative	
Provide evidence of organisational impact on completion of initiative	
Provide evidence of dialogue with colleagues (own team and across organisational boundaries) in developing/undertaking the initiative	
Identify further opportunities for learning on completion of learning initiative	
Provide evidence of learning that occurred to meet objectives	
Provide evidence that individual learning was captured and transferred throughout the organisation	

Now identify four actions to improve organisational learning relating to the initiative you have identified.

1.
2.
3.
4.

Conclusion

Undertaking a work-based learning course offers considerable opportunities to enhance your own professional and personal development and the organisation in which you learn and work. This chapter has outlined some of the ways in which you can do this. You have considered the ways in which you can identify yourself as a professional and a learner-worker, how you can develop your professionalism and how you can remain motivated by developing a growth mindset. You have also examined methods for identifying and assessing development/improvement opportunities in your organisation that have the potential to become work-based projects, and, how you can enhance organisational learning through work-based learning practices.

Summary

1   Develop yourself as a professional by proactively focusing on enhancing your *proficiency* and *conduct* relating to your area of professional practice.

2   Working and learning are interrelated – recognising yourself as a learner-worker will positively change the way you think about both learning and work.

3   Recognise that to achieve great success you must embrace failure, because it provides you with powerful a tool for improvement.

4   Nothing is gained without taking risks – don't just take safe easy options and be prepared to push yourself out of your comfort zone by choosing tasks that offer opportunities for learning something new.

5   Organisational SWOT analyses can be performed in a range of contexts to identify opportunities for organisational development

References

Boud, D. and Solomon, N. (2003) 'I don't think I am a learner: acts of naming learners at work', *Journal of Workplace Learning*, 15 (7–8), 326–331.

Dweck, C. S. (2006) *Mindset – How You Can Fulfill Your Potential* (New York: Random House).

Easterby-Smith, M., Araujo, L. and Burgoyne, J. (1999) *Organisational Learning and the Learning Organisation: Developments in Theory and Practice* (London: Sage).

Evans, L. (2008) 'Professionalism, professionality and the development of education professionals', *British Journal of Educational Studies*, 56 (1), 20–38.

Hager, P. (2001) 'Workplace judgement and conceptions of learning', *The Journal of Workplace Learning*, 13 (7/8), 352–359.

Ions, K. and Minton, A. (2012) 'Can work-based learning programmes help companies to become learning organisations?', *Higher Education, Skills and Work-Based Learning*, 2 (1), 22–32.

Johnson, S. (2002) 'Lifelong learning and SMEs: issues for research and policy', *Journal of Small Business and Enterprise Development*, 9 (3), 285–295.

Kim, D. H. (1993) 'The link between individual and organisational learning', *Sloane Management Review*, 34 (1), 37–50.

MacIntosh, R., Beech, N., McQueen, J. and Reid, I. (2007) 'Overcoming change fatigue: lessons from Glasgow's National Health Service', *Journal of Business Strategy*, 28 (6), 18–24.

Marsick, V. J. and Watkins, K. (1990) *Informal and Incidental Learning in the Workplace* (London and New York: Routledge).

Ortenblad, A. (2001) 'On differences between organisational learning and learning organisation', *The Learning Organisation*, 8 (3), 125–133.

Sockett, H. T. (1996) 'Teachers for the 21st century: redefining professionalism', *NASSP Bulletin*, May, 22–29.

Solomon, N. (2005) 'Identity work and pedagogy: textually producing the learner-worker', *Journal of Vocational Education and Training*, 57 (1), 95–108.

Stanford Research Institute (2005) 'SWOT analysis for management consulting', *SRI Alumni Association Newsletter*, December 2005.

Suggested further reading

Elliot, A. J. and McGregor, H. A. (2001) 'A 2 x 2 achievement goal framework', *Journal of Personality and Social Psychology*, 80 (3), 501–519.

Firestone, J. M. and McElroy, M. W. (2004) 'Organizational learning and knowledge management: the relationship', *The Learning Organization*, 11 (2), 177–184.

Senge, P. M. (1992) *The Fifth Discipline: The Art and Practice of the Learning Organization* (London: Century Business).

White, T. (2012) 'Employer responsive provision: workforce development through work-based learning', *Higher Education, Skills and Work-Based Learning*, 2 (1), 6–21.

Chapter 4

Build your degree

Barbara Workman and Tracey White

In this chapter you will learn:

► how degree frameworks are constructed and what a framework can offer;
► what it means to study work-based learning as a subject in a degree framework;
► the benefits of flexible learning pathways when constructing your final award, from short courses to full degrees;
► how credits relate to the amount of time taken in study;
► the different levels of learning required within academic study and how they contribute to the stages of your degree.

Introduction

As a WBL student you will probably have a variety of formal and informal learning experiences, from different sources, which can be recognised as part of your work-based degree or university award. This means that your degree will be unusual, in that you, as the learner, are able to negotiate much of your own content and study pathway, within a structured university framework. The benefit of a structured framework is that it is devised to satisfy university rules and regulations, while still enabling *you* to build a customised, flexible and appropriate work-based degree. The framework gets its flexibility from its combination of 'empty' modules and different components, designed to be populated with content negotiated between you, your tutor and sometimes also your employer. Your HE award will ultimately meet both the university requirements and your professional development needs, due to its combination of previous work-based learning experiences with new university learning. Many WBL awards are created from units of study or modules which, when built together within a validated framework, enable a tailored and personalised approach, which encompasses your previous learning from experience; formal certificated learning; in-house training; and university modules.

University programmes focus on a subject discipline, which usually determines the core and optional topics of your programme; they are often prescribed either by a profession, such as medicine or engineering, or by experts in the subject area, such as geography or history scholars. For most subjects this is standardised within 'Subject Benchmark' statements, which set out expectations about degree standards and describe what gives a subject its coherence and identity, as well as defining the abilities and skills needed by a graduate to develop understanding or competence in the subject (QAA, 2014). See: http://www.qaa.ac.uk/assuring-standards-and-quality/the-quality-code/subject-benchmark-statements).

Some subject benchmarks include, or refer to, professional standards required by the external professional regulations of a discipline; these also ensure a level of consistency across UK universities in relation to subject content (QAA, 2014). A validated framework combines the subject discipline with the study components that together shape the content and structure of a university award. This can be visualised like a building scaffold, whereby each topic links into the next, or builds on the previous one, to create a cohesive structure. Such a scaffold or framework will allow you to create an award that meets your needs *and* is structured by the requirements of the university.

WBL is different from a university subject discipline as your own work activity and professional practice become the subject of study. Certain professions such as Art and Design or Medicine, for example, have a strong practice focus reflected in their university programmes, guided by the subject benchmarks, but for many of us our work is not guided by professional regulations, and therefore there are no subject benchmarks (see Figure 4.1).

WBL awards usually reflect their subject matter in the award titles, with names like: 'Professional Practice'; 'Integrated Professional Studies'; 'Work-Based Learning'; 'Work-Based Studies'; 'Professional Development Studies', or similar. These titles suggest that the subject of study is a combination of topics focusing on professional development and work-related learning, rather than a pure subject discipline in, for example, Arts or Science. In all HE degrees the units of study, often called modules, or courses, contain the academic components. The academic difficulty is expressed as levels; usually 4–8 at Higher Education (HE) level, with level 4 being the equivalent of year one if you were a traditional full-time undergraduate. How long you are expected to study a particular module, together with the form of assessment used (see Chapter 11), will also determine the level of difficulty associated with the learning. The academic topics tend to be divided into

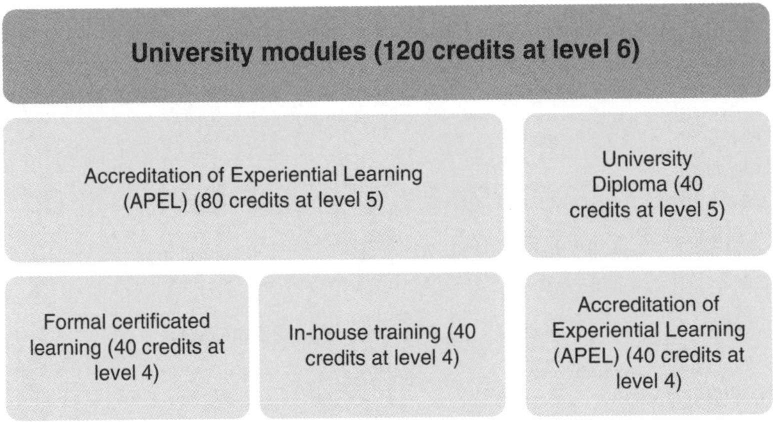

Figure 4.1 Example of a personalised WBL degree programme, constructed using a framework, incorporating study components from work, experience and university study into its existing format

several modules each academic year, reflecting the amount of teaching and learning time allocated and the subject complexity; this is then equated to credits per module. Universities therefore tend to divide each academic year into a series of modules, which can be, for example, 15, 20 or 30 credit sizes. They may be bigger than this, but the intention is to combine a number of modules, which add up to 120 credits per year. As you are a work-based learner you may not be studying in the traditional format of 120 credits per year, but your learning agreement (see Chapter 6) will state how you intend to gain the equivalent credits needed to pass your chosen qualification. Using a framework to gain your award allows you to use an equivalent route to a degree, or smaller award without the need for three years' full-time attendance at university. The example in Table 4.1 uses 20 credit modules, with the exception of the final module in the degree, the honours dissertation, which carries 40 credits, as it is often a larger component of the programme (see Chapter 12).

A WBL framework is designed so that you can use your learning from a variety of sources, provided it can be clearly evidenced as HE level, as part of your new university award. The sources you use might include: in-house training; Recognition of Prior Learning (RPL) (Chapter 5); Accreditation of Prior Experiential Learning (APEL) (Chapter 5); previous formal study such as HNCs (Higher National Certificates); HNDs (Higher National Diplomas); Professional Body awards such as CIPD (Chartered Institute of Personnel and Development); National Vocational Qualifications (NVQs); Higher Apprenticeships arising from National Occupational Standards (NOS), and more. A WBL degree will be based on the same number of credits and levels

Table 4.1   One example of a traditional undergraduate degree framework

Level	Core modules	Optional modules	Total credit required at each level
Level 4 Entry point Year 1	6 × 20 credits		120 at level 4
Level 5 Year 2	5 × 20 credits	1 × 20 credits	120 at level 5
Level 6 Year 3 Honours	2 × 20 credits 1 × 40 credits	2 × 20 credits	120 at level 6
Graduation			360 credits in total 120 at level 4 120 at level 5 120 at level 6

Table 4.2   Example of a work-based BSc (Hons) in Engineering Studies

Level	Core modules	Optional modules	Credit awarded	Credit	Total credit
Level 4			HNC Mechanical & Electrical Engineering	120	120 at level 4
Level 5	RPL module		Prior experiential learning claim HNC	20 40 60	120 at level 5
Level 6 Honours	Research Methods Continuing Professional Development Work-based projects × 2	Engineering Module		20 20 20 1 × 20 1 × 40	120 at level 6
Honours degree				120 at level 4 120 at level 5 120 at level 6 = 360 total	

as a traditional honours degree, but can be achieved in a variety of ways. For example, you may have already completed a HNC (approximately the equivalent of year 1, or 120 credits at level 4, of a traditional degree). To progress from your HNC you require further credits at levels 5 and 6 to achieve an honours degree, in a framework that usually includes specific WBL modules. You would also be able to include any relevant experiential learning, which you can provide evidence for, claiming these credits via RPL and APL (Chapter 5); your WBL might look like Table 4.2.

Case Study 4.1   Using your past learning within a degree

Robert lived in a mining community and left school with no formal qualifications. As was expected, he joined the local mine and became a coalmine worker. After five years he joined a rescue service, where he held his first management role. Over the next 20 years he worked in different areas of the business, taking the necessary training and development to support his career. For example, he was the Operations Manager responsible for overseeing the provision of services, ensuring that the organisation was running as smoothly and efficiently as possible. He also became the Management Representative for Quality, Environment and Health and Safety. Some years later Robert became the Commercial Manager for his organisation, thereby recognising his years of experience and proficiency of skills in the industry.

Robert was now at a stage in his career where he wanted to acknowledge his management skills in the workplace with a formal qualification. Given the wide range of his learning over the years Robert was able to make a substantial claim for recognition of prior experiential learning (RPL). Through discussion with his tutor he undertook an undergraduate degree pathway with an RPL claim for 240 credits, equivalent to the first and second year of an undergraduate degree (Chapter 5). Robert then went on to plan his studies for the final 120 credits he required at level 6 to obtain his degree (see Chapter 6 for a fuller discussion of learning agreements and Figure 4.2 below).

Figure 4.2   Recognising experiential learning within a degree (from Robert's Case Study 4.1)

Exercise 4.1   Learning from previous work and achievements

Read Chapter 5, about RPL/APL, to find out about making a claim. Reflect on what you have learned from your work history and experience, and what you think might form the basis of an RPL claim:

● What are the key learning and achievements that you have accomplished, particularly in the last five years?
● How did the learning that you gained through these activities inform future work or practice?
● What sort of evidence would demonstrate your learning, and how?
● How would you like to build on this learning in a university award?

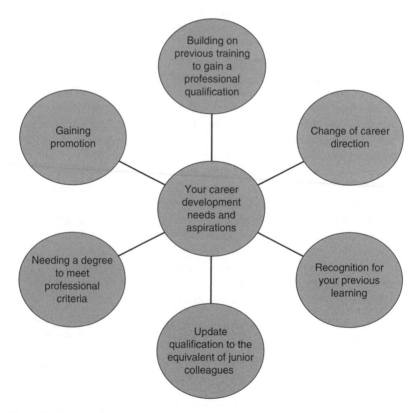

Figure 4.3   Reasons for studying for an HE award

Using a framework to get the qualification that you want

WBL awards come in a range of different sizes and levels from University Certificates, through to Foundation Degrees, Honours degrees and Postgraduate degrees, and many of these can be designed by using a framework. If you would like to use your previous formal learning to extend into a higher education award, you can start by reflecting on your career development needs (see Figure 4.3).

Exercise 4.2   Reflecting on further study

Reflect on why you are undertaking further study and make notes.

● What qualifications do you need for your role now or in the future?

_____

_____

● What are your career aspirations in five years' time?

_____

_____

● What skills do you need for your role now or in the future?

_____

_____

● What knowledge would you like to build on to equip you for the future?

_____

_____

● What level of study do you think you need?

_____

_____

Case Study 4.2   Introducing a WBL programme into the workplace

A private sector medium-sized enterprise made the development of its employees a Company Objective. Following an employee survey, they concluded that there were communication problems within the organisation due to employees working across six different branches throughout the United Kingdom. The organisation recognised that education was fundamental to meeting the business objectives and to improve efficiency. Communication skills were identified as vital for future business growth, and in supporting the expansion of the company.

The company worked with a university to develop a 30-credit programme leading to a Certificate of Achievement in Organisational Behaviour and Communications. It focused specifically on solving communication problems, and incorporated real-time work-based projects.

The findings were presented to the company directors and led to a greater understanding of the organisation's communication needs, resulting in the implementation of innovative new ideas. Participants on the programme were then able to use their Certificate of Achievement in a WBL framework when progressing to a work-based qualification.

Why are credits relevant?

Credits are transferable units, reflecting the amount of time you spend in study. One credit is equivalent to 10 hours' study, so an undergraduate full-time programme will have 120 credits every year, which is equivalent to studying for 30 weeks at 40 hours a week, which reflects an average university year. Part-time study tends to be between 60–90 credits per academic year, though some WBL courses offer 120 credits in a calendar year, which is about 25 hours of study per week for 48 weeks. Each credit includes study time spent in formal classes, (which could be online, at a distance or on campus), personal reading and study, and assessment preparation time.

So, a 20-credit module requires an average of 200 study hours over 10 weeks, leading to about 20 hours study a week. For WBL programmes this would also include time spent in the workplace undertaking project work or learning activities. Knowing how much time is required might help you to negotiate study time outside work to support your learning. It will also indicate to you how much time you should plan into your life in order to undertake a work-based degree. It is helpful if your manager knows you are studying so that you can undertake learning at work, whether this is through an independent project, discussions with colleagues or shadowing experienced staff while you learn specialist skills.

Exercise 4.3   Time commitments

Consider the time commitment that studying is going to require, and make some notes.
For example:

● Identify 20 hours of study in a timetable of your week – what might that look like?
Where would you fit it in?

_____

_____

● What might you have to give up temporarily?

_____

_____

● What would help motivate you to keep at the programme?

_____

_____

● How would you compensate if your weekly target slips?

_____

_____

● What support would you need at work and at home?

_____

_____

Every University Award is validated at a specific academic level from 4 to 8,
relating to the expected level of difficulty. Table 4.3 shows how the numbers
of credits and academic levels from level 4, 5, 6, 7 and 8 can create
qualifications ranging from a University Certificate through to a Doctorate
award in England and Scotland. These are being reviewed and updated at
the time of writing, but are not yet finalised. Current details regarding the
levels and credit combinations in other parts of the UK can be found at
http://www.qaa.ac.uk/en/Publications/Documents/Quality-Code-Part-A.pdf

Table 4.3   Credit distribution leading to main UK Framework for Higher Education Qualifications (as at June 2014)

HE qualifications in Framework for Higher Education Qualification	Levels	Total credits required for award
University Certificate	4	40
Certificate of Higher Education (Cert HE) Higher National Certificate (HNC)	4	120
University Diploma	5	40
Diploma in Higher Education (Dip HE) Foundation Degree (Fd) Higher National Diploma (HND)	4 & 5	240
University Advanced Diploma Graduate Certificate	6	60
Graduate Diploma	6	120
Bachelors Degree (Ordinary)	4, 5 & 6	300
Bachelors Degree (Honours)	4, 5 & 6	360
Post Graduate Certificate (PGC)	7	60
Post Graduate Diploma	7	120
Taught Master's Degrees (MA, MSc, MRes)	7	180
Professional Doctorates (credit-based) (EdE, DBA, DClinPsy, DProf)	7 & 8	540

Exercise 4.4   Counting your credits

If you have some formal qualifications, do you know what credits they are worth? Are they relevant for your current work role? Could you include them within a University Award? If you are not sure how many credits or what level they are at, seek advice from the college that awarded them to you. If you gained the qualifications abroad you can find out their value from NARIC (National Academic Recognition Information Centre), http://ecctis.co.uk/naric/.

Consider:

- Does this qualification contribute to my work?
- How can I build on it towards a formal university qualification?
- What is my next step in planning my qualification?

Table 4.4 shows the range of academic and intellectual skills that are required at each academic level, and should therefore be evidenced through your academic studies, within the framework of your chosen pathway. Many of these skills are integrated into your everyday work, but you may not have previously appreciated the range and complexity of intellectual skills that you employ on a daily basis. You may find it helpful to discuss your work role with a course tutor so that you can determine the equivalent academic level that you are already performing at. This will be useful when you gather evidence to make an RPL claim. By building your HE study programme within a WBL framework you can use this previous learning towards your new award, and it will help you to avoid repeating previous learning as you gather credits towards your chosen qualification.

These different academic levels in the framework are designed to develop your academic skills in relation to how information and knowledge are used. Level descriptors are used to describe characteristics of Higher Education qualifications and provide reference points from which to build a work-based curriculum. They are often written in a generic way so that they are useful in many different occupational contexts, professions or vocations (Workman and Maguire, 2011). These standards mean that you can be assured that your WBL degree is equivalent to a traditional programme of study, although focused on a different subject and often studied in a non-traditional way.

Table 4.4 summarises the academic skills at each level (see QAA and SEEC), your university will also have their own version to guide their qualifications that state how you can use the work-based framework to build your award. WBL descriptors have been included to show the types of work environment and contexts that you might be involved in when working at these academic levels.

Table 4.4   Summary of academic skills at each level

Academic levels	Description	WBL context descriptors (SEEC, 2010)
Level 4 – Certificate level	Develop a rigorous approach to the acquisition of a broad knowledge base; employ a range of specialised skills; evaluate information, using it to plan and develop investigative strategies and to determine solutions to a variety of unpredictable problems; operate in a range of varied and specific contexts, taking responsibility for the nature and quality of outputs.	Operates in a range of varied but predictable contexts that require the use of a specified range of techniques and information sources. Acts with limited autonomy, under direction or supervision, within defined guidelines. Takes responsibility for the nature and quality of outputs.

(continued)

Table 4.4   Continued

Academic levels	Description	WBL context descriptors (SEEC, 2010)
Level 5 – Diploma/ Foundation degree level	Generate ideas through the analysis of concepts at an abstract level with a command of specialised skills and the formulation of responses to well-defined and abstract problems; analyse and evaluate information; exercise significant judgement across a broad range of functions; accept responsibility for determining and achieving personal and/or group outcomes	Operates in situations of varying complexity and predictability requiring the application of a wide range of techniques and information sources. Acts with limited supervision and direction, within defined guidelines accepting responsibility for achieving personal and/or group outcomes and/ or outputs.
Level 6 Bachelors degree with honours	Critically review, consolidate and extend a systematic and coherent body of knowledge, utilising specialised skills across an area of study; critically evaluate concepts and evidence from a range of sources; transfer and apply diagnostic and creative skills and exercise significant judgement in a range of situations; accept accountability for determining and achieving personal and/or group outcomes	Operates in complex and unpredictable contexts, requiring selection and application from a range of largely standard techniques and information sources. Acts with minimal supervision or direction, within agreed guidelines, taking responsibility for accessing support and accepts accountability for determining and achieving personal and/or group outcomes.
Level 7 Postgraduate and Masters level	Display mastery of a complex and specialised area of knowledge and skills, employ advanced skills to conduct research, or advanced technical or professional activity, accept accountability for related decision-making, including use of supervision	Operates in complex and unpredictable and/or specialised contexts, requiring selection and application from a wide range of advanced techniques and information sources. Acts with initiative in decision-making and accessing support, within professional or given guidelines, accepting full accountability for outcomes.

(continued)

Table 4.4   Continued

Academic levels	Description	WBL context descriptors (SEEC, 2010)
Level 8 Doctoral level	Make a significant and original contribution to a specialised field of inquiry, demonstrate a command of methodological issues and engage in critical dialogue with peers; accept full accountability for outcomes	Operates in complex and unpredictable and/or specialised contexts at the forefront of knowledge. Acts autonomously and with initiative, often in a professional capacity with responsibility for self and often others.

Source: www.qaa.ac.uk/en.

Are work-based award frameworks equivalent to traditional degrees?

Most work-based studies programmes use their own university's 'Level Descriptors' (see also Chapters 1 and 11) to build WBL programmes. These are designed to ensure that their programmes are robust and adequately challenging, and framework-style programmes are no exception. They are usually based upon those suggested by the QAA (above) and are designed to consider the context in which learning occurs, so are particularly appropriate when describing learning at work and the types of skills and knowledge required for practice. SEEC also provide useful guidance in this area (SEEC, 2010), identifying key types of learning:

- knowledge and understanding: the subject and context knowledge;
- cognitive and intellectual skills: ability to analyse, synthesis and evaluate information;
- practical skills: problem-solving, action planning, project design;
- key graduate and transferable skills: team-working, communication and interpersonal skills.

These fit into the UK higher education requirements, which are described in the Framework for Higher Education Qualifications (FHEQ) (QAA, 2008), and so reflect equivalence to traditional programmes in terms of difficulty and amount of study required. The FHEQ also aligns to the National Qualifications Framework (http://www.ofqual.gov.uk), demonstrating equivalence against UK qualifications. The Level Descriptors have been mapped against European Standards to demonstrate parity and equivalence with European qualifications. If you have gained some of your experience outside the UK the learning from this experience may be relevant within your current programme of study, and European Standards mean that you can use it towards a UK qualification. The relationship between the FHEQ and European qualifications is provided by the QAA at www.qaa.ac.uk/en. Alternatively, if you have studied in the UK and wish to take your university award abroad, these guidelines will inform you of the equivalent qualification abroad.

Getting started on a work-based award

WBL frameworks enable professional qualifications and learning from prior work experience to become the building blocks of your degree. It may be that a work-based programme will start in your organisation with a smaller award than a degree as a way of introducing higher education-level study, particularly if you have not studied for a long time. For example, participants on a University Certificate may not have traditional higher education entry qualifications, so a certificate introduces higher education in an accessible way. Some universities offer in-house professional training to businesses, including assignments meeting university requirements, thereby recognising and building on your learning from work, when, perhaps, these certificates are accepted into a larger qualification as a progression route. Training in your organisation may be accredited by a local university that will award credits to those who have completed the training successfully. Academic credits may be used within future appropriate qualifications (usually for about five years), so it is worth checking whether any training you have undertaken at work was accredited and furthermore can now be incorporated into the WBL framework's study topics that you intend following. If you have several professional qualifications to claim for, such as apprenticeships, management training or National Vocational Qualifications you will find that there is not so much opportunity to also claim for your prior experiential learning as there needs to be a balance between your claims for previous learning and your new learning on the programme (see Figure 4.4).

Figure 4.4   Building on a Degree Framework to progress from Foundation Degree to Honours Degree

Case Study 4.3   Using the HE Framework to change sectors

Jay is a Mechanical and Electrical Project Manager in the public sector. He came out of the Armed Forces with a Foundation Degree in Building Services Engineering. While in the forces he focused on professional developmental courses rather than a degree as these would make him an effective work-based engineer, and enable him to gain Incorporated Engineer status.

   When Jay left the forces he built on his military experiences with further study and CPD, leading to a work-based distance learning top-up degree in Engineering Management. This degree framework allowed him the flexibility to utilise real engineering projects in his new organisation. This enabled him to gain the qualification and use work-based project assessments in his new workplace.

You might choose an alternative entry route to a WBL award, for example, through an Apprenticeship or Higher Apprenticeship. These involve a professional qualification and recognition of credits gained through WBL, which can then be 'topped up' to a higher education qualification such as a Foundation degree (240 credits) or Honours degree (360 credits).

Case Study 4.4   How building blocks work: A Foundation Degree for Professional Practice in Construction Operations Management

The professional body the Construction Industry Training Board (CITB) wanted to provide a professional development pathway for apprentices who were skilled in technical construction skills and were looking to develop their careers in managing construction sites.

   A Foundation Degree (FD) in Construction Operations Management was created to meet this need, and students entered the programme from three possible routes: Advanced Apprentice; A Levels/ BTEC Level 3 qualifications; or experience in the sector.

   Undertaking the programme required support from their employer and a workplace mentor. Figure 4.5 demonstrates how the programme was designed to include modules at each academic level to allow 'stepping off' points with university awards, or to progress to the next level towards the full foundation degree.

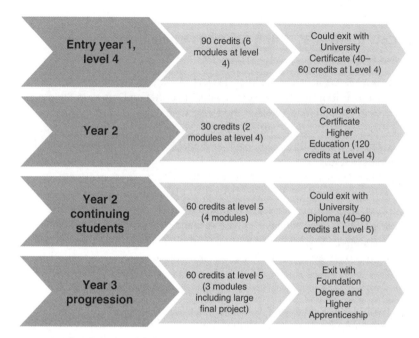

Figure 4.5 Part-time Foundation Degree Professional Practice in Construction Operations Management, pathway leading to a joint award with a Higher Apprenticeship (see Case Study 4.4)

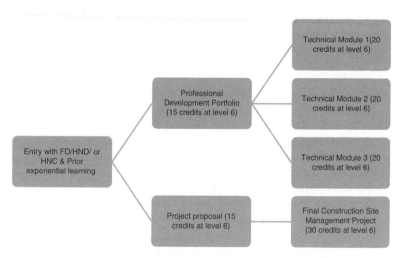

Figure 4.6 Progression on to graduate programme to gain BA (Hons) Professional Practice in Construction Site Management

This example shows how a WBL university framework provides stepping-off points for smaller higher education awards. This enables you to learn professional skills for the workplace at a pace and with a relevance that fits into your work and learning requirements.

Case Study 4.5   Progression from Foundation Degree to Honours Degree

After completion of the FD the students in Case study 4.4 are able to progress to the Honours Degree, Professional Practice in Construction Site Management:

Entry routes:

- FD Construction Operations Management;
- HND Construction-related award;
- HNC with appropriate experiential learning in the sector demonstrated in an RPL/APL portfolio (see Figure 4.6).

All participants are:

- sponsored by their employer;
- provided with a work-based mentor;
- given appropriate experience in the workplace to develop their skills and knowledge.

The programme is devised to run over 12–18 months, part-time, alongside the practice-based learning that is supported by the employer and mentor.

The construction degree programme (in Case Studies 4.4 and 4.5) demonstrates how a Foundation Degree, which was designed with employers and the professional body, includes academic studies and workplace learning and provides a stepping-stone to a degree by using a work-based framework and building blocks.

Designing your learning pathway using a framework

You may know what you want to study, but not how it will fit together; discuss this with your university or college tutors and find out how a framework could enable you to customise your own WBL award. Consider talking to your manager at work to see how your employer could support you, whether through study time, mentoring, help with fees or sponsoring you for a professional programme. For example, there could be additional government funding for Higher Apprenticeships (University level) becoming available in 2015, and you and your employer may be able to benefit from this. More importantly, your employer may wish to influence the study topics you choose to fill your framework with, especially if your employer is supporting your study financially. Explaining to your employer how your WBL framework operates is a good idea; they may not have heard about this kind of flexible programme and may presume that you need to attend the campus more than you actually do, as well as maybe being tied to inappropriate modules. The benefits of studying in this way could well be a selling point, so make sure you share the details.

Case Study 4.6   Building a part-time degree pathway

Kate has been a Care Manager working in a residential care home for the elderly for six years. She has already undertaken the statutory training in Care Management; this carries 120 credits at level 4. Due to her many years of experience it makes sense for Kate to undertake an RPL claim. The learning from this experience results in an additional 120 credits at level 5, for staff management and staff training, taken together with a module on care of the dying.

This gives Kate a total of 240 credits on which to build her programme. It took her a semester to put the RPL claim together, during which time she didn't undertake any other study.

This meant she chose to study 40 credits for each of the following academic semesters, allowing her time for her demanding job and other commitments. Figure 4.7 shows how she used specialist work-based projects within the Framework to complete her award over two academic years (the figure shows details of content).

Her employer funded her original Care Management statutory training, and then allowed her some paid study time to attend college and undertake private study to complete her award. The employer benefited because Kate was able to improve the standard of care where she worked, to the extent that the care home gained an excellence rating with the Care Home Inspectorate.

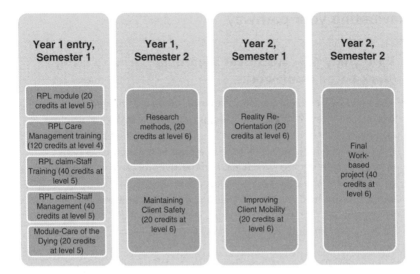

Figure 4.7   Kate's part-time pathway for a BA (Hons) Work-based Learning (Care Management)

Exercise 4.5   Choosing your professional programme

Are you studying an award to gain a professional qualification? Do you need to take an 'approved' course? You may want to use a WBL route so that you can afford to study as well as work, but check that the programme you choose will give you the right type and level of qualification.

Consider the following and make some notes:

- What programme options are available at your chosen university and what are your alternatives?
- Can you use your past learning to complete more quickly?
- How will this course prepare you for your choice of your career or consolidate your learning to date?
- What options are the most appropriate for you at this time?

Navigating your pathway

> ### Case Study 4.7   A student's learning pathway using a work-based framework
>
> Anisa had been working as a manager for 10 years. She realised that new starters were coming into the business with formal qualifications and overtaking her, so she decided to get a qualification to progress her career. As she worked full-time in a busy role she chose a WBL undergraduate degree, which allowed her to combine work with study, while also undertaking real work-based assessments to elevate her skills and profile in the business. Anisa also changed her role to become the company's Commercial Manager. Her studies could then support her new position and develop the way the company carried out its business.
>
> Anisa designed her own degree using the WBL Framework and negotiated learning contracts. Following discussions with her tutor, she incorporated a mix of RPL, existing modules and negotiated work-based projects. Her employer was involved in shaping the work-based projects, which were aligned to Anisa's objectives for her new role, as well as the future strategy of the company. Her degree was entitled 'Managing a Commercial Environment' (see Figure 4.8). RPL figured significantly as her previous learning experiences were included, while new work-based projects enabled her to gain further learning in her role in order to build on her past and existing knowledge and expertise.
>
> For Anisa, this journey of personal development was critical to her role and her ability to influence the organisation. She changed her learning methods from being 'taught' didactically in the past to being investigative and self-driven to succeed in her degree. The flexible framework enabled her to choose the content focus and link to real workplace issues, so informing her practice. The impact on the business from her studies helped to shape her role and responsibilities, and gave her more influence with the company. Anisa now has a greater understanding of the commercial environment, improved management skills, and a deeper knowledge of the complexities and interrelationships of business management with which to support current and future business activities as well as undertake her own development needs.

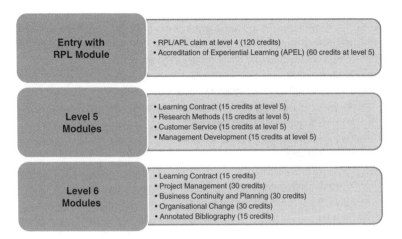

Figure 4.8 Anisa's pathway using a WBL Framework: BA (Hons) Managing a Commercial Environment (see Case Study 4.7)

What are the benefits of using a work-based learning framework?

Like Anisa in Case Study 4.7, the framework allows you to become increasingly independent as a learner, deciding when and how you will study and what topics you want to pursue. You can choose the pace of learning, which is usually part-time, so that you can work and study. You can negotiate the subject matter to reflect your needs in the workplace, and you can gain recognition of your previous learning, and, as a consequence, reduce the overall study time required. Being able to bring previous experience and certificated learning into your programme also means your award may be cheaper and quicker than a traditional degree, although the university standards, subject benchmarks and framework regulations ensure that it is an equivalent standard. The style of teaching on your WBL programme will probably differ from your previous experiences, in school or college, or even some other university courses.

TIP Inquiring about your work-based framework

- What type of WBL is your course? Will the work-based framework incorporate all your different learning experiences?
- Is your preferred programme accredited by a professional body? Some courses include professional requirements, and supervised work placements, to meet the required knowledge within specific areas. If this is the case, you should ensure that you can meet the necessary requirements.

- How is the framework delivered, and does this fit in with your work and lifestyle? For example, do you need a computer and internet connection to access online resources? Some courses may require attendance at classes: is this feasible?
- How does the framework structure enable your studies?
  - What is compulsory and what can you negotiate?
  - How do you negotiate your choices?
- Do you need any specific skills, such as
  - report writing,
  - giving presentations,
  - basic computing skills?
- How will you be tutored and supported?
- What methods of communication will be used
  - between you,
  - your tutor,
  - other students?

The impact of University Regulations on Framework requirements

When your programme of study is constructed through a Framework, the University Regulations guide the combinations of study components that you are allowed, and what is compulsory or optional. It is important that you are aware of these because your study choices, although flexible, will be structured and facilitated by the Regulations. Regulations at universities differ but they all govern:

- qualification standards;
- the construction of and processes involved in achieving a qualification;
- the admissions process to the courses;
- assessment of your work;
- progression requirements from one component of study to the next;
- your responsibilities and conduct as a student;
- the university's responsibilities for your learning;
- regulations concerning fee payments;
- attendance requirements.

When you enrol on a programme you are signing a written undertaking to follow the regulations in force during your period of study. All universities have a commitment to academic excellence and to assuring the quality of learning, teaching and supervision. The QAA and the UK Quality Code guide this for Higher Education by specifying academic standards and quality requirements. Further information about higher education quality requirements can be found at: www.qaa.ac.uk/assuring-standards-and-quality/the-quality-code/quality-code-part-c

The flexibility of building blocks of study in a customised programme will allow you to be in control of when, what and how you learn, and can make a real impact in your workplace and job role. Being able to choose your programme's content to make it relevant to your work, to fit study into your work pattern and use your learning and experience in a relevant way to inform your future career and professional aspirations can make a big difference in how long it takes to complete a degree, and keep you motivated throughout your studies.

Summary

1   Work-based degree frameworks offer flexibility and negotiated learning opportunities and build on your experience.

2   You can decide what topics to study and which university is best for you.

3   Choose what your final award will be and how long it will take; can study be part-time or full-time?

4   Ask what is expected in terms of study hours; attendance at classes; independent study; study support and so on.

5   What is in place if your circumstances change and you need to adapt what you have chosen?

6   Choose the right academic level of study – is this to consolidate your career, or to take the next step?

7   Negotiate your learning pathway: this should reflect *your* choice of award; *your* preferred learning style; *your* work focus; and *your* available timeframe.

8   Find out how you will learn, be taught and be assessed; these will motivate you and keep you on track, so check they are the best ways for you.

9   If you need to meet professional body requirements, make sure your chosen course is accepted by the profession.

10   Ensure you understand what the course expects of you; what the University Framework offers you; how your programme will be structured; and what the compulsory course requirements are.

11   Most of all, enjoy the flexible learning opportunities WBL frameworks offer your studies!

References

Quality Assurance Agency (QAA) (2008). Available at http://www.qaa.ac.uk/Pages/default.aspx (accessed 12 April 2014).

QAA (2014) Subject Benchmark Statements. Available at http://www.qaa.ac.uk/assuringstandardsandquality/subject-guidance/pages/subject-benchmark-statements.aspx (accessed 6 April 2014).

SEEC (2010) SEEC Credit Level Descriptors. Available at http://www.seec.org.uk/seec-credit-level-descriptors-2010/ (accessed 11 March 2014).

Workman, B. and Maguire, A. (2011) Interpreting Academic Level Descriptors for Work Based Learning. In B. Dhillon et al. (2011) *Making Employer and University Partnerships Work* (Faringdon: Libri Publishing).

Suggested further reading

Gordon, N. (2014) *Flexible Pedagogies: Technology-Enhanced Learning* (Higher Education Academy). Available from http://www.heacademy.ac.uk/resources/detail/flexible-learning/flexiblepedagogies/tech_enhanced_learning/main_report.

Kettle, J. (2013) *Flexible Pedagogies: Employer Engagement and Work-based Learning* (Higher Education Academy). Available at http://www.heacademy.ac.uk/resources/details/flexible-learning/flexiblepedagogies/employerengagement/report.

NARIC (2014) UK home page. Available at http://ecctis.co.uk/naric/ (accessed 9 April 2014).

NQF (2012) The Qualifications and Credit Framework (QCF). Available at
http://www.accreditedqualifications.org.uk/qualifications-and-credit-
framework-qcf.html (accessed 12 April 2014).

QAA (2011) UK Quality Code for Higher Education (incorporates the QAA,
2008, and The Framework for Higher Education Qualifications in England,
Wales and Scotland and the framework for Qualifications of Higher
Education Institutions in Scotland (FQHEIS), published by QAA in 2001).
Available at http://www.qaa.ac.uk/Publications/InformationandGuidance/
Documents/Quality-code-Chapter-A1.pdf (accessed 19 May 2014).

Quality Assurance Agency (QAA) (2012) UK Quality Code for Higher
Education; Part C: Information about Higher Education Provision. Available
at http://www.qaa.ac.uk/AssuringStandardsAndQuality/qualitycode/Pages/
Quality-Code-Part-C.aspx (accessed 6 April 2014).

To find out more about the European Higher Education credits and levels,
read http://www.qaa.ac.uk/Publications/InformationandGuidance/
Documents/Quality-code-Chapter-A1.pdf.

Make your learning count: Recognition of Prior Learning (RPL)

David Perrin and Ruth Helyer

In this chapter you will learn:

▶ what the Recognition of Prior Learning (RPL) is;

▶ how to use the accreditation process to make a claim for academic credit;

▶ how to include your certificated and experiential learning in your claim;

▶ how to scope out your strengths and expertise as 'Areas of Learning' you can claim for;

▶ how to make and submit a claim for academic credit, with appropriate supporting evidence.

Recognition of Prior Learning (RPL): Context and background

The Recognition of Prior Learning (RPL) process is used widely across the Higher Education (HE) sector both in the UK and abroad, as a basis for 'recognising learning gained outside a defined (or formal) higher education programme ... in relation to prior learning applicable to two widely recognised forms: prior experiential (or informal) learning and prior certificated learning' (QAA, 2013:4).

What this means is that your university or college will have a process that allows you to add credits for your past relevant learning to your current profile. Many work-based learning (WBL) students state that without RPL they would never have gained their HE qualification. Your institution might refer to RPL as the Accreditation of Prior Learning (APL) – this is just a difference in terminology, and the philosophy of the process remains the same. Obviously a process that facilitates the granting of credit in HE for learning that has already taken place offers work-based learners a time-saving and empowering device: time-saving because if you have already learned something in the workplace (and can evidence that learning) you will not be asked to do it again as part of your HE course, and empowering because it is a method which helps you to see just how complex and challenging your work role actually is. By attaching HE-level credits to learning you have gained elsewhere the university can acknowledge your expertise, skills and rich experience. For whatever reason, you may have not had the opportunity to attend a university in the past but RPL can help to show you that you have amassed important knowledge from elsewhere. There is a lot to be said for lifelong learning and the 'University of Life', and the RPL process can actually transform your experience of learning into academic credit.

Accrediting your prior learning can take one of two forms – and you might find that both of these are applied to your claim:

- Accreditation of Prior Certificated Learning (sometimes called APCL or RPCL);
- Accreditation of Prior Experiential Learning (sometimes called APEL or RPCL).

As stated above, institutions differ in what they call these processes, but the basic process remains the same and you will have the opportunity to claim for both experiential and certificated learning.

Accreditation of Prior Certificated Learning (APCL)

Previous learning that has led to the award of a formal qualification, and probably a certificate, is called 'certificated learning' and, when this previously rewarded learning is used in a new programme of study it is often called Accreditation of Prior Certificated Learning (APCL). This is usually learning that has contemporary relevance and an obvious coherence with what you are proposing to study now. 'Credit transfer' is the name of the formal process by which credit that has been awarded for the learning achieved on one programme (the certificate you hold already) can be recognised and accepted as part of the overall credit requirements on another programme (your new WBL study route).

Accreditation of Prior Experiential Learning (APEL)

Prior learning also includes your learning *for which no award has previously been conferred at all* ('uncertificated learning'). This type of learning has often been acquired in your workplace and has not involved conventional forms of HE study or assessment. Instead it typically takes the form of what is called 'experiential learning' – that is, learning while doing your job (see also Chapter 1 and the 'Work-based learning terminologies' section). When this learning has academic credit attached to it via HE processes it is called the Accreditation of Prior Experiential Learning (APEL).

Recognising your prior learning usually has one of two purposes: either to admit you to an HE programme, for example, instead of the more standard entry requirements, such as 'A' levels; or for the purposes of awarding you credit towards a named award. RPL is usually dealt with at your point of admission to an educational institution, whichever of the two outcomes above you are aiming for. On negotiated programmes of WBL, however, RPL is often engaged with after your initial admission, and during the negotiation of your learning pathway or learning contract in your institution's version of a 'diagnostic' or 'negotiation of learning' module. One of the many advantages of negotiated WBL programmes for adult learners is the way in which RPL, especially prior experiential learning, is addressed systematically as an intrinsic part of the negotiation of the learning pathway. In this way you are made aware of its existence and its possibilities, and therefore do not miss out on the opportunities it offers. Many students do not even know that the RPL process exists, which is a pity and also a missed opportunity. So please don't be put off by how complex it might be sounding at the moment!

Exercise 5.1 Consider your existing learning

Think about any areas of your existing learning that may be relevant to your current programme of study.
Start to make a list (you will return to this later).

Existing Learning

Product branding

Training course at college

Customer relationship management

Market research

We can't leave this introductory section without first clarifying the difference between specific and general credit:

- *General credit* refers to the credit value attached to successful completion of a block of learning or a programme, and always reflects the amount/volume of learning concerned.

- *Specific credit* refers to credit awarded towards a specific route or award. It is 'specific' because it relates directly to the content of the course you will be following. In this sense, what you possess as general credit might not be applicable or allowable for your intended programme of study, or may be only partly allowable (for instance, if you hold a professional qualification rated as 60 credit points at Master's level you might not be able to bring all those points into a prescriptive course like an MBA as there might not be a sufficient 'match' between the learning outcomes of the two courses).

How is RPL facilitated practically? – the 'how'

Investigating how universities go about facilitating RPL in a practical sense reveals there is a variety of practice across the sector, and you really need to be aware of this when putting together your claim. Be sure you take your tutor's advice; whichever process is used, you should always be clear who it is you should speak to and consult about RPL – typically an academic member of university staff, often called an RPL or APL 'adviser' or 'tutor'.

Exercise 5.2   Find your own RPL expert

Who is it in your institution?
Find out their details and go and talk to them.
Their details should be on the university website, or in your student handbooks.

This designated person will certainly guide you through the credit-claiming process. There are various ways in which procedures can differ; for example, some programmes allow you to submit just one RPL claim, whereas others will allow multiple claims (especially for prior experiential learning). Alternatively, some WBL programmes encourage you to think about RPL claims in an initial 'diagnostic' or programme planning module; whereas other programmes facilitate RPL through the means of a credit-bearing and assessed module in its own right, usually with a title such as 'Recognising Your Learning'. In this type of module you get credit for the processes of identifying and planning your RPL claim, as well as credit for the claim itself – the module might carry, say, 20 credits, but the RPL claim you put together in that module will bring you extra credits, if successful.

Exercise 5.3   Some things to find out about RPL

- Will any credit you gain be graded? (it usually isn't)
- What is the minimum and maximum credit you can claim on your programme?
- Is there a fixed period of time in which you must submit any claim?
- Are you able to negotiate how your claim is assessed?
- How will you receive feedback on your formative ideas for areas of learning?
- How does the timing for making credit claims fit in with your taught modules? (if you are taking any).
- How and when will you find out the outcome of your credit claims?
- Where is the result of your credit claim recorded? (on your transcript, for example).

Universities look at RPL in differing ways (and even call it slightly different things!) – but the processes will always be similar:

- You will focus on current and recent working arrangements, skills and practices. For example, how you have been involved during your career or job role with company staff development issues; HR policies and practices; leading and managing projects and staff; and numerous other topics depending on your job and sector.
- You will need to think precisely about how your knowledge and talent has been built up over the years. This might be called a 'skills audit' and be a formal part of your course.
- Adult learners tend to undervalue their talents – you will be discouraged from using phrases such as 'I am only a nurse' or 'I am only a gardener', and will be encouraged instead to develop an awareness of the skills you possess, and to avoid taking your skills for granted.
- Your progression over the years represents considerable learning – much of which is probably *experiential* learning – 'hands-on' in the workplace; this will be teased out.
- The RPL guidance you receive will show you how to differentiate between this *experiential* learning and any *certificated* learning, and how you can potentially claim for either, or both.
- Areas of Learning (see section later in chapter) are a commonly used way of claiming for experiential learning – they are like short essays backed up with evidence.

Using certificated learning – the past

Exercise 5.4   Consider existing certificated learning

Remember your list of existing learning? (Exercise 5.1)
Return to that list and think about certificated learning.
What learning have you previously done that has led to a certificated award?
Refine your list in order to separate certificated learning from experiential learning.

Existing learning	Certificated learning	Evidence/details
Product branding	No	
Training course at college	Yes	FD Business and Marketing
Customer relationship management	No	
Market research	No	

TIP It's good to talk

- You must speak to your RPL adviser about any certificated learning you may have.
- There are a number of key considerations when prior certificated learning is being discussed; the most important are described in the steps below.

Step 1: Size – establish the academic learning level and credit value

Much certificated learning is useful and represents significant learning – but it may not necessarily be credit-rated in HE terms (because it is not at HE level or simply does not have recognisable credits/level). For example, City & Guilds qualifications are almost invariably pre-HE in nature and cannot, of themselves, be directly used towards HE awards. Another example is if you have a professional qualification or qualification from an international college, you will need to establish clarity about what this could be worth. National Vocational Qualifications (NVQs) in the UK are sometimes credit-rated but usually not; NVQ portfolios are more normally used as the basis for experiential learning claims, rather than certificated ones, as a result. It is usually up to you, as the student, to establish the level and credit-rating, if any, of your certificated learning (internet searches are useful, but nothing beats contacting the awarding body directly to establish level and credit points).

Step 2: Time – when did the learning happen?

This is important as most universities have rules concerning 'academic currency', meaning whether an academic award can be considered to be usefully still in date. Typically, this is five years, meaning that you should consult your RPL adviser about any credits you have that are over five years old. If credit is deemed to be 'out of date' in this way all is not lost – many universities (including most operating flexible WBL frameworks) will allow you to demonstrate currency with a reflective review and/or presentation of evidence concerning how the learning has been applied and updated since, usually through engagement in the workplace. A typical example would be a manager with a HND in Business awarded seven or eight years ago who is encouraged to put together a reflective commentary with evidence about how the key areas of learning in their HND have been applied and extended in the last three years (a general outline of the content of previous qualifications will help this process).

Step 3: Relevance – what was the learning for?

For instance, if you are now on a WBL programme, working as an office manager, but flunked a geography degree several years ago, you may struggle to demonstrate the relevance of any credits you achieved. Even if the credits, level and academic currency are clear, the relevance to a WBL programme in the field of current practice might not be. Here the notion of specific (rather than general) credit comes into its own. On a negotiated WBL programme it is possible to use credit creatively, much more so than on a traditional or prescriptive programme, where credit is required to very closely match modules in the programme concerned. This is because negotiated WBL allows you to work towards creating your own curriculum, within certain parameters. This design determines what is relevant and what is not. Many universities will only accept general credit at certain levels of study too, sometimes only Level 4 (undergraduate first-year equivalent).

Step 4: Evidence – what is appropriate evidence?

This usually takes the form of photocopies of certificates and any accompanying documentation referring to modules, credits and levels (such as a transcript from the university Registry).

'Scoping' Areas of Learning – the potential

You have a large role to play in the design of the curriculum for your WBL pathway; this is one of the key advantages of WBL, and using the recognition of prior experiential learning plays a large part in this. WBL is predicated on the notion that the workplace is an important site of knowledge generation and experiential learning (Armsby et al., 2006). Much of your learning will already have taken place before you enrol at university and will have undoubtedly informed your current workplace practice.

The process of 'claiming' credit should be considered to be just that – 'making a claim'. You are proactively claiming that learning you have previously acquired legitimately, but which has gone unrecognised at university level, is usable and useful. It is therefore helpful to not see RPL as a process of 'opting out' of learning but of 'opting in' – it is the (albeit retrospective) granting of credits for learning that is just as genuine and powerful as that acquired through a traditional university course. Indeed, the very process of identifying RPL opportunities, assembling a claim and reflecting on practice with a view to future enhancement is a valuable learning process in itself – so valuable in fact, that many universities dedicate a module to the process.

Whatever method your institution uses for acknowledging RPL claims, their aim will be the same – to assist you in outlining your main areas of learning so that a claim can realistically be made for credit – this is the 'scoping' referred to in the title of this section. The scoping process will either take place in your initial programme planning module, or in a dedicated RPL module. In order for your RPL adviser to ensure that you are able to identify appropriate, relevant areas of prior experiential learning to claim for (including providing evidence), you will need to engage fully with the process. RPL considerations need to sit alongside wider considerations about your pathway of learning as a whole; it is important that any negotiated pathway is coherent and is assembled in a way that will provide a meaningful and holistic learning experience.

Provisional areas of learning

Exercise 5.5 Consider existing experiential learning

Return to your list of existing learning (from Exercises 5.1 and 5.3)
Take it a step further by considering your experiential learning;
Start by compiling a list of provisional areas of learning.

Existing learning	Certificated learning	Experiential learning	Evidence/details
Product branding	No	Yes	
Training course at college	Yes	No	FD Business and Marketing
Customer relationship management	No	Yes	
Market research	No	No	

To complete Exercise 5.5 you will need to:

- look closely at your past and current achievements;
- from all this experience, select themes or areas in which you feel you have significant learning;
- focus on what can you provide evidence for – evidence of learning is very important, as without it you will not be able to make a claim;
- decide what has the most relevance to your new award's other proposed content, and its title;
- determine what you have done that you would like to progress or build on.

When scoping out potential claims for prior learning, your curriculum vitae and your job description (possibly previous job descriptions too) can be especially helpful. These documents structure experience in terms of roles and activities – they are about what you do and have done. Underlying and informing these duties are skills, abilities and knowledge that you have learned. Some of these generic and transferable to other occupations, like project management skills; some are specific to particular work roles, such as skills needed to teach – for example, being able to construct a viable lesson plan. In this way, areas of expertise can be categorised into themes or topics, which are often called 'Areas of Learning'.

Exercise 5.6   Areas of Learning – compiling a provisional list

Job title	Main areas of responsibilities	Potential area(s) of learning?
Classroom assistant	Supporting teaching, research, health and safety and so on	1. *Helping develop lesson plans* 2. *Truancy* 3. *Early years development*
Marketing manager	Key client account management, research, planning and so on	1. *Customer relationship management* 2. *Branding* 3. *Market research*
Technician	Repair, maintenance and technical support and so on	1. *Digital Media* 2. *Project Planning* 3. *Human/machine interface*

Look at the above examples and start to make a list of your own:

Your current job title	Areas of responsibilities (see job description)	1. 2. 3. 4. 5.

Developing a learning CV

When you are working on your CV you probably think about your work-based and other experience in a chronological way. When you are developing your list of possible areas of learning for an RPL claim, it is helpful to think more thematically about experiences and pick out recurring and/or significant themes of learning that you can group together into areas. For example, if you identify 'Teaching young adults' as a possible area of learning for your claim, you have probably developed this area of learning through a number of activities; these might be:

- teaching maths in a secondary school;
- running a youth club;
- teaching a son or daughter how to play a musical instrument.

Each of these activities may have enhanced and developed your teaching abilities over time, in a tangential, rather than necessarily linear, way. It is these key areas of knowledge and skill that are identified in the areas of learning, which are then turned into an RPL claim and assessed for credit, rather than the work activities listed in your usual CV or job description. Many work-based study routes ask you to create a further CV and job description that focus more clearly on your areas of expertise, what you do at work and what you have learned from that activity, and so on (see Appendices 1 and 2). Formulating a coherent list of your possible areas of learning usually involves looking back over experiences to date across your entire career pathway. You are likely to have developed a great deal of skill, ability and knowledge over the years that has accumulated and informed your current practice – so how do you decide what to use as areas of learning for your RPL claim(s)?

Narrowing down your list of provisional titles

There is no single straightforward answer, and you need to negotiate with your university RPL adviser; ideally, and as a general guide, chosen areas of learning should be:

- **C**apable of being clearly evidenced in terms of supporting workplace artefacts.
- **R**elevant to the chosen pathway of learning and award you have negotiated.
- **I**ndicative of the type of skills and knowledge that are appropriate for the level of HE study currently being pursued.
- **S**ubstantial enough to have had a significant effect on your development, professionally and/or personally.

Used as a memory guide, the acronym **CRIS** might help you to remember these important points.

It is vital that you get feedback on initial ideas before they are developed further. RPL advisers have experience of seeing a variety of claims from a range of students and occupation types over time, and will be able to tell you whether or not your ideas, at this stage, are likely to result in areas of learning of appropriate size, content and academic level.

TIP **Scoping experiential learning**

If you are still struggling to think of areas to claim for try the following:

- List the types of education and training necessary/currently provided for the type of job you do – list everything you can think of.
- Now list how *you* have attained knowledge and competence in the fields covered (perhaps not by traditionally studying – but how?).
- Identify the aspects of this learning you have never received formal academic recognition for (or which you have developed/added to significantly since gaining relevant qualifications).
- Think about whether there is knowledge and a body of skills that you possess that others typically entering into your type of role don't have.
- This approach can also be adopted in relation to other jobs you have had in the past.

Mapping against modules

At this 'scoping' stage you also need to decide whether RPL is going to be claimed:

- against existing modules (that is, specifically matched against their outcomes);
- as a 'block' of credit that is relevant to the pathway, and perhaps split into named sections, which all map comfortably on to the award that you and your advisers have planned out;
- as a combination of the two.

If you are undertaking a traditional degree you would be more typically guided towards claiming against existing, specific modules. This is because most HE programmes are largely prescriptive with a set modular pathway and limited choice. However, the experiential learning acquired by you in the workplace is rarely an exact match for the learning identified in existing university modules, which is precisely why increasing numbers of universities are now offering work-based study routes – in acknowledgement of the need to be more flexible and to recognise how much is being learned in the workplace – at HE level. The RPL process can be used to facilitate a claim being presented retrospectively, for example, to apply credits to a work-based project (Chapter 12) that has already been completed (Lester, 2007). Many universities have empty or 'shell' modules (see Chapter 4 regarding frameworks) that you can use for this purpose. These provide handy 'containers' for RPL credits and can help you to identify and define clear learning areas, which can then be claimed for separately, or added to an RPL portfolio.

Amount of credit claimed for experiential learning (volume)

Deciding on the level of credit is fairly straightforward as universities have their own established *level descriptors* (Chapters 1, 4 and 11), which elaborate on the discernible characteristics of each level of study, complete with many examples of how these levels might be attained and what kind of evidence will prove this attainment.

Exercise 5.7   Find your own level descriptors

- Do some research and find a copy of your learning institution's level descriptors – they will really help you to map your experiential learning against academic credit.
- Sometimes they are reproduced in your course handbooks.
- Often they are online.
- Ask your tutor.

However, deciding on the *volume* of credit to be legitimately claimed is more complex (Workman, 2008; Pokorny 2012). Generally in HE in the UK it is accepted that each credit represents 10 hours of notional learning, though, as very often with taught modules, an emphasis on the word 'notional' is required because exact measurements are usually near impossible. In other countries, the volume of learning in relation to credit points varies, so check with your institution. Quantifying learning time on a discrete project at work may be easier than when a claim is based on learning in a subject or skill area (say, for instance, presentation skills), which may cross-cut a variety of workplace activities and represent learning accrued over an uneven period of time. What is used as evidence is important too – a significant report written for the workplace is likely to underpin a far greater volume of credit than sketchier or less substantial evidence like minutes of meetings.

Determining appropriate volumes of credit for RPL is complex, and because of this some universities have broad indicative word count guidelines for experiential learning claims, as well as for conventional modules: this is explained in more detail later in this section. This has the advantage of clarity for you, though some critics have argued that it is an approach that places an undue emphasis on outputs rather than inputs (Prince, 2004). Some universities, and yours may be one, try to equate areas of learning to essay sizes, which may be used for other, more traditional modules. For example, if a module carrying 20 credits assesses its students with an essay of a certain word count, could some comparison be drawn between this and your

20-credit claim? This is not to say that you should also produce the same amount of words, but it provides something for your Area of Learning, plus its accompanying evidence, to be compared to, even if rather different. You also need to be aware that some universities rely almost solely on their assessors to determine RPL credit volume *after* submission (Workman, 2008), although this practice seems to be less common in HE than it was.

Case Study 5.1   RPL in practice

Below is a practical, recent example of a student from the University of Chester who entered the negotiated work-based learning framework at undergraduate Level 4 on the initial programme planning module, 'Self Review and Negotiation of Learning'. As part of her programme planning process she identified a number of likely areas of learning for RPL claims.

Davina is a health service manager in an NHS Trust who has risen 'through the ranks'. She has negotiated to work towards a work-based Honours degree in Health Service Management. She doesn't have any certificated learning that is relevant to gaining credits for her degree, but she *does* have a lot of experiential learning built up over recent years managing a unit in the local hospital. In consultation with her tutor she was able to identify the following significant areas of learning:

- She had set up a new committee, which she still chairs, into an important new area of working in the Trust related to clinical audit.
- She wrote a comprehensive set of patient admission procedures that is still in operation in the unit she manages.
- She investigated the impact of a new piece of Government legislation and disseminated her findings on its implications for hospital workers, giving presentations to staff at all levels and in all departments.

There were lots of other, smaller Areas of Learning too, but these were the main ones she was confident of making a claim for. Treating these areas of experiential learning as work-based projects (Chapter 12) she had already completed, she wrote claims (with supporting evidence) for each of these projects to show that she had met the learning outcomes of the undergraduate Level 4 Negotiated Experiential Learning Module. In consultation with her tutor regarding the amount of work and effort she had put into these projects, she decided to claim:

- *20 credits* for setting up and chairing the committee;
- *40 credits* for the new procedures, as this was a major piece of work that had probably taken as much as 400 hours of her time in

---

Case Study 5.1 (continued)

learning the things she needed, with copious evidence of how the
procedures had been drafted and developed;
- *40 credits* for the dissemination project to other staff, another
significant piece of work that she estimated was the equivalent of
around 400 hours learning, with a variety of written evidence plus a
video presentation.

When she submitted her prior learning claim with her Self Review
module (20 credits) she was hoping to gain 100 credits worth of RPL
(20 + 40 + 40) at Level 4, enough to complete that level of her degree
programme (120 credits in total). She was successful in her claim, and
the next module she signed up for started her on Level 5, thanks to
achieving almost an entire level's worth of accreditation for her prior
experiential learning.

Timing issues

Timing is crucial for your RPL claim both in terms of workload and in
maintaining momentum. Many universities prefer the presentation of an RPL
portfolio that contains all the prior experiential learning being claimed for,
so that RPL is assessed and dealt with all at once. This allows you to move on
beyond the RPL process to the next stage of your pathway in the knowledge
that your RPL credits have (hopefully) all been granted and that this part of
your learning pathway is complete. However, it can also mean you working
on very significant and often time-consuming claims before receiving credit
for any of them, and, in such circumstances, it is not uncommon for you to
become slightly nervous while awaiting the outcome of your submission and
even to find it difficult to carry on with other study until you know how much
credit you have been awarded.

Other universities allow you to submit a number of RPL claims over time,
especially those universities that invite learners to package their RPL into a
series of retrospective work-based projects or similar. This is a more piecemeal
approach but has the advantage that you can concentrate on one claim at
a time and progress in an incremental fashion, in keeping with the spirit of
modular programmes more generally and, indeed, with how you will most
likely complete the rest of your study, if your pathway is negotiated. You may
even take other modules (taught modules or current work-based projects)
alongside working on your RPL claims.

Compiling claims for prior experiential learning – the process

Once you have scoped out the areas of learning and agreed some timescales, the second stage of RPL begins – the writing and compiling of your claim(s). This is the really substantial (and exciting) part of any credit claim and comprises the specific identification of the prior experiential learning you are claiming for, usually in written form (though presentations and verbal assessments are also usefully deployed by some universities). It must also include your appropriate supporting evidence, drawn usually from workplace artefacts that you have generated. So the majority of RPL claims will include these two key elements as standard:

- a *written claim* about the learning;
- an *appendix of supporting evidence.*

In the written part of the claim, you are typically expected to clearly describe, in a short narrative or report:

- the prior learning you are claiming for;
- the particular learning and skills that you have acquired;
- the appropriate supporting evidence (cross-referenced).

You must be aware that the learning being claimed for *must not* be the same as any learning you are claiming via certificated learning, or contained in other modules you plan to take, and it must be relevant to your proposed pathway of learning and ultimate award; in other words, you have to make sure you are not going to repeat your learning or double-claim and that your learning is appropriate for your programme.

There are two distinct ways of constructing a claim for uncertificated, experiential learning. The *first* is when you wish to make a claim for taught modules that already exist, for instance, modules from other programmes at your university. To do this, you will need to choose the modules you think you can claim for in consultation with your tutor/RPL adviser (for example, if you have negotiated a pathway towards an award in Management, you might wish to look at the modules in existence at the appropriate academic level in your university's Business School or School of Management).

You will then need a copy of the relevant module details for each of these modules. This will be called something like a 'module descriptor' – some universities might have a slightly different name, but it is a printed, and usually also online, document that gives key information about the module or unit of study concerned (its aims, content, credit points value, method of assessment, and so on). It includes the module's learning outcomes, which describe the learning that you are expected to have achieved when you pass the assessment for the module.

Having digested what the specific modules require and entail, you will then need to demonstrate that you have met the relevant learning outcomes for each module (without actually taking the module) you are claiming for, through writing a claim that clearly identifies, describes and reflects on your learning, and which is cross-referenced with appropriate supporting evidence.

TIP Share your ideas and take advice

It is always a good idea to speak to the relevant module leader(s) to:
- explain to them why you think your experiential learning matches their module/s;
- get advice from them about how you can best demonstrate that your learning encapsulates that intended by their module/s.

A general guide adopted by some universities (again, you will need to ask your tutor) would be to write a claim for each module that is *no more than half* of what would normally be required for assessment purposes. If your institution expects something like an assessment with a notional word count in the region of 4,000 for an undergraduate 20-credit single module, then they might also expect learners writing an RPL claim for 20 credits to produce no more than 2,000 words, plus their evidence. To produce more than this starts to feel like defeating the object of the exercise!

The *second* type of experiential RPL claim is for learning that has been achieved in the workplace but which does not exactly match or fit existing taught modules, or which you simply do not wish to match in this way. It is now typical for the majority of negotiated WBL students claiming RPL to use this particular method. The most straightforward way to claim for prior learning in this manner is for you to treat it as a bundle of retrospective experiential learning projects or independent learning activities. Write your claim to demonstrate your achievement of learning outcomes (or associated university-level descriptors mentioned above) by writing a short claim for each module, cross-referenced with appropriate evidence that can support the learning claim (see Table 5.1).

Remember – the credit you will receive for any experiential RPL claim is for the *learning* from your experience, rather than just the experience itself.

Table 5.1   Template for mapping learning outcomes for specific areas of learning

Level 4 outcomes (linked to level descriptors)	Ways in which this is demonstrated in this Area of Learning
Ability to communicate clearly	Narrative and evidence: *for example, marketing leaflets produced*
Ability to initiate, plan and co-ordinate a project	Narrative and evidence: *for example, project plan and Gantt chart produced, minutes of co-ordinating committee*
Ability to work effectively in a team	Narrative and evidence: *for example, group presentation materials created*
And so on for all of the outcomes at levels, 4, 5 and 6.	

Exercise 5.8   Constructing your RPL claim

Make some notes under the following headings. This will help you to sort the learning from the experience.

Did I learn anything?	Focus on significant learning experiences
What did I learn?	Identifying your learning
How did I learn?	Your learning style and associated theory
How do I know that I've learnt?	With evidence and theory

You will need to:

- clearly identify the skills, knowledge and abilities claimed for;
- include reflection on how this learning was acquired, could have been approached differently, and how it has been applied since or built upon.

TIP **Don't say it twice!**

The more evidence you have of your learning – and the more obvious it is that this evidence demonstrates the type of skills and knowledge associated with the level concerned – the less wordy your claim will need to be.

By way of example, if the main piece of evidence for a postgraduate RPL submission is a research paper that has been written for delivery at a conference, then the claim that identifies the learning and puts it in context, may be quite short (perhaps just several bullet points) as the level of academic engagement will be demonstrated by the piece of evidence itself. However, if the evidence you assemble for your RPL submission demonstrates the *content* of your learning but not necessarily its *level* (and this is quite often the case), then the written claim part of your submission will need to demonstrate the type of skills and knowledge required for the level concerned; this will almost certainly be with reflection on the learning achieved, supported by some academic referencing. Exactly how substantial this 'claim' part of the submission needs to be, within the suggested word count limit above – and how sophisticated academically – is an issue that should be discussed with your tutor/RPL adviser.

How the written claim is structured can vary according to the nature of the claim and the demands of particular universities. The example shown in Box 5.1 is typical.

Box 5.1   The structure of an experiential RPL claim

Introduction
Make sure that you clearly state the general area of learning to be claimed for, the volume of credit claimed, along with the level of study – and how your learning relates to what is expected at that level of study.

Bulleted table of the main knowledge and skills
The main knowledge and skills gained need to be identified in your Area of Learning and cross-referenced to module learning outcomes or level descriptors, if necessary.

An elaboration of the learning processes behind the claim
- how the learning came about;
- why particular approaches were taken;

Box 5.1 (continued)

- what worked well and less well;
- what could have been done differently and so on.

References
Cross-reference the presented evidence in the appendices:

- to relevant bodies of work;
- to academic books, journals, publications (include online publications if appropriate);
- to in-house manuals, procedures and guidance;
- your learning CV and job description;
- other areas of learning you may be submitting.

Be very clear which piece of evidence refers to which item of learning. One piece of evidence can be used for several items, so this will need to be cross-referenced with clear signposting for the assessor.

Conclusion
In your conclusion consider how the learning could be applied or adapted in the future, perhaps with an action plan, if appropriate.

When constructing the written element of an RPL claim, it is vital to remember that assessors are primarily interested in your *personal* learning at work – RPL claims should not consist of extended quotations from theoretical texts about learning, or be driven by discussions of theory. By their very nature, RPL claims are concerned with learning via experience, what you have learned by actively 'doing', not just reading about. This will have already taken place. Academic theory is primarily used in RPL claims as a useful external point of reference and to contextualise knowledge. Indeed, RPL assessors will typically know when you have understood a theory when you have successfully *applied* it, rather than just described it.

What makes good evidence? – the proof

What you use to evidence what you have learned, and thereby link to what you are claiming for, is of the utmost importance. All items in your appendices of evidence should be clearly labelled for ease of reference, and an appendix contents page included. You may well ask: *what form is the evidence of experiential learning likely to take?* The following is a guide to the type of evidence typically offered in support of prior experiential learning, though it is not an exhaustive list:

- Any of your assessment material that has not led to certificated learning.
- Reports and handbooks that you have produced.
- Similarly, presentation materials like PowerPoint slides, video recordings and so on, produced by you.
- Online evidence – such as Blogs, websites and Twitter feeds authored by you.
- Appraisals, testimonials and reports of your performance in the workplace.
- Any correspondence that provides evidence of your involvement.
- Products and artefacts that you have made/constructed.
- Minutes from meetings with actions assigned to you.
- Budgets or forecasts that have been put together by you.
- Briefing papers that you have written.
- Drafts and plans that you have produced.
- An academic paper or article that you may have written.
- Details of project work, procedures developed and so on.

Exercise 5.9   Making the links

- What evidence do you have?
- Think about the evidence you have to support your areas of learning and start your collection.
- Quality is more important than quantity – but at first gather anything you think helps – you can always prune back.
- Ask your tutor – and your fellow students and work colleagues, who might think of things that you have forgotten or taken for granted.

It is important that you abide by *ethical* considerations when assembling your evidence (and writing your claim) so as to ensure personal and business confidentiality where this could be an issue. If there is any doubt, it is worth consulting with your line manager about the suitability of material you intend presenting and discussing (sometimes it might just be a matter of blanking out certain confidential information in copies of documents).

Make sure that all your pieces of evidence are *appropriate;* just because a particular document exists and relates to an area of learning does not mean you have to include it. You may have already adequately evidenced the learning you are claiming for with other material. It is important that you select carefully and do not just include everything you can find – your assessor may tire of picking through irrelevant, repetitive, cumbersome material. Evidence should not be included just on the basis that it exists or is something you have done or produced – *its main job is to be relevant to the particular claim being made.*

Evidence must be *authentic.* Any claims you are making as to work undertaken on projects and so on in the workplace and your precise contributions to such projects needs to clearly and concisely backed up by testimonials and statements of authorship or authenticity from your line manager and/or mentor. You would do well to consider the advice of Wailey (2002), who has suggested that when putting together an RPL claim there are widely accepted criteria to adhere to; the key elements are:

- *validity* – the evidence and the learning outcomes claimed have a coherent match;
- *sufficiency* – the evidence, including reflection, has sufficient breadth to demonstrate *all* the outcomes claimed;
- *currency* – the evidence is capable of proving that the learning is of contemporary relevance or has a current application;
- *quality* – the evidence demonstrates the required *level* of learning achievement.

You could add currency and authenticity to this list; currency we have discussed already, but you also must ensure that the evidence you submit only relates to your own efforts and accomplishments. Wailey (2002) and Johnson (2002) outline and examine best practice in the field of RPL and its assessment at HE level, discussing techniques commonly used to facilitate prior experiential learning claims in particular. While these texts were not primarily written with learners on negotiated WBL programmes in mind, they are definitely *recommended reading* for you as you pursue your HE-level claim for prior learning.

Summary

1   If you have significant 'on the job' experiential learning (or certificated learning that might be difficult to 'fit' other programmes) you have much to gain from RPL.

2   WBL frameworks are ideal for helping you gain recognition for your prior learning (RPL).

3   Even if you have commenced your study it is worth enquiring about RPL to ensure that you achieve maximum impact both for prior certificated and experiential learning.

4   Remember to check if your general credit will be counted towards your degree or award.

5   Universities are still approaching this issue in different ways – a significant help in constructing your claim will be getting to understand your university's system (and terminology). Always seek advice from the tutor(s) responsible prior to submitting anything.

References

Armsby, P., Costley, C. and Garnett, J. (2006) 'The legitimisation of knowledge: a work based learning perspective of APEL', *International Journal of Lifelong Learning Education*, 25 (4), 369–383.

Johnson, B. (2002) *Models of APEL and Quality Assurance* (London: SEEC).

Lester, S. (2007) 'Professional Practice Projects: APEL or Development?'. *Journal of Workplace Learning*, 19 (3), 182–202.

Pokorny, H (2012) 'Assessing prior experiential learning: issues of authority, authorship and identity', *Journal of Workplace Learning*, 24 (2), 119–132.

Prince, C. (2004) 'University Accreditation and the Corporate Learning Agenda', *Journal of Management Development*, 23(3), 256–269.

Quality Assurance Agency (QAA) for Higher Education (2013) *UK Quality Code: Chapter B6: Assessment of students and the recognition of prior learning.* Available at http://www.qaa.ac.uk/Publications/InformationAndGuidance/Documents/B6.pdf (accessed 7 January 2014).

Wailey, T. (2002) *How to Do AP[E]L* (London: SEEC).

Workman, B. (2008) 'beyond boundaries: value and assessing experiential learning outside module templates'. In J. Garnett and D. Young (eds), *Work Based Learning Futures 2* (Bolton: UVAC), 72–83.

Suggested further reading

Armsby, P. and Helyer, R. (2015) 'Recognising and accrediting prior experiential learning'. In R. Helyer (ed.), *Facilitating Work-based Learning: A Handbook for Tutors* (London: Palgrave).

Challis, M. (1993) *Introducing APEL* (London: Routledge).

London Lifelong Learning Networks (nd) *Accreditation of Prior Learning (APL): Using Your Previous Learning and/or Experience to Enter Higher Education* Available at http://www.bbk.ac.uk/linkinglondon/resources/

apel-credit-resources/leaflet_PanLondonAPELLearner.pdf (accessed 7 January 2014).

McKelvey, C. and Peters, H. (1993) *APL: Equal Opportunities for All?* (London: Routledge).

Merrifield, J., McIntyre, D. and Osaigbovo, R. (2000) *Mapping APEL: Accreditation of Prior and Experiential Learning in English Higher Education* (London: Learning From Experience Trust).

Nyatanga, L., Forman, D. and Fox, J. (1998) *Good Practice in the Accreditation of Prior Learning* (London: Cassell).

Qualifications and Curriculum Development Agency (2006) *The National Qualifications Framework: Helping Learners Make Informed Decisions.* Available at http://www.qcda.gov.uk/libraryAssets/media/qca-06–2298-nqf-web.pdf (accessed 7 January 2014).

Quality Assurance Agency for Higher Education (2004) *Guidelines on the Accreditation of Prior Learning.* Available at http://www.qaa.ac.uk/Publications/ InformationAndGuidance/Pages/Guidelines-on-the-accreditation-of-prior-learning-September-2004.aspx (accessed 7 January 2014).

Quality Assurance Agency for Higher Education (2008) *Higher Education Credit Framework for England: Guidance on Academic Credit Arrangements in Higher Education in England.* Available at http://www.qaa.ac.uk/publications/ informationandguidance/pages/higher-education-credit-framework-for-england-guidance-on-academic-credit-arrangements-in-higher-education-in-england-augu.aspx (accessed 7 January 2014).

Wilcox, J. and Brown, R. (2003) [on UK Centre for Material Education] *Accreditation of Prior and Experiential Learning: A Student Guide* (online). Available at http://www.materials.ac.uk/resources/library/apelstudents.pdf (accessed 7 January 2014).

Planning and negotiating your learning

Elaine Hooker and Ruth Helyer

In this chapter you will learn:

► about some of the main theories, concepts and themes of learning;
► the commonly used terms and processes, as you 'return to learning';
► how to put a Learning Contract together;
► how to develop autonomy in your learning;
► the value of personal and professional development planning (PPDP) and continuing professional development (CPD);
► ways to cope with change.

Self-analysis, learning styles and some of the associated theory

As you embark upon your learning journey you need to consider your learning style; if you have been away from formal learning for sometime this is probably something you haven't given a lot of thought to. Learning styles are different approaches to, or ways of, learning. Most of us have a preference and use a particular way of taking in and processing information. The idea that we learn via individualised learning styles has gathered momentum since the 1970s, and much has been written and proposed (for example, Felder and Brent, 2005; Hattie and Yates, 2014; Honey and Mumford, 1982, 1984, 2006; Kolb, 1984). Learning styles are not foolproof, nor are they set in stone, but they can be a useful aid to understanding learning and are certainly a valuable first step and practical start for those returning to learning.

At the beginning of your work-based learning programme there will be an emphasis on self-analysis and audit, and learning styles will be an important part of these processes, which will involve you reflecting on not only what you have learned already through experience (experiential learning) but also *how* you learned. Many work-based programmes include a module focusing on just this. Undertaking guided self-analysis helps you work towards one of the biggest aims of WBL programmes: creating autonomous learners. Becoming an autonomous learner will see you take responsibility for, and control of, your own learning. This is a gradual process, usually starting with tutor encouragement, support and some formal learning. However, as the learning directly concerns you and your work role, and as your knowledge of the pedagogy and process involved with your learning matures, and subsequently your confidence, it will become easier to take ownership and develop into a successful, self-directed learner.

Psychometric tests are often used to assess learning styles, doing this by analysing personality traits, attitudes, abilities and knowledge. Many employers utilise similar tests especially for recruitment procedures; they measure and assess:

- your *personality traits* (The Big Five Test, Myers Briggs Type Indicator – MBTI), with more information at http://www.makeuseof.com/tag/ top-8-websites-with-cool-free-tests-that-measure-your-personality-traits/
- how you behave in a *team role* – http://www.belbin.info/
- how you behave as an *individual* (rather than measuring your personality type); and these can gauge how you may react in a given context using Neuro-Linguistic Programming and Neuro-Semantics – www. neurosemantics.com
- how you can improve both your business performance and your behaviour through *Emotional Intelligence* at Work – www.6seconds.org/ business

Revisit the results of your learning style assessment (and similar test results) on a regular basis to evaluate the changing nature of your preferred learning style, and examine the influence of various conditions on this established style. The most commonly used example is probably David Kolb's 1984 model based on his experiential learning theory and used extensively in education and training.

Kolb's model (Figure 6.1) focuses on two learning actions: 'perception' (how you take in information) and 'processing' (how you deal with that information).

Perception is divided into concrete experience and its polar opposite, abstract conceptualisation:

- *concrete experience* uses feelings and senses, for example, seeing, hearing and touching;
- *abstract conceptualisation* uses thought processes.

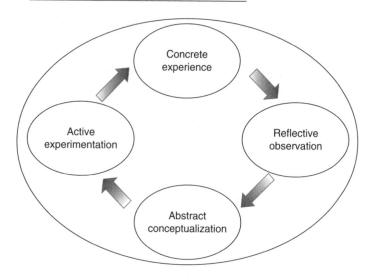

Figure 6.1   Kolb's learning cycle
Source: Kolb, 1984.

Information is perceived, then processed, often in one of two ways:

- *reflective observation* – thinking about the information;
- *active experimentation* – doing something with the information.

The *concrete experience* part of this cycle can be any learning experience that makes you reflect on things differently and can come from many diverse sources, for example, information and skills gathered from working with others, reading about something or having to deal with something for the first time. A good example is the notional learning hours attached to modules you are undertaking. The total of these hours is often in excess of 100 – causing many new students to gulp – this almost certainly will not come entirely from time spent 'with your nose in a book'; it will be a combination of the sources of learning suggested above, and others.

    At the *reflective observation* stage *concrete experience* is transformed into learning, because you think/reflect and consider the experience and ask yourself, 'How can I use this information?' and 'How will it help with my daily work tasks and enhance my work role?' The *active experiment* stage is the testing stage, where you work out and decide how the learning can be applied to become part of your skills and knowledge base. In reality Kolb's cycle need not be used in such a cyclical manner, following each step, neatly, from experience to experimentation, for although the model is often reproduced numbered one (experience) to four (experimentation), the cycle is actually continuous, which allows you to start at any stage.

Exercise 6.1   Why don't you try it?

Think about a new work task you have recently undertaken and the different stages that you went through to finish the task and achieve an outcome.

Kolb went on to develop the Learning Style Inventory (see http://www.infed. org/biblio/b-explrn.htm), an assessment method for individuals to assess and determine their own learning styles using four major categories:

- *Accommodator* – prefers concrete experience and active experimentation;
- *Converger* – favours abstract conceptualisation and active experimentation;
- *Assimilator* – tends towards abstract conceptualisation and reflective observation;
- *Diverger* – characterised by using concrete experience and reflective observation.

Kolb's learning theories have inspired a great deal of other work around how we learn, resulting in various student-friendly adaptations of these ideas being widely used. One good example is the categories suggested by Honey and Mumford (1982/1984):

- *Activist* – actively seeking through experience;
- *Reflector* – using thoughtful reflection to review the experience;
- *Theorist* – understanding the lessons learnt from the experience;
- *Pragmatist* – planning how to translate the experience into actions.

Although learning preferences might be considered intrinsic to your personality you *can* consciously adapt them. This ability to adapt is useful in a work situation, for example, see Figure 6.2.

To put Figure 6.2 into context:

- A learning experience (activist) could be managing a project for the first time.
- Thinking about the experience (reflector) might raise the point that several key things went wrong.
- Learning from the experience (theorist): there is evidence suggesting that most of the errors could be traced back to lack of communication.
- Going forward better informed (pragmatist): there are concrete actions to take to tackle this – instigate staff development training in this area for self and team.

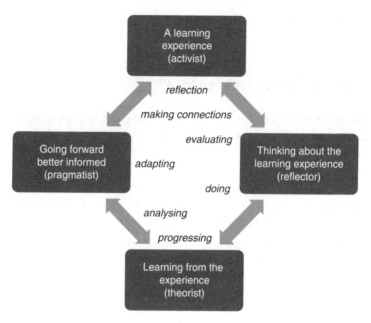

Figure 6.2   Adapting learning preferences

Adapting to different styles may not always be comfortable, but it will help you to actively seek out and learn in different ways and better recognise your areas for development. It might help to understand this concept if you compare it to something that may be more familiar to you as an employed learner – the process of Training Needs Analysis (TNA):

- TNAs focus on the learning required to accomplish a job role.
- They 'flag up' any gaps in an employee's knowledge or skills with regard to completing this job role.
- They use these gaps to indicate training needs.
- The aim of a personal TNA is to then identify appropriate training.
- TNAs can also continually evaluate the effectiveness of training.

Just as you have been asked to reflect upon and identify your own learning strengths and preferences, and the gaps this also draws attention to, a TNA reflects upon and defines the needs of a whole business or organisation to implement training, but then also attempts to evaluate and determine the effectiveness of that learning/training. Analysing your preferred learning style can be usefully perceived as a TNA at individual level (see Appendix 3, and Chapter 3).

What is an autonomous learner?

An autonomous learner is someone who controls his or her own learning. As you make your own choices about what you learn and how you learn it, you become an autonomous learner and have much more responsibility for planning, organising and 'doing' your own learning.

Throughout your learning journey you will be aware of certain characteristics developing. Some of these really indicate that you are becoming an autonomous learner, for example, your instances of self-awareness will increase and you will notice that your motivation to learn is increasingly coming from within you, rather than waiting for someone else to tell you. As your self-motivated learning, and willingness to take responsibility for your own learning journey, grow you will gain confidence in your own ability to plan and manage your personal learning. Part of this is 'knowing how the system operates', in other words, understanding the requirements and procedures of your programme. The next step is asking questions, as you begin to possess the critical thinking skills, as well as the research and information skills, necessary to pursue lines of enquiry. As you learn more about your own discipline, subject or specialism, and furthermore how knowledge has been, and is, created in your subject area, you become ever more autonomous. Your interdependence – the ability to work well with your peers, and to recognise when support and guidance from tutors and peers will be helpful to you – will improve enormously.

Being autonomous is not the same as being left alone to cope with everything. Your university or college will have support mechanisms in place (Chapter 7) to assist you, and these will include clear induction and guidance processes regarding institutional structures, guidelines and regulations, to, hopefully, demystify HE. Skills training and support, and the provision of opportunities for negotiated learning, for example, through the use of learning agreements or contracts, will also be provided. Project-based learning (Chapter 12) will allow you to hone your problem-solving techniques while managing your own projects, and independent study modules will improve your self-assessment and self-evaluation skills. One of the most important skills for an autonomous learner is reflection (Chapter 2); your skills of reflection will be improved enormously by the use of learning journals and diaries.

Autonomous learning definitely requires support, and some of this will come through electronic and technological means. Communities of learners that do not have the opportunity to come together as often as traditional students depend upon a programme that includes some blended and distance learning. The use of blogs and tweets to keep in touch with your peers becomes essential as you move from relative dependence to autonomy (Chapters 8 and 9).

Exercise 6.2   Becoming an autonomous learner

Questions	Response
Have you decided what you are going to learn?	*Yes/no/working towards*
Have you decided how you will study (including logistics)?	*Yes/no/working towards*
Have you considered the practicalities of your study?	*Yes/no/working towards*

- **Make a plan to facilitate your learning.**
- Create a means of creating your progress that
  - makes best use of your time;
  - issues reminders;
  - you will use;
  - is electronically based (possibly).
- Maximise on your own learning preferences:
  - times of day;
  - others present;
  - help needed.
- Be aware of the learning in life and work experience.
- Proactively look for problems and solutions.
- Consciously use your imagination and creativity.
- Constantly try to develop your communication skills.

Developing a detailed learning agreement (see next section) will really help you with achieving some of the above.

Negotiating your learning contract (also called learning agreements and learning proposals)

As a work-based learner tailoring your learning experience is very important in how you learn, what you learn, and in the attainment of a successful outcome; it also allows you to develop a sense of ownership and responsibility for your learning that brings commitment, added enthusiasm and satisfaction. The use of learning contracts across HE, and also in training, has become common practice in recent years; they can take the form of a written, therefore considered binding, contract between a tutor, learner/employee, and employer (or some combination of these). Whether printed, formal documents and/or online, interactive documents they will confirm:

- what you will learn;
- how you will learn;
- how you will be able to apply your learning to your job role;
- timescales involved;
- methods for evaluating and reviewing your learning.

There are many advantages in having a learning contract:

- you manage your own learning and can prioritise your preferred learning style;
- you become a self-directed, self-managed learner;
- you use your own work experience and job role to initiate new learning;
- very clear objectives, identified with your tutor, provide a direct pathway;
- they provide a formal record;
- their tailored learning outcomes are more relevant than standardised assignments;
- negotiation and communication between you, your tutor and your employer, are prioritised.

Review your learning contract on a regular basis to ensure that your learning matches your plan (and that your plan is still appropriate). Planning your 'programme of study' may well be embedded in a formal planning and development module; usually carrying credit and usually called something like, 'Individual Programme Planning'. Whether it is part of a module, or part of your own preparation, when writing your learning agreement you will need to identify: your development needs; your career aims; the needs of your employer; and your HEI's criteria for an approved programme of study. You might not have expected to plan your own programme in this way, but ultimately the process empowers you tremendously by encouraging the development of your reflective processes, and in turn your independent learning; for example, you may opt to include taught modules, work-based projects, distance learning, modules from other universities and so on. It also serves as an aide-memoire for module details and timings.

TIP **Completing a learning agreement (check your own institution's rules)**

- Which core modules does your award require you to undertake?
- Check the start dates for the modules you select.

TIP
- Plan work-based projects in advance so you can ensure they fit in.
- Usually you must study Research Methods (may be called Practitioner Enquiry) before you can embark upon a work-based project.
- Provide a full rationale of how your RPL/APL credits are relevant.
- Do your chosen modules have any pre- or co-requisites? It is compulsory that these are completed first.
- If you are including modules from other universities, check your HEI's rules around this.
- Similarly, check the rules around the balance between credit awarded for prior experiential and/or certificated learning and new study

Box 6.1 is a sample of what you might choose in the planning stages of completing your learning agreement.

Box 6.1   Sample learning agreement

Name:	Module:		Tutor:	
Objectives	Resources and Strategy	Timing	Evidence	Verification
What are you going to learn?	How are you going to learn it?	Dates to complete	How are you going to know that you have learned it?	How are you going to prove that learning has taken place?
Research Methods-	Enrol on and undertake research module at HE Level 6 at Summer University	September 2014	Achieving module learning outcomes. Application of the learning to job role – research and analytical skills	Assessment and learning review
Continuing Professional Development (CPD)	Undertake CPD module Level 6	September 2014 to March 2015	Understanding theory of CPD and applying learning to job/personal goals	Assessment and updated CPD plan and log

Box 6.1 (continued)

Name:	Module:		Tutor:	
Objectives	Resources and Strategy	Timing	Evidence	Verification
Work-based Project (WBP)	*Undertaking research methods module will allow me to determine the subject for my work-based project. Will register for WBP and liaise with my supervisor regularly to undertake a WBP*	*September 2014 to September 2015*	*Using knowledge gained and actual research skills to carry out a WBP Using both quantitative and qualitative methods to answer a research question*	*Assessment, dissemination and consultation with employer re WBP Leading to implementation of processes identified through WBP into the workplace*

Box 6.2 is an example of a completed learning agreement.

Box 6.2   Example of a learning agreement

Module	Level 4	Level 5	Level 6	Credits achieved	Date
RPL/APL – Areas of Learning completed	*100*	*100*		*100, 100*	*May 2014*
Research Methods completed			*20*	*20*	*July 2015*
Returning to Learning	*10*				*In progress*
Managing own Learning			*10*		*In progress*
Planned modules					
English module		*20*			*February 2016*
Information Handling	*10*				*February 2016*
English module			*20*		*July 2016*
Mentoring in practice			*20*		*September 2016*

Box 6.2 (continued)				

Module	Level 4	Level 5	Level 6	Credits achieved	Date
Work-based Project			40		*September 2016*
Level 6 area of learning			10		*February 2017*
Total credits	120	120	120	220 / 360	Complete degree

The information in Boxes 6.1 and 6.2 will help complete your own learning agreement (Exercise 6.3)

Exercise 6.3 Planning for the future

Scope out information for a learning agreement for your proposed study route, including:

- Title of your award.
- Area of focus of your study.
- Total number of credits required.
- Credit gained through RPL, either experiential or certificated, and why it is relevant to your programme (see Chapter 5)
- Credits gained elsewhere, for example, from modules.
- A status code for your modules, for example: Planned (P); Completed (C); In-Progress (IP).
- A record of Levels, Semesters and Years.

You are now prepared with your own version of a learning agreement, and a better understanding of what one is.

Personal and professional development planning (PPDP)

Personal and professional development planning (PPDP) has become an essential part of WBL, as a 'structured and supported process undertaken by an individual to reflect upon their own learning, performance and/ or achievement and to plan for their personal, educational and career development' (QAA, 2001). Exercise 6.4 provides some ways to kick-start your thinking.

Exercise 6.4   Kick-start your thinking

- How would you like your life to develop? Write a couple of detailed paragraphs about your thoughts and ideas.
- Write down several statements that begin with 'I want to'.
- Now list what might be the barriers to the above wish list (especially focus on where your learning and development could help).
- Write about what you would like to achieve in the next 12 months.
- Finally, write about what you would like to achieve in your career.

Completing Exercise 6.4 will help you to identify your personal strengths, weaknesses and what is important to you, in order to concentrate upon your training and development needs. You are now in a better position to start on the process of PPDP and to begin to map out some specific aims and outcomes for your educational, personal and career development, such as:

- What do I want to learn?
- How will I achieve this?
- What resources will I need to help me?
- How will I measure my success?
- What timeframe will I need to achieve my outcomes?

The primary objective for PPDP is to improve the capacity of individuals to understand what and how they learn and to review, plan and take responsibility for their own learning. This helps you to:

- become more effective, independent and confident as a self-directed learner;
- understand how you are learning and make connections to relate that learning to a wider context;
- improve your general skills for study and career management;
- articulate personal goals and evaluate progress towards what you want to achieve;
- adopt a positive attitude towards lifelong learning;
- strengthen your reflective skills (see also Chapter 2) and become more self-aware;
- become more analytical and more strategic about learning opportunities, including maximising on any overlap between personal strengths and professional ambitions.

The last bullet point is an interesting one, as you will sometimes find the acronym PDP used interchangeably for Personal Development Portfolio (or Plan), and Professional Development Portfolio (or Plan). There may be a requirement in your course, or one of your modules, for you to produce one of these, and good preparation for either is to create a portfolio containing your:

- Personal statement:

  Throughout history humans have kept diaries and journals to consign to print our thoughts, feelings, memories and goals, and this should be the start of your learning journey. Write a personal statement (which might well grow into a diary or journal) to describe where you have come from, in order to provide an account of how you have arrived at this time in your life and explain your ambitions for the future. Many different factors may have made you decide that this is the right moment for you to undertake a programme of study at university. Write about these factors, but also what you want to achieve from learning. This will be a useful self-analysis/ self-reflection tool (see Appendix 4 for an example of a personal statement from a WBL student).

- Curriculum vitae (CV):

  You need to develop a learning CV, which will provide an overall picture of your past learning achievements, similar to the more familiar CV that provides an overall picture of your previous job roles and responsibilities. However, your learning CV will give contextualising information on your past learning achievements *linked* to your job role and employment. Do not forget any voluntary or unpaid work that is sure to have learning involved (see Appendix 1 for an example of a learning CV from a WBL student).

- Job description (JD):

  As with your CV, the JD should provide a clear picture of your current roles, responsibilities and achievements. You should think of the term 'job description' as one that encompasses *the work you do*. A formal job description provided by an employer may be a useful starting point – but you will need to add to this formal document to ensure that it gives as full, accurate and realistic picture of your work role as possible. Remember you are not just listing your 'duties' at work – this is about what you know, as well as what you do. (see Appendix 2 for an example of a job description written for this purpose by a WBL student).

Preparing this basic content for your PDP moves you towards a greater understanding of your own strengths and development areas. These areas can also be identified or confirmed using various self-analysis tools, such as a SWOT or PEST (political, economic, social and technological) analysis. A PEST analysis tends to be the broader of the two as it aims to examine the external business environment impacting on you, whereas a SWOT analysis should be much more narrowly focused, in this case, on you in particular. A SWOT analysis is a well-established self-evaluation technique, aiming to identify the critical issues and enable you to come up with a sound approach to self-development planning which supports you in dealing with them. As with most self-analysis exercises SWOT will not, on its own, give you any specific answers but it will help you to organise the information required to develop your learning plan. Introduced in Chapter 3 as an organisational tool, we are now going to use SWOT for your personal reflection (see Figure 6.3).

Undertaking a SWOT analysis as part of your planning will allow you to:

- Consider your *Strengths* – honestly. Try to look at this from a third-party perspective: what strengths can an outsider see? How can those strengths and attributes help you to achieve your objective?
- Consider or reflect on any *Weaknesses* (or 'areas for development'). These will be those attributes that will be harmful or impede your performance, and will, in turn, limit your skills or your capability to achieve your objective(s).
- Use *Opportunities* for learning – these usually arrive from external origins, but can provide real learning opportunities. The trick is being able to identify (and seize) them when they come along. They can come from changes in our job role, secondments, promotion or participation in different working groups – in fact anything that gives an opportunity for learning ultimately leads to achieving your objective.
- Ensure that you counter any *Threats*, which can be explained as anything that will stop you from achieving your objective. Generally these are

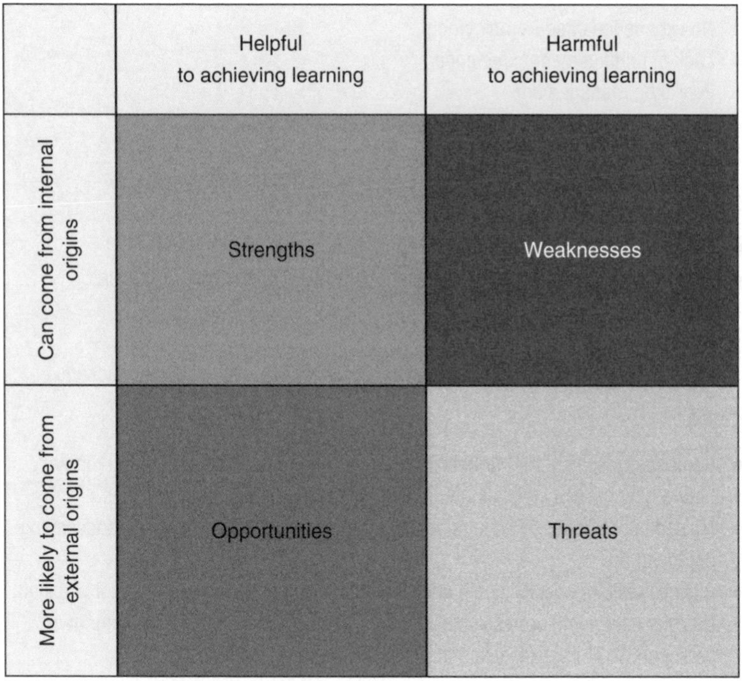

	Helpful to achieving learning	Harmful to achieving learning
Can come from internal origins	Strengths	Weaknesses
More likely to come from external origins	Opportunities	Threats

Figure 6.3   SWOT analysis chart

external factors, but not always: for example, they could include time management skills, personal problems, blockages that hinder your learning, lack of funding or clashing opinions in the management team.

Exercise 6.5   Be part of the SWOT team

SWOT analysis example: Seb the Landscape Gardener, who specialises in water features and aims to become self-employed.

Strengths:

- Technical expertise.
- Good communicator.
- Commitment to work long hours.
- Able to set realistic goals.
- Not afraid to ask for advice.
- Researched market thoroughly.
- Support of family and friends.

Weaknesses:

- Limited financial accounting knowledge.
- No experience of selling.
- No experience of self-employment.
- Lack of management experience.
- Poor time management.
- Technical expertise limited to a specific area – water gardens.

Opportunities:

- A growing market.
- University/college courses in horticulture to open up new markets.
- Courses/workshops to attend to gain knowledge in other areas – finances, management.
- Use home as office – saving costs.
- Practise artwork for designs – even computerise them with software package.

Threats:

- Competitors seeing the market opportunities and the need to be 'first to market'.
- Future government legislation (Europe/local/national) might hinder plans.
- Missed opportunities, if training in up-to-date methods/other areas of landscaping not taken up.
- Business failure possibilities if knowledge in business/ administration not widened.
- Designs need to be professionally drawn – not expert in this. Now do your own personal SWOT analysis using the same format.

Having now completed a personal SWOT analysis, you can combine this with your personal statement, CV and job description within your growing PDP to help identify the skills and knowledge that you most frequently use and any gaps; it is often these gaps that will prevent your progression, and it is worth spending sometime thinking about what they are.

Exercise 6.6   Mind the gap

Spend sometime identifying what factors may be stopping you from moving forward, and list them. Can these be easily resolved, and if so how? This will identify ideas for your development planning that you should include in your PDP.

Continuing professional development (CPD) and lifelong learning

CPD and lifelong learning are a holistic commitment to structured skills enhancement and personal or professional competence. They concern the conscious updating of professional knowledge and the improvement of professional competence throughout a person's working life. This is a commitment to being professional, keeping up to date and continuously seeking to improve. It is the key to optimising a person's career opportunities, both today and for the future (see www.cipd.co.uk/).

Continuing professional development, or CPD as it is commonly known, is used to varying degrees across employment roles and sectors. In any given group of work-based learners levels of engagement with CPD in the workplace will be wide-ranging. If CPD is taking place in your working life then it will without doubt be providing you with learning experiences and opportunities that you should record in your PDP. Those familiar with CPD have often gained that familiarity through necessity as many professions require that a certain amount of CPD is undertaken every year in order that practising employees retain their membership or fellowship of an association or other body (often represented by a set of letters after your name). A major bonus of being part of such an association is the community of practice this can provide (see Chapter 9), and alongside the obligation placed upon you to improve, expand and sustain the learning, skills and knowledge vital in your professional life, you will also probably be presented with ways in which you might do this, because of the networking and support opportunities a community of practice embodies.

Within groups of work-based learning students those undertaking regular CPD activities are usually from professions such as engineering, teaching, nursing and high-level managers, often from multinational corporations. However, given its obvious benefits, CPD is now also widely used within the public sector and within education. Employers value employees who are prepared to take responsibility for their own development and use the principles of CPD to aid the retention of the best staff. The spread and acceptance of WBL in recent years has also positively influenced the take-up of CPD activity, with its focus on self-development and ongoing learning. There are many overlaps, and a shared ethos, with PPDP, which is a process work-based learners rapidly become familiar with, and see the point of. These overlaps:

- place you at the centre of your own learning destiny;
- encourage you to examine any skills that may be dormant;
- build on the talent and skills that you already have in all areas of your life;
- develop new knowledge and skills, and therefore develop you;
- help you to recognise and achieve your potential;
- help you to respond to a rapidly changing world;
- develop your self-reflection and critical reasoning skills;
- above all, encourage lifelong learning, which, in the challenging world of work, will keep you, with your knowledge, skills, experience and added awareness of possible development areas, at the forefront of your profession, which in turn will keep you employed and employable.

The benefits of becoming a lifelong learner extend beyond the individual to the employer and company, and more widely to the colleges and universities where the learning is being facilitated. Sometimes one of the unexpected consequences of learning, because it encourages curiosity and reflection, and questions the need for change, is that you begin to think you are in the wrong job. Often, in busy working lives there is neither the time nor the inclination to pause and analyse what is happening – but learning encourages you to find time for self-development analysis, so be prepared!

Many universities and colleges deliver CPD and tailor this learning to the individual along with ensuring that you record your progress. You might find that some of your university's CPD offer fits very well into your own learning plan, and you should make enquiries as to whether you can use those modules. The CPD modules may well be unaccredited – this is often the case as those choosing to take them are not trying to obtain a degree or other award, but rather to keep up their professional standing. However, in the RPL/ APL process this is not a problem (see Chapter 5). The CPD modules that universities and colleges deliver really enhance their curriculum by providing a strong context between job role and learning.

Figure 6.4   The CPD continuum

Exercise 6.7   How the CPD continuum works

Examine the CPD continuum in Figure 6.4 and apply it to where you are now in your development or, even better, bring it to life by reflecting upon a situation, using these headings, especially taking notice of the overlaps between the quadrants. Using this in real life you will see – as suggested above – that learning doesn't consistently flow in one direction.

Becoming skilled with your own learning development needs via PPDP and CPD practices will help you to become an accomplished and confident learner. You will become expert at not only recognising your learning needs but also recognising learning solutions and opportunities, and as a consequence you will become more relaxed about taking risks, being creative and coping with change.

Coping with change

Much of this chapter has been about the benefits of planning, but, inevitably, given the pace of modern life sometimes your plans will have to change, often because of circumstances beyond your control. Change is both unavoidable and constant, yet individuals can react to it very differently. Some people seem impervious to change, and enjoy the challenges and opportunities it offers by embracing the adjustments that accompany new learning experiences, new job roles and new responsibilities.

On the other hand, others find change very difficult to deal with and can expend a good deal of wasted energy resisting inevitable changes and all that accompanies them. These people tend not to view any changes as offering opportunities, instead only seeing negative challenges. As your learning journey continues you will find yourself having to cope with increasing change, because learning is a disruptive process and what you learn changes and develops you as a person and as an employee; you need to pay attention to the transitional stages of change brought about during your learning journey, rather than merely focusing on the end product.

One much used coping strategy is to work through the 'Change Curve' suggested by Kubler-Ross (2014). Adapting Kubler-Ross's headings can suggest the phases of change as:

1. Shock
2. Denial
3. Anger
4. Depression
5. Acceptance
6. Integration

The original work from 1969 was based upon victims of grief. However, the ups and downs suggested are applicable to dealing with any kind of change.

Exercise 6.8   Coping with change

Think about the emotions that accompanied any change you have been through. Was the order above the same as the order of your emotions when met with change or were they different?

Whether you perceive change as a threat or an opportunity depends upon how prepared for change you are, your personality and the resource you have available to you for coping with change; sometimes changes that are out of your control can be frustrating, because although you can see the potential opportunities you are not in the position to make the most of them.

TIP Coping with change

- Information helps – if you hold that information be open and honest – if you need the information, ask for it.
- Don't let rumour and speculation take over – respond to facts.
- Look for choices within the change – but be honest about the possible consequences of those choices.
- If there is loss, try to think what might replace what is to be lost.
- Keep observing good practice.
- Make the most of both formal and informal discussion and feedback.
- Try to make connections between past, present and future practice.
- Look back to other periods of change – where hopefully there were some good outcomes.

We already know that job roles will change, probably more in this century than ever before. New job roles and new sectors are appearing all of the time, and people in the workforce must keep ahead of that change by constantly learning to update their skills and develop new expertise and knowledge. Learning is transformative and a vehicle for change; coping successfully with change and continually improving are intrinsically linked. As a work-based learner you are in a good position to see the world of work as it is now and know that, although impossible to predict, the future will be better if you are resilient, adaptable and equipped for change. Self-analysis, reflection and 'learning to learn' (see Chapter 2) all help you prepare for change by ensuring that you become more flexible. Learning through work can help you to cope with, or at least handle, change; the notion of a job for life has become an unfamiliar concept to the modern workforce, who are increasingly striving to develop themselves to possess the skills required at that moment in time for the job role they are undertaking, as multi-skilled individuals – in a rapidly changing society employees need to be adaptable and multi-faceted (Helyer, 2007; Helyer and Lee, 2012; Helyer and Lee, 2014). In this scenario it seems obvious that change management is a key skill.

There are five basic elements involved with change management, and being aware of what they are should help you to cope with change better, but also will help you to deal sympathetically with your colleagues:

- Different people react differently to change – there is no right or wrong way, but we can definitely get better at it.

- Everyone has basic needs that have to be met; any changes impacting on these have serious implications.
- Change often involves a feeling of loss and perhaps nostalgia – this is 'the good old days' scenario, and sometimes all that will support a new way of behaving is sufficient time passing to prove its worth and validity.
- Expectations need to be managed realistically; for example, objections to change might be selfishly motivated.
- Fears have to be dealt with. Examples of past successful change might help here – to dispel unfounded fears.

Adapting to change is part of the learning journey and will give you more confidence moving forward. However, planning, evaluating and negotiating your learning will put you firmly in control.

Summary

1 Examine all available resources to get to know your preferred learning style.

2 Plan your learning programme using PPDP and CPD (with those involved); use learning contracts as a mechanism to formalise your learning strategy.

3 Remember that you are a different type of learner from the traditional HE student; you will be working, predominantly, on your own. Maximise this opportunity to become an autonomous, self-directed learner.

4 Embrace the opportunities that arise from change; be prepared to adapt by developing your own learning tactics.

5 And don't forget, revisit your self-analysis exercises – you could be surprised at how much you can change and develop.

References

Belbin Team Role, *Frequently Asked Questions*. Available at http://www.belbin. info/, (accessed 28 May 2014).

Chartered Institute of Personnel and Development, *Development Plan and CPD Templates*. Available at http://www.cipd.co.uk/cpd/guidance/ CPDrecordandplan.htm (accessed 28 May 2014).

Felder, R.M. and Brent, R. (2005) 'Understanding student differences', *Journal of Engineering Education*, 94 (1), 57–72.

Hattie, J. and Yates, G. (2014) *Visible Learning and the Science of How We Learn* (Abingdon: Routledge).

Helyer, R. (2007) 'What is employability? Reflecting on the postmodern challenges of Work-based Learning', *Journal of Employability and the Humanities*, vol. 1 (Lancashire: University of Central Lancashire).

Helyer, R. and Lee, D. (2012) 'The 21st century multiple generation workforce: overlaps and differences but also challenges and benefits', *Education + Training*, 54 (7), 545–578.

Helyer, R. and Lee, D. (2014) 'The Role of Work Experience in the Future Employability of Higher Education Graduates', *Higher Education Quarterly*, 68 (3), 348–372.

Honey, P. and Mumford, A. (1982) *The Manual of Learning Styles* (Maidenhead: Peter Honey Publications).

Honey, P. and Mumford, A. (1984) *Using Your Learning Styles* (Maidenhead: Peter Honey Publications).

Honey, P. and Mumford, A. (2006) *The Learning Styles Questionnaire,* rev. edn (Maidenhead: Peter Honey Publications).

International Society of Neuro-Semantics, Welcome *to the World of Neuro Semantics.* Available at http://www.neurosemantics.com (accessed 28 May 2014).

Kolb, D. (1984) *Experiential Learning: Experience as the Source of Learning and Development* (London: Prentice-Hall).

Kubler-Ross, E. (2014) *On Death and Dying* (Scribner: New York).

Myers and Briggs Foundation (http://www.myersbriggs.org/my-mbti-personality-type/mbti-basics/) (accessed 28 May 2014).

Quality Assurance Agency (2001) *Guidelines for HE progress Files.* Available at http://www.qaa.ac.uk/Publications/informationAndGuidance/Pages/Guidelines-for-HE-Progress-Files.aspx (accessed 28 May 2014).

Suggested further reading

Billett, S. (2001) *Learning in the Workplace: Strategies for Effective Practice* (Sydney, Australia: Allen & Unwin).

Brown, P. C., Roediger, H. L. and McDaniel, M. A. (2014) *Make It Stick: The Science of Successful Learning* (Cambridge, MA: Harvard University Press).

Deakin Crick, R., Stringer, C. and Ren, K. (2014) *Learning to Learn: International Perspectives from Theory and Practice* (Abingdon: Routledge).

Merriam, S. B. and Bierema, L. L. (2013) *Adult Learning: Linking Theory and Practice* (San Francisco, CA: Jossey-Bass).

Rogers, J. (2007) *Adults Learning*, 4th edn (Buckingham: Open University Press).

Watkins, C., Wagner, P., Carnell, E., Lodge, C. and Whalley, C. (2000) *Learning about Learning: Resources for Supporting Effective Learning* (Abingdon: Routledge).

Chapter 7

Support and guidance for work-based learning students

Jenny Naish and Ann Minton

In this chapter you will learn:

- ► about the support available to you as a work-based learning student;
- ► how this might differ between institutions and companies;
- ► what a workplace mentor might do for you;
- ► the role of tutors on work-based programmes;
- ► the potential triangulation of employer – employee – university;
- ► what resources you need to support yourself as a work-based learner;
- ► questions to ask yourself to ensure you are prepared for the journey ahead;
- ► how to develop, enhance and motivate yourself.

Work-based Learning (WBL) is often considered to be a tripartite relationship, between you, your employer and your university. If this is so then you, the learner, are at the heart of this relationship, and as the central person it is important that you familiarise yourself with the various support mechanisms available to you. Your employer and the university have a range of support to offer you, which will be outlined in your programme or module handbook, provided at the beginning of the course. This is a useful reference document, signposting key support in a range of areas, often providing links to other documentation or areas where support is available, and giving specific guidance about the programme and assessment. It will contain the key contact details for your tutor and others who are involved in supporting you on your programme.

Work-based learning programmes are focused on your personal and professional development; they enable you to use your work activity to learn more about your role and to become an agent for change within your

organisation. This means that you are in control of your learning journey –
you are in the driving seat, your tutor and your employer will provide
maps, helpful guides and signposts (they may even pay for the journey!),
but ultimately you decide how you are to get to your destination. Use the
guidance that is provided and don't forget to ask if you need help.

Supporting yourself

When you undertake any formal learning, understanding your own
motivation for doing so is important, as is acknowledging what support you
need from yourself to meet those aspirations. You must acknowledge that
there are key differences between the motivation you put into the public
domain – 'I've always wanted a degree', for example – and the context for
why that motivator is your key driver – 'I didn't do well enough at school
to go to university when I was 18'. The deeper drivers are likely to remain
unspoken and may even be subliminal.

WBL means that a lot of your studies will be at work and possibly not in
lecture rooms. However, while a lot of the thinking, listening and planning
can take place in this way, the actual writing up of your work will have to
be in your own time and own space. Have you got that space organised,
and with access to appropriate ICT equipment? If you have to share that
equipment with anyone else, what deals have to be done for equitable
sharing? The majority of work-based learners report a huge learning curve
with ICT. Help yourself by pre-empting that learning curve and familiarising
yourself with the software that you need and by also attending in-house/
university IT courses (with some HEIs they will be free once you are a
registered student). Can your family, or the others that you are sharing the
equipment with, help you with this?

Intellectual agility and stamina

Under what circumstances (state of mind and mental alertness) are you at
your best for real hard reading, thinking and writing? If your best 'brain time'
is early in the morning, then do all you practically can to ensure that when
you have a big piece of work to do you can block out morning time to do it.
How accustomed are you with concentrating for long periods of time –
reading, note taking and writing, for instance? You will need to build up
that intellectual stamina, and that will include your own inner resilience and
perseverance for writing, rewriting and rewriting where necessary, to ensure
you are doing full justice to your capability and potential. The university will
have all sorts of practical and motivational ways of supporting and guiding
you – make the most of them and above all raise your levels of self-awareness

of what works for you and, equally, what does not! (Chapter 8 will provide you with some insights into using technology to help to keep you motivated).

How do your previous experiences of formal learning influence your hopes and expectations of WBL? Do you know what your preferred 'learning style' is? For example, use Honey and Mumford, 2006 (see Chapter 6), or indeed do you have any 'blocks' to learning effectively and successfully that you need to address? It is very useful to know what your likely strengths and weakness may be as a learner and to prepare for that. Given the emphasis within WBL on reflective practice (see Chapter 2), we recommend that you actively develop your reflective abilities (Moon, 1999; Walsh, 2008), as reflection on learning and then being able to apply that learning to your practice is one of the essences of WBL.

TIP Consider your potential stakeholder group

Let's consider the range, scale and scope of the support available to you from the differing stakeholders who have a role to play, and a vested interest in your success as a work-based learner.

Support from stakeholders is complex and varied.

Some you will use more regularly than others, and the support that they provide surrounds you, the work-based learner.

Everyone's stakeholder group is different and never static; your personal stakeholder group (employer, tutor, mentor and so on) represents just a few of the influences and therefore supporters of your WBL. There will be others, fellow students, fellow workers and a diverse group of professionals, not forgetting your family and friends. You will find it beneficial to think carefully about the level, extent and quality of influence these different groupings of people have on you, and indeed how much you choose to be influenced by them. In doing so you will probably find it helpful to remind yourself of the multiplicity of professional, and indeed personal, roles you occupy in your life: as friend, partner, employee, employer, student and learner, for instance.

Now you have thought about this, take some further time to consider who your stakeholders are and how you can maximise the combined strengths and opportunities of your stakeholders. What resources already exist (internal and external, psychological and practical), which enable you to support yourself? Remember that some stakeholders will be able to provide more support than others (for example, tutor), and that some support may be related to a specific aspects of your studies. This is a somewhat simplistic representation of your stakeholder group, but it is designed to help you to start to think about the nature and type of help that a variety of people can offer. You may like to revisit Figure 7.1 during the course of your studies, as new learning needs and objectives occur, and as you meet more people within your network.

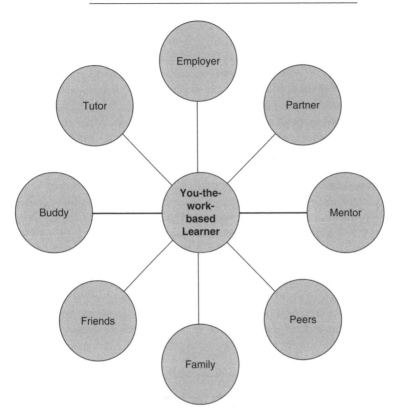

Figure 7.1   Your potential stakeholder group

Exercise 7.1   Considering your stakeholders

Stakeholder (for example)	Strengths	Opportunities	Resources	Practical
Tutor				
Line manager				
Team				
Peers				
Friends				
Family				

Be very mindful that the dual role of being both an employee and a learner within your own organisation may bring with it a number of advantages and disadvantages. How you make yourself aware of any tensions and/ or dichotomies the dual role of worker and learner may bring and your management of them could be crucial in your learning journey, especially once you are planning for and engaged in work-based projects (see Chapter 12).

A major advantage of being a learner within your own organisation has to be your in-depth knowledge of the organisation itself and your proficiency in your own job, together with the specialist knowledge that comes with that. One of your key characteristics as a WBL student will be your existing expertise; however, it is not always straightforward how you will draw on this. Are you too close to the issues and/or influenced by the values that come with them to see your work environment critically and analytically? You are likely to have close working relationships with colleagues who are highly supportive of what you are doing, but just suppose that through your studies an evaluation of your work environment is academically critical of that environment: how might you manage that, and would it be a tension for you? Thinking through the duality of your rights, roles and responsibilities as both a learner and a worker in your organisation, and both a student and an expert, and how you might support yourself is perhaps one of the most vital elements in preparing to deal with the duality of your roles in an analytical but also reflective way.

Exercise 7.2   Try to quantify the influence of your personal stakeholder group

Take sometime to review your own stakeholder group, and consider the direction of power and influence (it is unlikely to be solely one way).

- What does this look and feel like to you?
- Is the influence 'authoritative', for instance, or is it 'personal' or 'expert' (you might like to use different types of arrow – dotted, dashed, continuous for this)?
- How does your stakeholder group change over time?

Exploring this and revisiting it at various times during your study (but especially when you are doing your project) will enable you to consider the shifting dynamics of the group in relation to yourself, and therefore how you can make choices about how to gain the support you want from the stakeholder group members.

Figure 7.2 might give you a helpful framework for this process as it shows some of the different stakeholder groups, with arrows to indicate that the relationships and influences will be two-way. Some arrows will be larger at

Figure 7.2 Your personal stakeholder group

one end than the other as the influence is not equally balanced – remember that this may change at different times during your studies. Think about the quality and quantity of influence in these relationships; it will be uneven and not necessarily linear. You also need to consider the extent to which the 'power' components feel comfortable for you. Embolden or underline those that are more powerful than others.

TIP How much do you know?

Consider what you know in relation to Figure 7.2, but use some different ways of thinking about knowledge to do so:

- Know what?
- Know why?
- Know how?
- Know when?
- Know where?
- Know who?
- Know the context?
- Know for what purpose?
- Know with what consequences?

Key to this list of tips is 'know the context', because if you know the context (which as a work-based learner you are in a strong position to) then you can usually answer the other 'knows' even if only in outline, and it is useful to acknowledge the varying degrees of knowledge that you have for different events/occasions/scenarios and to ask yourself – 'is this sufficient?'

Case Study 7.1   Know the context

A group of managers working in the retail sector were all embarking on their work-based projects. Each one was different but all were within the context of food retail. As these were experienced managers they could use their contextual knowledge to shortcut a number of the 'know' questions. Some of the managers were doing projects related to training and development, with a high-level strategic objective of reducing food wastage on the shopfloor. This is a fundamental characteristic of food retail through factors such as:

- sell by and use by date;
- damage;
- deterioration;
- faulty packing.

Because these managers knew the context they also knew 'with what consequences' food wastage might be reduced, and the significant impact this would have on product turnover and consequently on bottomline profit and loss, as well as on stock management. They also knew that the 'know where' had implications at store level, backstage storage, regional distribution centres and centred on intelligent use of electronic point-of-sale product ordering. You may find it helpful to think about your own work-based project in the terms of the question you are seeking to explore, and then asking yourself the 'know' questions, starting with 'know the context'.

Support from your university

The university is there to support and guide you, and has a range of support mechanisms to help you. You should use them when required. One of the key characteristics of university learning is being an 'autonomous' learner. This doesn't mean that you are expected to do everything alone; it simply means that you should ask for and use the many means of support and guidance available to you when you need help.

One of the most important aspects of support from the university is access to the library. Most universities offer online facilities for students who are studying away from the campus. Librarians are information retrieval and knowledge management experts, who can guide you to the search mechanisms you need and also provide access to a range of study skills resources, including study buddies.

It is important that you access the library services and refer to academic books and journal articles to underpin the knowledge and experience you have gained through work, so that you can reflect upon and evaluate your experiences – this is another characteristic of university learning, and differentiates Higher Education WBL from other vocational forms of learning such as NVQs.

Librarians are often willing to help students in identifying key sources of literature to support their studies; a reading list will be available in your course handbook to give you a start. You should make the most of this and ask whether your university's library enables you to order books, journals, articles and so on online, and if these can be posted to you direct. You may also be able access to reciprocal rights facilities if you are working away from home, for example, in another town with a university.

The university will have a virtual learning environment (VLE), for example Blackboard or Moodle, which will host a variety of learning support materials. This often includes copies of presentations from face-to-face sessions, access to specialist software relating to your area of study, recommended reading and links to interesting and useful online resources. Sometimes the assessment for your modules will be hosted online or will provide access to discussion boards or other social media sites to enable interaction with your peers (see Chapter 8).

Universities also offer a range of in-depth support for all students. WBL students with specific learning difficulties such as dyslexia or disabilities such as hearing impairment should take the opportunity to discuss their needs as soon as possible with their tutor (perhaps even before the course starts), who may well refer them to specialist advisors, or counselling and other pastoral support services. It is important to discuss any specific needs with the university, in order that you are able to access the appropriate support to enable you to succeed.

Case Study 7.2   Always ask for extra help

Amanda is undertaking a work-based programme, designed with her employer. She has dyslexia. She discusses this with her tutor, who refers her for guidance to specialist support within the university. A plan is prepared that helps Amanda with access to equipment to help her, together with guidance for her tutor on the layout of hand outs

Case Study 7.2 (continued)

that will support her. This is held in Amanda's file on a confidential basis but enables her tutor to be able to note this in terms of possible extenuating circumstances at assessment.

If your organisation is sponsoring you in your studies, there may be a formal contractual relationship between your organisation and the university. However, the university also has a contract with you as a student, which covers things such as confidentiality and your access to support services. You may never need these, but the knowledge that you have access to free counselling, information, advice and guidance beyond your employer is an additional resource to you, especially if you do not wish your employer to be aware of, or involved in, such support. Think of these as additional layers to your networking resources both professionally and personally and, as such, make the most of them.

Support from your tutor

In WBL programmes your relationship with your tutor is unconventional in comparison to the tutor/student relationships on traditional degree programmes; communicating as equals in the learning process is key (see 'Learning conversations', below). Even though you may have no experience of traditional higher education we are sure that you have ideas and images in your mind that sum it up for you (see Exercise 1.2 in Chapter 1).

Here is a quick summary of some of the typical characteristics of a work-based tutor:

- Provides a first rate academic service to you.
- Assists in maintaining positive and purposeful relationships with your managers and senior staff (some of whom may well be looking for tangible proof of your success/progress).
- Is likely to have a diverse academic and professional background.
- Will tend to 'facilitate learning' rather than adopt 'directive teaching'.
- Feels more like a peer/colleague with different expertise to yourself.
- Will regard you as an expert in your own field and respect your existing knowledge.
- Will support you in the articulation of that knowledge (help to make it explicit).

A major aspect of WBL programmes is negotiation of study with your employer and the university. Supporting this process requires high levels of teaching skills from your tutor, which are applied within sensitive organisational environments to ensure academic rigour, while simultaneously meeting your organisation's needs. This is almost always underpinned by a formal learning agreement/plan/contract (see Chapter 6).

Telling stories

A good way to build rapport with your WBL tutor is to think about the professional 'stories' you could tell each other to illustrate your approaches to your job, and your experiences of WBL. Storytelling within a professional context is a powerful tool. It is often used to help teams to bond and to create a 'vocabulary of change', used to describe how small changes in ideas can bring about transformations for you, your team and your company.

Exercise 7.3 Using 'storytelling' in day-to-day activities

Think of the stories you might tell to introduce yourself in a new group.

Don't just mention your title and job role – try to talk about why you are there.

To further this, try referring to yourself in the third person – introduce yourself as that other person.

Once you begin to think about yourself by your name – rather than as 'I' – you will want to also say something about personality, motivation, likes and dislikes. This is the richer picture.

'Telling your own story' is good background work for writing the personal statement that you would put in an application form, or in your WBL portfolio (see Chapter 6).

TIP What storytelling does for you

- Builds your credibility and confidence.
- Develops your perspective.
- Helps with bonding.
- Enables you to say not just who you are, but why you are present.
- Can provide a vehicle for your hopes and expectations about WBL.
- Brings structure – a plot, a protagonist, a journey and an ending.
- Can give a framework (and some distance) for exploring difficult and controversial topics.

A major emphasis of your WBL programme will be for you to critically reflect (see Chapter 2) on your learning. This critical reflection encourages an analytical style of narrative and gives you an opportunity to tell the 'story' of your learning. Your reflective narratives will provide your tutor with a wealth of information about your professional knowledge and give the kind of context that enables your tutor to learn about you and your role quickly.

Learning conversations

You should be getting the picture by now that communication is vital to your relationship with your WBL tutor(s). Much of this communication could be termed 'learning conversations' (Naish, 2006, building on Pedler et al., 1991).

Case Study 7.3   How to use learning conversations

Jenny developed the notion of learning conversations when she was working with groups of mature master's-level WBL students. These students were highly intelligent, capable people, with vast amounts of expertise in their own areas. They worked together in many ways, but always as equals, not in traditional 'teacher' and 'student' roles:

'Learning conversations, which made it explicit that we were talking about learning, made it possible for me to learn as much about these students' contexts as possible.'

This facilitated learning processes, and the acquisition of further knowledge, using appropriate methods such as:

- formal lectures;
- workshops;
- master-classes;
- distance learning materials both in hard and soft copy (for example, on a VLE, a virtual learning environment);
- group discussions and seminars (actual and/or virtual);
- directed own reading.

In thinking about these learning conversations (which also include those with your student peers), you might want to think about yourself as a professional adult who is also in a learning role. How you and your tutor(s) and/or supervisors communicate with one another has an impact on the support you seek, and on your achievements; the term 'learning conversations' is very much based on the equality of these conversations, adult to adult, while acknowledging that you and your tutor are likely to have differing levels of expertise on different subjects/topics/processes and so on. Traditionally the relationship between tutors and students is not one of equality, but rather the tutor 'teaching' the student things they 'need' to learn. This is very different from the 'facilitation of learning' style that works best for WBL. An excellent WBL tutor will be very aware of your existing knowledge and expertise, which is often going to be very different from their own, and will not only be keen to learn *about* you, but also *from* you, as the more in-depth understanding they have of your specialisms and environment the more effective they can be in supporting you.

Making the most of your tutor

One of the distinctive features of WBL programmes is the intention to develop autonomous learners. This is a complex topic, which is substantiated by theory (for example, Candy, 1991: 13). The support your tutor gives you will be designed to encourage you to become more autonomous, and that might feel as if they are becoming increasingly 'hands off'. You might notice them not giving you a specific answer to your questions; giving you a range of options that may not always be clear cut; returning the question to you and asking you what you think the answer is and so on. This feels quite uncomfortable at first, as you may previously have experienced quite a lot of very 'hands on' and almost directive support from your tutors. You should see this as being a positive transition into a greater level of autonomy.

TIP **In order to help you develop this autonomy in your relationship with your tutor:**

- Prepare well for your tutorial – What do you want to get out of the meeting? Is this about scoping a project, refining an idea, or 'unpicking' a difficult concept? Try to let your tutor know in advance what it is that you want to discuss, then they can also prepare.
- Have a list of questions and issues ready – This will help you to marshal your thoughts and ideas.
- Make notes of your tutor's response during the tutorial – If you are trying to clarify a difficult concept, it may be useful to bring a list of reading with you, to help your tutor see where your thinking has come from.
- Send drafts of your work to your tutor in good time prior to the tutorial – This will enable them to read it and reflect on it to give you some in-depth formative feedback. It can also be helpful to use 'comments' boxes to highlight particular areas that you are unsure of.

TIP
- Use 'track changes' or highlight the specific area for review – This can be useful if you have acted upon feedback received, and are seeking to clarify that you have understood and revised your work appropriately,
- Check the regulations about reading and reviewing drafts of work with your tutor.

Feedback from your tutor

Your tutors will give you feedback on your draft work throughout your studies. (All university WBL programmes are slightly different in terms of how and when feedback is given, but feedback mechanisms and timing will be pointed out to you). Good feedback is about building you up and supporting you, by highlighting what you have done well and why, and offering ideas on what to do to improve your work. Take time to reflect on the feedback and act positively upon it, asking for clarification if you are unsure of what it means.

Feedback mechanisms vary but might include:

- Comments written directly on to your work.
- Feedback via email on soft copies you have sent.
- Spoken feedback in tutorials at pre-arranged times and locations.
- Feedback placed on a protected area of a virtual learning environment (VLE) (for example, Blackboard).
- Group feedback in an actual or virtual seminar setting (for example, a discussion group on Blackboard).

There is further discussion around feedback in Chapter 11, which focuses on assessment.

Your tutor will indicate areas where your work is good; reread these areas and highlight what it is that you have done well, and remember to build on these good points in your future pieces of work. There may also be areas where your tutor feels that you need to pay more attention to; reread these areas and spend a little time thinking about how you feel you could have improved them.

TIP **Common areas of improvement**

The application of theory to practice
- Don't simply write about the theory and then write about your practice. Illustrate your understanding of theory by using examples from your own practice, but avoid long descriptions.

TIP **Inadequate reference to theory**
- You must demonstrate that your work has an evidence base, or is underpinned by theory. Reference to literature enables you to analyse your practice in the light of theory and to highlight areas for change or development, from a sound evidence base.

Inaccurate referencing
- Check in your course handbook, or with your tutor, which referencing system you are expected to use and then follow exactly the guidelines available to you. Most university libraries carry guides to referencing; follow the conventions carefully, both in your written text and in your list of references.

If you experience difficulties

WB Learners are by their very nature busy people – combining working, studying and often busy family lives can cause time pressures, which are sometimes unforeseeable and insurmountable. In these circumstances, it is important to recognise that support is available and to use it, rather than simply give up. Universities have mechanisms to enable students who have extenuating circumstances that arise during the programme, to apply for additional time to complete a particular assignment or, if the issue is going to take sometime to resolve then it may be necessary for you to 'hit the pause button' on your studies for a while (sometimes called an authorised break from study, or intercalation). In either circumstance, don't panic or pretend it's not happening. Speak to your tutor early so that they can offer you support and advice about making the appropriate application.

Case Study 7.4   Using real workplace issues

Tim is undertaking a work-based programme co-designed by his employer, a large manufacturer, and is progressing well. Midway through the programme a serious issue arises on the production line that Tim is responsible for, which requires his immediate undivided attention. Tim discusses the situation with his tutor, noting that it is likely to be a month before the problem is rectified and the situation returns to normal. Tim's tutor suggests that he can apply for an extension to his deadline to enable him to complete his assignment,

Case Study 7.4 (continued)

and include the valuable learning that he has experienced while dealing with the manufacturing problem. The extension is granted to cover the four weeks lost from his studies while dealing with the production issue, and Tim produces a very interesting piece of work, which demonstrates how the learning from his programme had helped him to solve the production problem.

Tangible self-development

One way of demonstrating your learning is to develop not only as an autonomous learner but also as an autonomous thinker. You will find that your confidence grows alongside your ability to back up your findings, by referring to literature and comparing it to your own experience. Try to express your views and opinions more assertively as your growing data and evidence enables you to be more courageous in your analysis and interpretation. Don't be afraid to disagree with the literature, if your data supports your argument.

If you are undertaking a major award, for example, a foundation degree, degree or master's, a large work-based project is normally the final piece of work you would be expected to complete for your award. By that stage in your programme you are likely to know all the assessment grades or marks you have achieved so far. Therefore you are also likely to know what kind of grade or mark you need to achieve the award classification (first class, 2:1 and so on) you are aspiring to. Your tutor can advise you about what kinds of approaches you would need to take in order to aim for a realistic classification within the scale and scope of your capability, and often this will have been indicated in the formal feedback from your previous pieces of work.

Support from your employer

The findings of WBL students' work are often taken up and used by their employers – indeed, this is often why employers choose the WBL approach for their learning programmes.

Case Study 7.5   Problems make good projects

A healthcare company sponsored 15 of its managers to undertake a WBL programme. Candidates made presentations of their final projects to a group of senior managers and their tutor. The projects dealt with a

> ### Case Study 7.5 (continued)
>
> range of pressing company issues related to communication, including the development of a companywide induction programme and an improved system for stock control within the warehouse. The senior managers were delighted with the outcome of the projects, which not only demonstrated cost savings, but were immediately applicable and useful because the managers' inside knowledge of the detailed context of their work brought in-depth understanding and analysis of the whole situation, including consideration of how to overcome barriers to implementation (Ions and Minton, 2012).

The role your employer may take in supporting your WBL can be diverse, and range from co-designing the programme and funding, or part-funding, your studies, through to helping you to get the most out of your studies in terms of project advice or even co-supervision. The amount and quality of the support you receive from your employer will depend on a number of factors, but especially on the nature of any agreement your employer has with the university at which you are studying.

Managing your employer's involvement with your WBL

If your employer has 'sent' you on this WBL programme it is important to know why. Is the course compulsory to your job role? If you do not know why you have been sent, then your human resources or staff development teams at work are your best first point of contact via your line manager. It is also worthwhile noting that some employers will ask you to sign an agreement confirming that you will reimburse any fees paid by them if you leave the organisation within a set period of time.

If you are part of a group of students from the same company, there will probably be a designated person within your organisation who acts as the programme liaison officer with the university – make sure you know who this is. The university may also ask that a student representative be elected, to provide feedback to the course team on progress and support.

You need to understand your employer's expectations of your studying and whether there are any specific areas that they wish you to investigate as a part of your studies. This may usefully be outlined as a part of the development review process within your organisation, or during a one-to-one meeting with your manager.

Learning agreements

All WBL programmes are designed to help you develop professionally within the context of your work role, enabling you to contribute more fully to your organisation achieving its objectives. In order to facilitate this, most universities running WBL programmes require students to complete a learning agreement/contract/plan (see Chapter 6) in which you will negotiate the specific learning you intend to do, usually with both the university and your employer. As your learning agreement may have to be signed by your line manager or other senior person in the organisation who understands your programme, then allowing time for that process within the framework of deadlines from the university is important for you to manage.

As part of a learning agreement you would need to discuss (normally with your line manager) the content of any work-based projects you are planning to do as part of your programme to ensure that, as well as meeting your learning needs, they are going to be of benefit to the organisation. It is important therefore for you to understand what your line manager's hopes, expectations and aspirations are for your role and that you make the most of these by aligning them to your learning. This is a vital and very dynamic interaction between you, your employer and the university, and it is important that you initiate the discussions to progress this and take the lead in the decision-making and the nature and level of support your employers will provide (Chapter 12 is dedicated to work-based projects).

Accepting support and guidance (while avoiding being railroaded)

Your focus should be very largely your decision, in negotiation with your organisation and the university. Take on a topic that will engage you and be current, and that both you and your line manager are enthusiastic about. It could be a project from an ongoing list of problems that you and your team face. Your motivation and feelings of ownership towards the activity are significantly higher if the work you are doing is of your choice, is of interest to you and you can see will be of real benefit to you in the future.

Some of your learning comes from going through the process of deciding on a suitable topic, so embrace this process. Early topic ideas often have to be refined and even discarded until all parties agree on a suitable topic – look at this as formative and useful. Where programmes have been designed with employers, line managers or company tutors will have been briefed about the programme and the expectations. If your line manager or you are unsure about the suitability of a topic, then seek advice together from your tutor.

Work-based mentors

Mentors can be drawn from your colleagues, line managers, HR directors – the number and position differs from organisation to organisation. If your programme has been jointly designed by the university and your employer, then a group of mentors from within the organisation may have been identified and trained specifically to help and support you through the programme. Their role is often to act as a 'sounding board', for you to explore your ideas with someone who understands the business and may be able to suggest enhancements to your plans, or to introduce you to others within the organisation who can help you with access to information.

Case Study 7.6   Mentorship in action

A local authority developed a programme for its managers to understand how to manage a mobile workforce. A group of well-respected and experienced staff, who had experience of HE WBL programmes, were trained as mentors to support the students, who had a number of questions about applying the learning in the context of their own specialism.

The mentoring programme, as well as introducing models and theories of mentoring, included discussions about understanding how people learn, the expectations of HE, from both the learner and tutor's perspective, and tools and techniques to support learners when the 'going gets tough'. The mentors, because they were familiar to, and embedded within, the organisation, were able to signpost and facilitate access to key information within the organisation. They were aware of what other directorates were planning and could highlight topics where students could support each other, sharing resources as well as 'troubleshoot' some key IT issues.

Most importantly, they attended team meetings, challenged negative and outdated thinking in a supportive manner and provided a motivational force, without which the programme would have struggled to have the lasting benefits that are being identified even several years after the programme has finished.

You, the work-based learner

Finally, we return to the heart of WBL, and that heart is you, the person, the learner, the student, the employee. You will want to get the most out of your WBL programme, and only you and those closest to you will know what 'most' means in terms of what it will look and feel like when you have got there. In thinking about this the experience of WBL is often profound, motivating, non-linear and can be life-changing. All in the best possible way – but you will wish to ask yourself how you feel about such powerful statements and their reality for your own professional and personal development. Try to make sure that you find the learning opportunities that arise from your everyday work that can be aligned to the learning outcomes of the course. In this way you will be enhancing the work that you already do, rather than taking on additional work. You will also discover that learning can occur in many ways, and that opportunities to learn are plentiful. One of the most profound effects of the experience of WBL is that it transforms you into a lifelong learner – one who finds and takes opportunities to learn in every aspect of their life.

In making the most of your WBL programme, remember that you are the 'driver' on the journey, so take charge of the route – don't be afraid to follow new ideas, and use the signposts and guidance that are on offer when and if you need them. Independent and autonomous learning does not mean that you are alone – enjoy the trip!

Summary

1   Be proactive – ask about the full range of support available to you from your university and your employer.

2   Make SMART (Specific, Measureable, Aspirational, Realistic and Timely) choices about how, why and when you need to make use of this support.

3   Remember that you might wish to use university support with some employer-related matters and vice versa.

4   Help your tutor to support you – turn up on time for tutorials; send work in advance if you expect feedback; be clear about what you need.

5   Have upfront negotiations with family and friends – don't just presume they are there to support you.

6   Support yourself by networking effectively within your stakeholder group.

References

Candy, P. (1991) *Self-Direction for Lifelong Learning: A Comprehensive Guide to Theory and Practice* (San Francisco, CA: Jossey-Bass).

Honey, P. and Mumford, A. (2006) *Learning Style Questionnaire*, rev. edn (Maidenhead: Peter Honey Publications).

Ions, K. and Minton, A. (2012) 'Can work-based learning programmes help companies to become learning organisations?', *Higher Education Skills and Work-based Learning*, 2 (1), 22–32.

Moon, J. (1999) *Reflection in Learning and Professional Development* (London: Kogan Page).

Naish, J. (2006) 'Application to the Higher Education Academy for a National Teaching Fellowship', unpublished.

Pedler, M., Burgoyne, J. and Boydell, T. (1991, 1996) *The Learning Company. A Strategy for Sustainable Development* (London: McGraw-Hill).

Walsh, A. (2008) 'What Is Distinctive about Work-based Knowledge and Learning?' In *Workforce Development: Connections, Frameworks and Processes* (York: The Higher Education Academy).

Suggested further reading

Carpentier, V., Pachler, N., Evans, K. and Daly, C. (2011) 'Work–Learn–Educate: The WLE Centre for Excellence's conceptualisation of work-based learning', *Higher Education, Skills and Work-based Learning*, 1 (3), 216–230.

Liyanage, L., Strachan, R., Penlington, R. and Casselden, B. (2013) 'Design of educational systems for work based learning (WBL): the learner experience', *Higher Education, Skills and Work-based Learning*, 3 (1), 51–61.

McDury, J. and Alterio, M. (2003) *Learning through Storytelling in Higher Education: Using Reflection and Experience to Improve Learning* (London: Kogan Page).

Moore, L. J. (2007) 'Ethical and organisational tensions for Work-based Learners', *Journal of Workplace Learning*, 19 (3), 161–172.

Ogilvie, C. and Homan, G. (2012) 'Everybody wins? Using the workplace as an arena for learning', *Higher Education, Skills and Work-based Learning*, 2 (2), 102–120.

Zachary, L. J. and Fischler, L. A. (2009) *The Mentee's Guide: Making Mentoring Work for You* (San Francisco, CA: Jossey-Bass).

What can social media (SoMe) do for me?

Conor Moss and Matt Bromley

In this chapter you will learn:

► how the exponential rise of social media has changed how we interact, work and learn;
► how you can use different technologies and tools to support your learning development;
► about the technologies and tools that are available to help you research and organise your learning;
► what tools you can use to collaborate with other learners;
► how you can use technology to present and share your learning;
► what digital literacy is and how you can build up a personal brand.

The evolution of social media?

Social media is a phrase used to describe interaction between people, where information and ideas are created, shared or exchanged in virtual communities and networks. Kaplan and Haenlein (2010) define social media as 'a group of internet-based applications that build on the ideological and technological foundations of Web 2.0, and that allow for the creation and exchange of user generated content'.

In the early days of the World Wide Web (Web 1.0), users passively viewed, read and published static pages. In 1999 Darcy DiNucci introduced the term Web 2.0 (Prandini and Ramilli, 2012), describing it as the development of the static web into an interactive medium available on different devices such as your computer, phone, TV or games console. Kaplan and Haenlein (2010) suggest that this development was 'the platform for the evolution of Social Media … whereby content and applications are no longer created and published by individuals, but instead are continuously modified by all users in a participatory and collaborative fashion'. One of the best examples of this is Wikipedia, a website built on the collaborations of over 21 million individuals.

These technologies allow for user-generated content (UGC) development, whereby the exchange of information and collaboration is undertaken in real time through global, social and virtual communities. Technologies and tools include forums, weblogs, microblogging, social networks, video, images, social bookmarking, wikis and podcasts. These are explored in detail later in the chapter, along with how they can enhance your learning and experience as a work-based learner.

The evolution of social media and mobile technology has changed behaviours and how we interact in many ways; people nowadays:

- are able to work in many different environments;
- consume and upload content such as video 'on the go'.

In addition, this evolution has transferred power over information and knowledge from the institution to users. Think again about Wikipedia – everyone has the ability to interact with this free source of information, add to it, correct it or clarify it. The information then has the potential to become more accurate, relevant and ultimately more valuable as collaboration occurs. In addition, the development of technology means that anyone with expertise can become a teacher and share knowledge with others. It is also easier for people to engage with learning. The rise (in the last five years) of Massive Open Online Courses (MOOCs) that are offered by many universities and other companies, such as Udemy, Coursera, Futurelearn and iTunes U, is testament to this. While the content of these courses is comparable to traditional university programmes, the courses are free, for unlimited numbers of participants to engage in collaborative learning via the web. Most courses do not use assessment although, some, such as Coursera, may offer an assessment and a Statement of Accomplishment. The discussion and support largely comes from your community of fellow learners using forums and other interactions.

Before using these social tools it is important to consider your digital identity ('personal brand') that is constructed by your online reputation, image values and the people you associate with. Case Study 8.1 provides an example of how to create a good digital identity.

Case Study 8.1   10 top tips to create a digital identity

by Victoria Tomlinson, chief executive, Northern Lights PR and author of *From Student to Salary with Social Media* **and** *How to Write a Top-Ranked Blog.*

Case Study 8.1 (continued)

Why would you want a digital identity?
It is a fast, cheap and effective way to demonstrate your expertise, passion, engage with peers in your sector, contribute to innovation and learning relevant to your research or job and get really good-quality answers to whatever problem you are facing.

How do you create a digital identity?

1. **Your personal brand**
   First of all, decide what your personal brand is. What do you want to be known for – the best event organiser, creative thinker on business problems, the history of churches or the least terrifying dentist?
   The more niche and focused you are, the more successful your digital identity will be.

2. **Who do you want to know about you?**
   This could be colleagues internally, academics, future employers or the world's gurus on your specialism. These are the people to build relationships with online.

3. **What keywords and phrases?**
   Think about your expertise – what problems and questions do people have that you could help with? Taking the above examples these could be
   - eight tips to help kids overcome fear of the dentist.
   - What are the most beautiful churches in London?
   - How to motivate colleagues to be creative thinkers.
   - Industry insights into organising a great event.

4. **Keywords in your profile**
   Your profiles should reflect your expertise – include your keywords in your Twitter profile, your LinkedIn summary and the description of your blog.

5. **Create a blog**
   A blog should be the core to your digital identity. This is where you can pose questions, give tips showing your expertise and invite guest blogs from the people you most admire.

6. **Engage with others**
   Social media is social. Find the people you want to know. Follow them, start conversations, retweet things you admire.

7. **Promote your blog**
   Post questions and comments on LinkedIn, Twitter, Facebook and Google+ with links to your blog.

8. **Measure what gets the best response**
   Use bit.ly to shorten the blog link – and look at the stats on what gets most clicks and when.

Case Study 8.1 (continued)

9. **Do research online**
   When you have a genuine question that you want to get views on, post it online. Help others when you spot them posting questions.
10. **Keep your profile professional**
    Keep your identity focused. Maybe keep Facebook for personal and the rest for your 'professional identity'.

Social media and work-based learning

As a WBL student, more so than for a full-time student, you must self-organise your learning. Whichever institution or route you choose for your study programme, no-one can manage self-organised learning *for* you (McClenaghan and Young, 2010). For this reason you are likely to be relying more on technology and the flexible access to university systems to fit around your work and personal commitments. This is where social media can really help. Although at first it may take time to experiment with different tools, once you establish how and when to use social media tools they will help you to organise and manage your learning more effectively, whether you are on a negotiated learning route, taught on-campus modules or pure e-learning modules. What is more, social media will help you develop your knowledge with new levels of agility, through your work, through your personal learning network (see later in the chapter) and through opportunities for more traditional learning such as a programme of study.

Social media tools for learning

Why would you use social tools as a work-based learner? Social tools are about people, human interaction, sharing knowledge and information, and working and learning collaboratively. Some of these tools are now household names: you will probably have heard of blogs, wikis, Twitter and social media, and networking sites such as Delicious, Facebook, YouTube, and so on.

The main functions for these tools include:

- communication (for example, Twitter);
- collaboration (for example, Wikis);
- networking (for example, LinkedIn);
- sharing (for example, YouTube).

The range of social media tools is growing and extends far beyond those discussed in this chapter. Within this chapter we have selected the most appropriate tools for you and categorised them in relation to how you might use them as a work-based learner.

Social networks and microblogging

There has been a radical shift in the number of communication-based apps available, many of which enable us to communicate and network in ways we couldn't have imagined 10 years ago. The most popular platforms include Facebook, LinkedIn, Twitter, Snapchat, Whatsapp and Yammer.

Facebook

Facebook is a social networking site that allows users to create profiles, upload photos and videos, send messages and posts information. In 2014 *The Guardian* estimated Facebook had over 1.2 billion active users (Sedghi, 2014).

TIP Using Facebook in WBL

- Create study groups and exchange information and updates.
- Create multiple groups, for study, for friends, for professional acquaintances and so on.
- Set groups to be open for everyone to join: or alternatively make them invitation-only.
- Develop your digital identity in your selected sector through your Facebook profile.
- Your university may use it to support you during your first weeks, to provide a platform for you to meet other students and provide information.
- As Facebook is open, some universities prefer to use more secure and private spaces for social networking with students, often within their own VLE.

Getting started: https://www.facebook.com/help/364458366957655/

LinkedIn

LinkedIn is an online professional network that lets you create and manage your professional identity online. It enables you to connect with professionals around the globe, extend and keep track of your contacts and seek out expertise in specific subject matter areas. LinkedIn estimates that it has over 277 million members worldwide, with 65 million professional members in Europe alone (LinkedIn, 2014).

TIP **Using LinkedIn in your personal and professional development**

- Join special interest groups with people that have a shared interest, post questions to other people in your professional field and therefore network with people to advance your career.
- Develop your Skills and Expertise profile; your professional network can endorse you on the site for projects you have delivered. In future endorsements from achievements elsewhere will be added to this facility, such as passing MOOC assessments.

Getting started: http://help.linkedin.com/app/home

Twitter

Twitter is a micro-blogging social network site, which allows users to create a profile, send and read short (maximum 140 characters) messages known as 'Tweets'. Users 'follow' people they are interested in to read messages and can 'retweet' (share) messages they have found interesting.

In 2013 Twitter had been number 1 in the top 100 learning tools for the previous five years (Hart, 2013) and it is widely regarded as a useful tool for both personal and professional development because it enables you to stimulate debate, follow discussions (via a hashtag #), engage in conversations and exchange ideas and information with your personal learning network.

TIP **Using Twitter as part of WBL**

- Search for organisations and people related to your work, as with all social media tools you will only benefit personally and professionally if you follow the right people.
- Consider how you would like to use Twitter: some people like to:
  - observe at the start by following others;
  - then work their way into retweeting/reposting other people's tweets;
  - then form their own tweets.
- Use Twitter to start conversations with peers or people in your personal learning network.
- Post links to questionnaires you want completed as part of your research.

  The setting up of a Twitter account is very straightforward and relatively intuitive, although the following links may help understand some of the jargon and get started:

  http://support.twitter.com/groups/50-welcome-to-twitter#topic_203
  http://support.twitter.com/articles/215585-getting-started-with-twitter

Exercise 8.1   Setting up a Twitter account

Create a Twitter account; if you already have a personal account then set up an account related to your studies; and follow relevant people and organisations. Remember to select people or organisations that will add to both your personal and professional development.

Getting started: http://support.twitter.com/articles/215585-getting-started-with-twitter

How can you use social networks for your learning?

Communities of Practice (CoPs) and Virtual Communities of Practice (VCoPs) provide a common way for people to share a common interest or profession; they are a great way for individuals to share information and experiences and learn from each other (see Chapter 9). Personal Learning Networks (PLN) are a natural extension of CoPs and VCoPs, in that an individual can collaborate with their PLN and build relationships with people who have common interests in a particular subject, industry or specialism.

As a work-based learner you can use PLNs to:

- Research topics relevant to your subject.
- Discuss and debate topics with individuals who have similar interests.
- Communicate with subject matter experts.
- Collaborate and connect with a range of individuals outside your usual domain.
- Bookmark interesting content for use in formal assessments.
- Curate content from a range of sources and present it appropriately.

It is argued that PLNs are less formal, and by contrast less effective, than formal CoPs; Communities of Practice usually involve active practitioners and are something that you work your way into by demonstrating your expertise, whereas PLNs can involve anyone regardless of expertise, and you are at the centre of the network from the start (Wheeler, 2013). That said, the shift in technology has opened many opportunities to collaborate with more people from around the world sharing experiences and engaging in stimulating debate on a particular theme. For many, the key aspect of social networks is their immediateness and quick collaboration via mobile devices or computers. They can be used as a platform for discussion, debate and professional development. As a work-based learner using PLNs and CoPs/VCoPs in conjunction with social media can enhance and support your studies. To maximise the impact of social media networks for WBL you should follow these simple steps.

TIP **Setting up your social network**

- Look outside your workplace for inspiration.
- Connect with others from similar and related specialisms.
- Consider what you post and retweet.
- Link your account to a bookmarking tool (more on this later).
- Focus on your personal brand.
- Be more than a broadcasting channel.
- Build relationships and knowledge by engaging in conversations.
- Ask your community for help, advice and guidance.
- Share your insights and thoughts on blogs, articles and curated content.
- Be yourself and have fun !

Exercise 8.2   Establishing a Personal Learning Network (PLN)

Think about your work, education and social networks, and write a list of 10 people/organisations in each area that you believe could enhance your Personal Learning Network.

Once you have established the list consider the various social tools you could use to follow these people or organisations.

	Work contacts	Social network tool	Education contacts	Social network tool	Social network contacts	Social network tool
Name/ Organisation	*Skills Unlimited*	*LinkedIn*	*Jessica*	*Facebook*	*Ryan*	*Twitter*

Blogs, bloggers and blogging

The term 'blog' comes from the words 'web log'; simply put, a blog is an online writing tool. A blog has a variety of functions and can be used as:

- a tool for publishing information online;
- a private and personal diary;

- a collaborative space where you share your entries and allow comments from other people.

A blog (usually written in chronological order, with the most recent first) can be:

- a couple of succinct paragraphs, or a more detailed entry on a chosen topic;
- words and/or images – can include images, videos and embedded links, referencing external sources (for example, journal articles or other blogs);
- personal or political;
- focused on a topic, subject, expertise or area of interest;
- often be linked to other material of interest and relevance.

The activity of writing a blog is called blogging, and someone who keeps a blog is called a blogger.

Blogging platforms

Like social networks, blogs are now used more frequently. Some of the best blogging tools include:

Wordpress

Wordpress enables you to write blogs and develop a fully functional website; it is relatively easy to set up and use. There are opportunities to add a range of plugins (software or applications developed by third parties), administer the blog from a mobile phone and develop your own personal website. In 2013 Wordpress had been in the top 10 in the top 100 tools for the previous five years (Hart, 2013).

Tumblr

Tumblr is a multifunctional micro-blogging site that allows users to share photos, videos, music, chat and blogs. It is estimated that in 2014 160 million people were using Tumblr, with some 113 million Tumblelogs per day (Tumblr, 2014). Easily accessible via a mobile device, Tumblr is a less formal way of blogging. With some of the same functionality as Twitter, you can 'retweet' other people's blogs and 'like' their updates. Tumblr is a perfect way to use a variety of media to research, curate and reflect on your learning in short, less formal blogs.

TIP　**Using blogging as a work-based learner**

The basics of Wordpress are relatively straightforward; however the following links may help:

http://codex.wordpress.org/FAQ_New_to_WordPress
http://codex.wordpress.org/Getting_Started_with_WordPress

TIP Similarly the following links may help you get started with Tumblr:
http://www.tumblr.com/about
http://www.tumblr.com/docs/en/pages
http://www.tumblr.com/docs/en/pages#troubleshooting

The blogging tools are outlined above, but how can you and why should you, as a work-based learner, use blogs? There are in fact a number of reasons:

- They are often used within a university's virtual learning environment or VLE (and this can provide a private and safe environment for you to perfect your blogging skills, before using a specific blogging tool).
- It is quite common now to use blogs or online journals as part of modules, which means that your journal is open for comments between you and your tutor or your fellow students, and you can learn from each other through discussion and feedback.
- You can use a blog as a reflective journal or a learning log as it offers plenty of room for you to express yourself and grow in understanding.

Case Study 8.2 illustrates how the various social media tools can be used in unison to maximise impact, as well as the value of using social media and how it is changing the way we work, communicate and learn.

Case Study 8.2   Creating a Global Personal Learning Network – the power of social media by blogging and Twitter

NZLEAD is a social media-based HR community that was started at the beginning of 2013 by two New Zealand-based HR practitioners, Amanda Sterling and Tash Pieterse. It has since grown into a community of over 200+ members with international participation from Australia, the UK, USA, India, and Singapore. NZLEAD provides an opportunity for HR professionals from New Zealand and around the world to connect, collaborate and share knowledge using social media tools.

NZLEAD had its origins in a leadership development course that Amanda designed in 2010 for a company with no training budget. She did this using free resources readily available through the internet and local libraries. This led her to conclude that all the information you ever needed was out there on the internet. You've just got to know where to find it and how to identify its quality.

Case Study 8.2 (continued)

Throughout the course the weekly tweet chat had become popular. HR practitioners and leadership development experts from around the world were participating in the discussion, sharing resources, learning and ask questions. Amanda and Tash paired up with a view to continue the tweet chat discussions but target it at HR professionals. NZLEAD was born.

The original premise of NZLEAD was simple: to co-ordinate guest contributors from around the world to provide tweet chat topics. The NZLEAD blog site (www.nzlead.com) provided an introduction to the topic. Four questions were asked during a Twitter-based chat (7pm Thursday NZ time using #NZLEAD). The guest contributor then provided a recap of the chat with their key learnings.

Over 2013 NZLEAD grew from a weekly tweet chat to a community sharing blogs, provoking each other's thinking (sometimes controversially), collaborating on projects and meeting in real life (IRL). The scope of NZLEAD became so much more than a tweet chat. Business connections were made, employment offers negotiated, and fundamental principles about what HR is and how it adds value to the business were debated and applied.

What has seen NZLEAD become successful are the same things the original leadership course lacked. Firstly, people need to be connected to learn from each other. This means creating a community that is not just based on professionalism but also authentic personal interaction. Secondly, people need to know how to effectively use social tools in order to learn. With these learnings in mind, NZLEAD is growing the HR community by working with HR professionals to increase their skills in using technology and create communities where people can connect and learn. The possibilities are now endless thanks to the connections created through social technology.

@TashTasticNZ   @sterling_amanda

Exercise 8.3   Dive in and follow

Blogs have a number of functions, but remember there are blogs on any topic, so be selective:

- Now that you have set up a Twitter account, use hashtags (#) to follow proceedings from conferences and events relevant to your subject/sector or area of study/expertise.

Exercise 8.3 (continued)

- Select an area related to your study or workplace and type it into a search engine adding the term 'blog'. You will find that there is a range of related blogs – choose blogs that contribute to your personal and professional development and enhance your personal learning network (PLN).
- Select at least two bloggers to follow, either through their blog site or on Twitter.
- Search for 'top Student Bloggers'. Use these examples to write a reflective or learning journal.

Collaboration and content curation

The technology revolution facilitates the circulation of more information than we can take in. Consider, for example, a one-day professional conference – there may be hundreds of people in attendance, all collaborating in formal and informal settings, learning from each other and the keynote speakers, tracking 'backchannels' from Twitter feeds and so on. Conference attendees may reflect on their new knowledge and learning experience via a blog or Twitter. The problem is: how do you stay up to date with and consolidate your learning from the event? Content curation, using social tools, is part of the answer.

Using content curation for WBL

Content curation is the art of discovering, gathering and presenting information around a particular topic or event; it is a bit like a curator in a museum who is a specialist in their field, but today there are tools that enable this to be done more easily than ever before. Using content curation as a work-based learner can help you in a number of ways:

- Researching:
  - to define topics and sources;
  - to research a particular topic.
- Making sense:
  - to organise huge amounts of information from one topic;
  - to make sense of a topic;
  - to demonstrate your understanding of a topic.
- Sharing:
  - to develop your social media network;
  - to demonstrate employability skills and your connectedness to your profession.

Federman (2012) suggests that the skills learners need have evolved from reading, writing and arithmetic to include the 4Cs of learning, that is to say, Connotation, Complexity, Context and Connection. Wheeler (2012) adapted the model, applying the principles to the skills we need for learning in a technology age. You can see Wheeler's adaptation on his blog at http://steve-wheeler.blogspot.co.uk/2012/11/skills-for-learning-20.html?m=1#!/2012/11/skills-for-learning-20.html.

Firstly, content curation can help you to make *connections* with subject experts; secondly, it can provide you with some *context* to the knowledge or information being discussed; thirdly, it can help aggregate and validate the *complexity* of a topic; and finally, through *connotation* the individual can then make meaning from the information and develop their own content in the form of blogs, tweets and e-portfolios.

Collaboration and content curation tools

Wikis

The term 'wiki' comes from the Hawaiian word for 'quick', and most wikis use relatively simple technology, making them quick and easy to create and use. A wiki consists of a cluster of web pages, used as collaborative writing space; you can add and edit written content, documents, links, embed videos and sound. Wikis offer a good place to consolidate a project as it is easy for users to build up information around a defined subject.

Wikis are useful to work-based learners as they can be used as:

- a source of knowledge: for example, Wikipedia is the world's largest encyclopaedia – albeit anyone can edit an entry, therefore the information may not be totally accurate or reliable;
- a home for a group project – this ensures that individual's contributions can be tracked and attributed, as well as the various iterations of the project archived;
- a place to develop project ideas, and collect background information;
- an organising and presentation tool for your work-based project (see Chapter 12);
- the vehicle for a glossary of terms or FAQs on a particular subject.

Storify

Storify helps registered users 'tell a story' by curating content from a range of social media tools, for example, Twitter, Google+, Facebook, YouTube and Instagram. Storify allows you to 'drag and drop' status updates, photos or videos to bring together the social media elements that will best illustrate your 'story'. Additionally, you can reorder the elements of what you produce, or delete them if you find something more useful. You can return to the story later to edit it.

As a work-based learner, Storify can help you:

- curate (collate in one place) tweets, images, links and videos events/conferences into one area;
- make sense of the content by annotating and commenting on the conference/event;
- reflect on your learning and its potential application to your workplace.

Exercise 8.4   Become a curator

- Think of a conference or event you have attended. Use Storify to curate the related tweets, images, links and videos from the conference into one area'
- Annotate the content and comment on the conference/event.
- Finally, write your own blog reflecting on your learning and its potential application to your workplace.

Paper.li

Paper.li is a content curation service that enables users to set parameters for the service to monitor content from blogs, websites and sharing apps. The content is presented as a newspaper in one place, saving you from manually finding content from around the web. As a work-based learner Paper.li helps you:

- set parameters for the kind of content you would like to review;
- annotate content to inform your essay, report or blog as part of your programme.

Exercise 8.5   Become a publisher

- Register for Paper.li or similar.
- Choose a topic around a particular subject or theme related to your studies.
- Set parameters for the kind of content you would like to review.
- Annotate the content and use it to inform a piece of work, report or blog as part of your programme.

TIP   **Using content curation in WBL**

- * Wikis

  Some of the most popular wiki tools are:

    Wikispaces: https://help.wikispaces.com
    Mediawiki: http://www.mediawiki.org/wiki/Extension:GettingStarted
    Dokuwiki – https://www.dokuwiki.org/tips:tailorwikirules

- Storify

  The following links may be useful to help you get started with Storify:
  http://storify.com/storifyfaq/frequently-asked-questions
  http://storify.com/tour

- Paper.li

  These links may be useful:
  http://support.paper.li/categories/20028282-Using-Paper-li-
  http://support.paper.li/entries/25771107-Paper-li-glossary

As a professional you could miss the multitude of blogs published on a daily basis in your area. Case Study 8.3 offers a good example of the power of social learning, in particular highlighting how collaboration, social learning and content curation can come together to produce a collection of works in one meaningful publication.

Case Study 8.3   The Book of Blogs – A content curated book of blogs for Human Resources Professionals

In 2013 I [David D'Souza] decided to try and create an HR book using collaborative technology to crowd-source its production. The concept was to utilise Twitter to attract multiple writers and bloggers to contribute individual chapters and for the result to be published on Kindle. It was to be a creative forum for people to share ideas – a safe 'white space' for individuals to write about subjects they are passionate about. All proceeds were going to charity; the motivation for individuals was a chance to express themselves and to be published authors.

I'd recently started using Twitter and blogging, so I tweeted the idea in an attempt to understand the likelihood of it being successful.

Case Study 8.3 (continued)

The response was overwhelming. My target was to get 30 authors involved, and I met this target by the end of the first week. We ended up with over 50 authors involved and a truly international project. I say 'we', because as soon as the project was launched it became a group enterprise, not an individual's work. The idea captured people's imagination and was shared rapidly. I deliberately had no strategy; my experiment was to test what could be created organically, with as little in terms of rules and restrictions as possible. It became clear that this was an approach that people were unaccustomed to (they expected far more direction), but one that people warmed to once they became more comfortable with the opportunity and choices that presented them with.

I wanted to have as little input as possible, as it was about sharing other people's work, and aside from adjustment of the order of chapters I left most work as it was submitted – and as the author intended. We encouraged community ownership: from PR, to design of the cover, to copywriting all elements of producing the book were executed free of charge by volunteers. Even the title 'Humane, Resourced' was chosen from a list of suggestions from the authors.

The book was floated as an idea in the middle of July and published on Kindle in early November. It topped the Bestseller list for HR books in the UK for over a month. For the first week of release it was in the Top 10 selling business books in the UK and it entered the Top 100 Nonfiction titles. It received press coverage as far away as New Zealand and the support of the CIPD [Chartered Institute of Personnel and Development], with Peter Cheese, CEO, agreeing to write the foreword. All of this was achieved through informal means – with no money invested.

If you reflect on the process as a whole there are a few key lessons:

- The ability of technology to enable networks and therefore accelerate the process of making productive connections.
- The ability of technology to support aggregation and production of content enables work to take place of a type and nature not possible only a few years ago – at a lower cost.
- The willingness of individuals to contribute time and effort to a project (without monetary incentives) where the objectives align with their own.

David D'Souza (@dds180)

Social bookmarking

As mentioned previously there is an overwhelming amount of information available via the internet. Social bookmarking is a way to store relevant stories, documents and blogs online; you can also tag them and share with your networks. Basically links are listed on a platform, and whoever has access can then search keywords to find relevant information on the topic. In simple terms, the concept is akin to personal bookmarks or favourites lists, and they can be used to categorise blogs, news and articles related to your subject specialism or as a way of sharing bookmarks with your network.

Tags, notes and comments can be added to bookmarks, and these might offer you some indication as to whether an item is going to be useful to you or not. As with most Web 2.0 tools, you can combine this service with other tools such as subscribing to blogs and social media feeds of individual bookmarks that you find interesting; this makes it easier to keep up with their new entries.

As a work-based learner a bookmarking tool can help you to:

- expand on a university course or module reading list;
- share bookmarks with other students, and your Personal Learning Network (PLN);
- save interesting articles from your social media feeds using tags (labels) to make it easy to narrow your search down;
- share your knowledge of this useful tool with your family, friends and colleagues at work.

Social bookmarking tools

A variety of social bookmarking tools are available. Two of the easiest to access are detailed below.

Delicious

Delicious is a free social bookmarking tool that in 2013 regularly featured in the Top 100 learning tools (Hart, 2013); it provides a virtual place where you can store and manage your bookmarks and share them with other people. There are bookmarking tools with more features but Delicious is very easy to use and has a strong community, which means it has an enormous collection of bookmarks for you to search.

Evernote

Evernote is a multifunctional application that helps you to takes notes, set reminders and bookmark or clip articles from websites. Your Evernote account is easily accessible across all computers and mobile devices.

As a work-based learner you could use Evernote to:

- take notes in class, take photos of activities in your workplace and bookmark content relevant to your subject;
- establish a folder for each module/course, so that when you find content on the web related to the module you can tag it to the respective folder;
- filter your notes and bookmarks, using tags, according to topic, for easy access when writing a blog or your assignment;
- develop a portfolio of evidence that you can access across platforms and share with your group/tutor;
- set reminders for your submission dates so you don't have the last-minute rush to submit!

TIP **Using social bookmarking as a work-based learner**

- Delicious

Useful websites to get you started with Delicious include:

https://delicious.com/help
http://blog.delicious.com

Exercise 8.6   Exploring social bookmarking

A good way to find out how social bookmarking can help you as a work-based learner is to find out what others have done.

Enter the following search terms into a search engine:

- 'social bookmarking for students';
- 'Evernote for students';
- 'using social bookmarking in education'.

Read what others who are studying have used these tools for and note down your observations.

E-portfolios – sharing and presenting

E-portfolios are used to bring together digital evidence or artefacts. Similar to other content curation tools, e-portfolios may contain text, images, graphics, hyperlinks, digital files and other multimedia such as videos. E-portfolios tend to be developed over a period of time and are often available within university VLEs.

How can you use e-portfolios as a work-based learner?

E-portfolios are often used to evidence learning by bringing together a range of different digital materials or artefacts. By developing an e-portfolio, you can reflect on a range of material, illustrate how you have developed over a period of time or showcase some of your work. Ultimately the aim of the e-portfolio is to demonstrate how you have met the learning outcomes for a module.

E-portfolio tools

There are a range of e-portfolio tools available, some of which are free:

PebblePad
PebblePad is one of the best-known proprietary e-portfolio tools and is used extensively by universities and other education providers. It provides learners with a learning space to reflect on learning experiences, create learning records for development and evidence your digital artefacts.
Free e-portfolios
There is a range of free e-portfolios built on the Mahara open source software that have much of the functionality of PebblePad.

Prezi is not a typical e-portfolio; instead it provides you with an excellent way of presenting your work in an engaging and informative way. You can create a Prezi using a range of templates that allow you to tell a story in a non-linear way; in addition, you can easily import images from Google and videos from YouTube.

TIP **Setting up an e-portfolio**

- Use a search engine (terms may include 'e-portfolios for starters' or 'using e-portfolios for assessment') to identify best practice.
- Explore the tools outlined above by searching for 'using Prezi as a portfolio' or 'best practice PebblePad'.
- Consider how you would use an e-portfolio in your WBL studies.

Getting started: Other useful websites to get you started are:

http://www.pepplepad.co.uk/l/faq.aspx
http://ww.pepplepad.co.uk/l/casestudies.aspx
https://wiki.mahara.org/index.php/Mahara_Wiki
http://prezi.com/support/
http://prezi.zendesk.com/entries/23448918-Get-Started-with-Prezi

---

The future of learning and social media

As demonstrated throughout this chapter, technology is changing rapidly, and this is having wide-ranging impacts on the way we work, learn and interact. It is anticipated that computers will soon be able to analyse and act on information found rather than this being undertaken by humans. Furthermore, Higher Education may well ultimately transcend university buildings and campus learning environments where Moodle and Blackboard are used, and instead utilise the emerging 'tools and services that enable us to personalise our learning, and these will be aggregated more easily too' (Wheeler, 2013). This means that the individual work-based learner will choose the range of technologies and tools most appropriate to their own situation or workplace, such as the tools discussed in this chapter, and the boundaries between formal and informal learning will increasingly blur.

The suggestions above may well become reality, and while we cannot see the future, the economy and the different working roles available, what we can predict is that digital technologies will still be central to life, and we will need to be digitally literate to get the best out of using technology to communicate, collaborate and engage in lifelong learning. To make the most of these technologies and tools, you need to develop the skills required to make use of and harness the power of different technologies, including how you find, use, create, evaluate and communicate information digitally. By developing your digital literacy skills (individual and social skills needed to effectively interpret, manage, share and create meaning in the growing range of digital communication channels [Dudeney et al., 2013]), you will be able to quickly understand and use new technologies in your learning, as and when they are developed in the future.

Summary

1 Technology and social media are changing the way we learn and work.

2 Technology and social media provide powerful ways to harness your thinking and learning, and help you share this with others.

3 Developing your Personal Learning Network (PLN) will allow you to connect with others and provide collaborative learning opportunities.

4 Social learning tools can help you to curate content relevant to your studies.

> 5   Try to use different tools and technologies in your learning
>   to further develop this range of skills – it may save you time!
>
> 6   Digital literacy encompasses an increasingly important set
>   of skills that you will need in order to engage with current
>   and future technologies.

References

Dudeney, G., Hockly, N. and Pegrum, M. (2013) *Digital Literacy* (Harlow: Pearson Education).

Federman, M. (2012) '21st century skills'. In Mobile Learning and Creativity Workshop at the International EC-TEL 2012 Conference, Saarbruecken, Germany, 18–21 September 2012.

Hart, J. (2013) *Top 100 Tools for Learning*. Available at http://c4lpt.co.uk/top100tools/ (accessed 12 May 2014).

Kaplan, A. M. and Haenlein, M. (2010) 'Users of the world, unite! The challenges and opportunities of social media', *Business Horizons*, 53 (1), pp. 59–68.

LinkedIn (2014) Press Information. Available at http://press.linkedin.com/about/ (accessed 24 March 2014).

McClenaghan, K. and Young, D. (2010) The Technology Revolution: Online Support for Work-based Learning. In R. Helyer (ed.) (2010) *The Work-based learning student handbook* (Basingstoke: Palgrave Macmillan).

Prandini, M. and Ramilli, M. (2012) 'Raising risk awareness on the adoption of Web 2.0 technologies in decision making processes', *Future Internet*, 4 (3), pp. 700–718.

Sedghi, A. (2014) 'Facebook: 10 years of social networking, in numbers', *The Guardian datablog*, 4 February. Available at http://www.theguardian.com/news/datablog/2014/feb/04/facebook-in-numbers-statistics (accessed 24 March 2014).

Tumblr (2014) Press Information. Available at http://www.tumblr.com/press (accessed 24 March 2014).

Wheeler, S. (2012) *Skills for Learning 2.0. Learning with 'e's' Blog, November 2012*. Available at http://steve-wheeler.blogspot.com/2012/11/skills-for-learning-20.html (accessed 20 May 2014).

Wheeler, S. (2013) *E-learning 3.0 Learning with 'e's' Blog, April 2013* Available at http://steve-wheeler.blogspot.co.uk/2009/04/learning-30.html (accessed 23 May 2014).

Suggested further reading

Bonk, C. J. (2009) *The World is Open: How Web Technology is Revolutionizing Education* (San Francisco, CA: Jossey-Bass).

Connor, M., Bingham, T. and Pink, D. H. (2010) *The New Social Learning: A Guide to Transforming Organizations Through Social Media* (San Francisco, CA: Berrett-Koehler).

Mahoney, S. (2012) *The Rough Guide to Social Media for Beginners: Getting Started with Facebook, Twitter and Google+* (London: Rough Guides).

Selwyn, N. (2011) *Education and Technology: Key Issues and Debates* (London: Continuum).

Thompson, C. (2013) *Smarter than You Think: How Technology Is Changing Our Minds for the Better* (New York: Penguin Press).

Social learning: Supporting yourself and your peers

Susan Smith and Laurie Smith

In this chapter you will learn:

► about what social learning is and why this is relevant to work-based (WB) learners;
► how to learn from multiple situations all around you;
► what experiential learning is and how to use this for your own learning;
► why peer learning is important for WB learners;
► what Communities of Practice are and how you can learn from them;
► how to create ongoing opportunities for learning and applying your learning to and from your own practice.

Making learning salient

Other chapters have said this already, but it is worth repeating, that as a WB learner you won't fit the traditional profile of an 18-year-old studying in higher education; for one thing, you will have more life experiences. The fact that you are working also means that you have many learning opportunities all around you. Some of these you will be aware of, and others may be hidden gems, waiting to be discovered. The aim of this chapter is to help you realise and exploit these learning opportunities, in other words, make learning more salient to you. So, what do we mean by salient? In this context salience equates to prominence. For example, your name is salient to you. Let us explain. Read the thought experiment below and place yourself in it.

Exercise 9.1   What is salient to you?

Imagine yourself in a room engaged in a conversation with a couple of friends. Behind you is another group of people who are also deep in their own conversation. You are involved in your own conversation so do not really hear (or are necessarily interested in) what is being said behind you.

Now imagine that you hear your name mentioned by someone in the group behind you. Suddenly, you are aware that your name has been said, and you may now be interested in what is being said behind you. Your name is salient to you, which is why from what was 'noise' behind you, the mention of your name – which you identify with – has sharpened your focus and made you interested in the conversation behind you. That is not to say that this group of people were actually talking about you, but your name has prominence and you tune in to this new conversation because your attention is drawn that way.

This may seem like a trivial example, but this is what we want to happen in relation to learning. We want learning opportunities to become salient to you so that you see them everywhere. And once you see these learning opportunities and they become salient to you, learning will become even more of an ongoing, everyday experience.

Exercise 9.2   Looking for the learning

As learning becomes increasingly salient to you, so will you be able to filter out what learning opportunities are relevant to your own context. Try this activity out:

Questions	Answer (example from a WB learner)
Think of something you have done recently at work that you feel you could have done differently.	*In a recent team meeting, a problem was being discussed. I came up with an answer and I didn't consult anyone else's thoughts.*
If you had the opportunity to do it again, what small thing would you change?	*I would gather ideas from the whole team.*
Why would you do it differently?	*My solution to the problem didn't work and, in hindsight, it would have been better to have a number of ideas and possible solutions.*

Exercise 9.2 (continued)

Questions	Answer (example from a WB learner)
What would it look like? How would it make you feel to do it differently?	*The team would have been more involved and we would have had many more ideas. I would feel like we were working together and that the team would have had ownership of this problem.*
If a similar opportunity arises in the future, how will you know you have approached (or are approaching) this thing differently?	*I will ask the team for input. I will know this is a different approach because I always try to fix problems on my own.*
What, if anything, can you learn from this?	*A problem shared is a problem halved! It is better to have more options from different perspectives rather than just mine.*

Using Exercise 9.2 above, try to get into the habit of analysing your own work practice and be aware of things that you would change and why. In the future, if you are faced with a similar situation and you do have the opportunity to approach it differently, be aware that you are doing this. Chapter 2 talked about reflecting forwards; as a WB learner you will be encouraged to reflect backwards and forwards on your experiences. Exercise 9.2 gives you some simple questions to ask yourself to help you reflect forwards into a new situation. By doing this a few times, this practice will become second nature to you.

TIP Observing other people

- You can also use the questions in Exercise 9.2 when observing someone else in action. We can learn from the experience of observing other people.

Another useful and very simple framework to help with increasing the salience of learning (and one that can easily be remembered) is 'Stop, Start, Continue', which considers what you should stop doing, what you should start doing and what you should continue to do.

Exercise 9.3   Stop, start, continue

Have a go at creating your own stop, start, continue framework.

Stop	Start	Continue
• What should you stop doing? • What would be the consequences/benefit?	• What should you start doing? • What would be the consequences/benefit?	• What is working well and should be continued? • What would be the consequences/benefits?
Example – *Stop talking over people in a meeting*	Example – *Gather colleagues' feedback*	Example – *Adopt same approach to running meetings*
Bigger issue relating to an aspect of your workload	*Change the way you communicate*	*Continue to use the same institutional policy*

Social learning

So, by making learning more salient to you, you will be able to see learning opportunities where you hadn't overtly realised there could be any. To help you with this further, we want to get you to think about learning and knowledge slightly differently. Chapter 1 discussed the liberating nature of WB learning, especially when viewed through a postmodern approach, without a set structure or order. We would like to introduce you to the concept of social learning to help you with what can at first seem like a daunting situation; viewing learning not as a structured activity but as something that can happen at any time, in any place.

Exercise 9.4   Learning socially

- What does the term 'social learning' conjure up for you?
- Identify a few instances or situations where you think you are learning 'socially'.

Do your examples above include other people? Quite often the phrase 'social learning' immediately invokes ideas of sociability and being with other people. This is very true, and theories of social learning indeed argue that learning is achieved through participation with other people, in a social context. However, they are rooted in something even deeper than this. Philosophically, they reject the view that knowledge is 'out there', a finite thing that can be delivered from a knowledgeable source to someone lacking that information (see Gherardi, 1995; Gherardi et al., 1998).

The social context for learning doesn't have to be somewhere where we socialise. It just means with other people (not necessarily being out at the pub or socialising with friends). This social context then can be the workplace, or anywhere where there are people. Gherardi et al. (1998: 277) argue that if we apply a social perspective to learning, attention shifts from the processing of information and the modifying of cognitive structure to the processes of participation and interaction that provide and sustain a good context for learning.

Exercise 9.5   Looking for learning opportunities

Now you have an understanding of social learning, try the exercise below.

Where are you involved in social learning (try to identify 2–3 examples)?	Who else is involved?	What learning opportunities do you think there are in this context?
I meet colleagues from a different department at work for lunch every Tuesday.	*Three friends.*	*Some of our conversation is about communication with our own teams. I can learn from them about how they communicate and how I might approach similar situations (or not).*

One of the key tenets of social learning theories is that learning takes place with engagement in everyday activities. As a work-based learner you have many opportunities for learning through your own practice in the workplace. In the 1980s Rogoff and Lave (1984) went as far as proposing that it is activity that structures cognition, meaning that thinking is structured by the activities that engage you. Typically, social learning theories stress that any activity is situated in a collective practice.

TIP **Social learning – get involved**

- See learning as participation in everyday activities (whether these might be constructed learning activity; social activity leading to learning; or learning in the workplace).

TIP
- Involve other people.
- Reject the view that knowledge is 'out there' waiting to be acquired from a knowledgeable source.
- See learning as socially constructed through social participation.
- View learning as a social process, which means that you will find (and see) learning opportunities wherever you are.

Peer learning as a framework for learning

Within WBL practice knowing is felt to be context-dependent, deliberately merging theory with practice and acknowledging the intersection of explicit and tacit forms of knowing (Raelin, 2007). As explained above, social learning is also about collective practice – with other people – and combines things you know explicitly with those that you take for granted (tacit knowledge). Collaboration and working with other people (peer learning) can provide frameworks for your learning experiences. Social learning theories question what kinds of social engagements provide the context for learning to take place. This is of particular relevance to your own learning, whether this is in the classroom, in the workplace or even in the family environment.

Things you take for granted can be made explicit and used as learning opportunities. Consider the example of learning to ride a bike. We take it for granted and don't really think about the processes we engage in when we are competent at riding a bike. However, you could stop and reflect on the very act of riding a bike and think about all the things you do to stay on and propel yourself forwards. If you were to now teach someone else, a child perhaps, how to ride a bike, you are able to make your tacit knowledge explicit in order to help them. As well as bringing your tacit knowledge to the fore, teaching someone else also involves peer learning.

Interaction with peers will naturally provide you with a framework for many learning opportunities. The exercises we suggest here can help make this more explicit to you and thus increase the salience of your learning in these situations. Giving and receiving feedback is vital for our learning and development, but all too often we focus on the negatives. Try Exercise 9.6 to practice giving feedback and to remind you of things you do well, and how to make those things happen more often.

Exercise 9.6   Sparkling moments

PART 1 – Sparkling Moments – an exercise with a partner

Say to your partner – 'Think of a time when you were at your best at work, when you really excelled (a sparkling moment). Spend two minutes describing it.'

Partner: Give as many observable, positive, concrete details as possible. You have two minutes.

Listen carefully and note key words that your partner says – you'll need these in a moment.

PART 2 – Giving affirming feedback/identifying resources for the future

Based on what your partner has just said, reflect for a few moments on what you now know about their excellent qualities, skills and resources as a person.

For two minutes give your partner feedback on what he/she said. The feedback should include your observations; for example, 'when you said *xxx*, your eyes really shone and you became very animated'. You have two minutes to feed back what you have heard.

Partner: Don't interrupt during the feedback.

Partner: Thanks you for the feedback.

PART 3 – Establish small actions

Ask your partner what small steps he/she can take to ensure Sparkling Moments like this happen more often.

Repeat the exercise, with your partner asking you for a Sparkling Moment.

Hopefully by encouraging you to focus on something you have done well, the exercise will also be action-oriented, resulting in you taking away a couple of small actions. Ask yourself these questions:

- How did you feel about this exercise?
- What was good about it?
- What was it like working with someone else to carry out this exercise?
- What have you learnt?

Communities of Practice

Working with other people can provide many opportunities for learning, whether it is through something structured, like the exercise above, or through everyday activities. The term 'Community of Practice' (CoP) was coined by Wenger (1998), and is based on a social theory of learning whereby learning is inextricably linked with practice. CoPs involve people who interact and develop relationships that enable them to address problems and share knowledge (Wenger, 2004). The premise is that learning accrues through participation in social, situated activity rather than is acquired from a more knowledgeable source.

A CoP is not a synonym for group, team or network. It is the mutual engagement of those who are members that defines the community, and whatever it takes to make this mutual engagement possible is an essential component of any practice. Examples of CoPs can apply to a street gang, whose members learn how to survive in a hostile world, or a set of engineers who learn how to design better devices, or a collection of civil servants who seek to improve services to citizens (www.wenger-trayner.com). A team, on the other hand, is held together by a task, and when the task is completed the team often disperses. A CoP is held together by the 'learning value' members find in their interaction, and although they may perform tasks together, the tasks do not define the community (www.wenger-trayner.com). Similarly, Swan et al. (2002: 480) argue that professions are not the same as CoPs as they are bounded by formal institutions and governance mechanisms that control membership.

Exercise 9.7   Identifying your own CoPs

Identify a CoP you are a member of by answering these questions:

- Are you involved in activities outside work, for example, as a sports coach, scout leader and so on? If so, do you meet up with, or communicate with other sports coaches, scout leaders and so on?
- At work, do you work across the organisation? Are there other people inside or outside your organisation with the same or similar job title? Do you ever meet up physically or virtually?
- Do you meet up or communicate with others who have a similar identity to you or who are involved in the same pursuit, for example, participating in a chat room with others who have a similar aim to you, or meeting up with people to pursue an interest?

The notion of a CoP returns knowledge back into its context. As a model for work-based learning it suggests that learning is built out of the materials of the local situation and that it is often collective (Raelin, 1997: 570). With this is mind, try Exercise 9.8.

Exercise 9.8 How you learn from your CoPs

Hopefully you will have identified one or more CoPs of which you are a member. Now, we would like to get you to think about how you learn, and can learn even more, from the CoPs you belong to:

- How do you share knowledge? Do you seek to make a difference to your practice? How do you do this?
- If you can answer those questions, think about how you can use your CoP(s) to make learning opportunities more salient to you. How will you know this? What will this look or feel like?
- How can you use your CoP(s) to help you learn more? What kind of conversation or questions will you be having with/asking your fellow members? How will this help your practice?

Case Study 9.1 Building meaningful relationships

A group of owner-managers of small businesses met on a leadership course at a university. Talking to one another at various tea breaks, they realised that they shared many of the same challenges and issues, despite their businesses being very different. It was the running of the business, as owner-managers, they had in common. During the leadership course they partook in small-group activities whereby real business issues were worked on using insightful, open questions. After the leadership course finished, the group of owner-managers decided to keep meeting. This was several years ago, and this group still meets once a month or so to help one another with real-life issues and challenges.

Wenger (1998) presents three 'dimensions' that give coherence to a CoP: mutual engagement; joint enterprise; and shared repertoire. In relation to the case study we can see the role of the three dimensions:

- Mutual engagement – Continuing to meet regularly.
- Joint enterprise – Helping one another with business challenges.
- Shared repertoire – Using insightful, open questions, based on experience to address real-life business issues.

Creating a CoP need not be onerous. For example, across our own organisation we created a CoP with people who share similar job roles.

The activity centres on meeting up for lunch once every six weeks and emailing one another in between if we need to seek help or advice. The point is that there is a rhythm to the activity and our focus is on how we can perform our own roles better; we aren't a team and we don't focus on a task. Nobody has instructed us to do this, and probably none of our superiors have requested this, but this activity will have an impact on the organisation as we are using collective knowledge to share ideas and address ongoing issues.

Exercise 9.9   Creating CoPs

- Who might you identify to create a CoP that is mutually beneficial for your collective learning?
- How could you do this?
- What will the mutual engagement, joint enterprise and shared repertoire be?

(You might not be able to identify all three but it is useful to think about them from the outset).

TIP CoPs – What they are and what they are not

- CoPs is not a synonym for a team or group.
- CoPs are made up of members who have a shared goal that doesn't focus around a task.

Communities of Practice theory has some very useful things to say about identity and learning that are relevant to work-based learning. Lave and Wenger (1991) use a concept called legitimate peripheral participation as a rubric for understanding the way we learn. Essentially, learning arises from participation in a community and gaining recognised membership within that community. Newcomers learn from old-timers, increasing their legitimacy within the group, and moving from peripheral participation to full participation as they identify more with the CoP in question (Lave and Wenger 1991). Lave and Wenger outline five case studies of CoPs to show how legitimate peripheral participation can be explained through an apprenticeship model of newcomers learning from masters (old-timers). The old-timers will have been newcomers once and will have also had to have learnt the practice that they will now be helping the newcomers to learn. We never stop learning, so even if you have completed formal training, for example, you will constantly be learning how to do your job.

Exercise 9.10   Think about your identity

So, how does this relate to WBL? Think about your own identity and your own practice, and use these questions to help you think about your own learning.

- How would you describe your work identity (for example, manager, nurse, consultant)?
- How did you learn to become this (for example, was it a formal training process or informally learning 'on the job'?)
- Who else was involved?
- Can you identify who the 'elders' are in your own context?

You may or may not be aware that you could be part of someone else's legitimate peripheral participation, that is, shaping someone else's professional identity. In this context you may be acting as an 'elder' for them to learn from you. Sometimes, and in some professions, this is clear; for example, apprenticeships are a model where this is made explicit. However, this is not always the case. We learn from others all the time, from the way they talk, carry themselves, what they say. We also learn from negative situations, learning from others about how we would not do something, especially when we see someone behaving in a way of which we disapprove, or think that we wouldn't have said or done a particular thing. Whether you are aware or not, your own colleagues, and people you meet in a professional context, will also be learning from your own behaviours.

Networking

We often hear that networking can be beneficial to our business practices. A network is different from a CoP in that a network is about meeting people, interactions, connections and exchanging knowledge, whereas a CoP (although it does many of the same things) is more about a shared identity and collective intention: the shared domain (see Wenger et al., 2002). However, that is not to say networks are less beneficial to us than CoPs. Networking can provide many opportunities for you as a WB learner. There are many networking events designed to provide a space for businesses to meet. Do you engage in any formal networking activities? This could be through work or organisations outside your work such as the Chamber of Commerce or a body relating to your profession. Networking can also mean something as simple as getting to know people: you are networking when you strike up a conversation or introduce yourself to someone new. However, you can be more strategic in your approach to networking in terms of thinking of it as a learning opportunity.

TIP **Networking – get involved**

- You already belong to many networks; make a list of the people in your networks (family, friends, colleagues, members of your sports club and so on).
- These networks will connect, some more than others. Who in these networks may be able to help with aspects of your WB learning?
- Look out for business networks that are relevant to your role/organisation (you could join the Chamber of Commerce or a trade body that is relevant to you, for example).
- Can you get involved in any volunteering activities in your local community? You never know where these networks may lead you.
- Are activities going on in your own organisation, for example, lunchtime seminars, training events?
- Networking opportunities are everywhere. Have a chat with your friends and family to see what they think about networking and how they do it.

Done well, networking can provide you with opportunities to exchange knowledge, learn about best practice, gain new perspectives, give and receive advice, collaborate, lead to new initiatives and create powerful synergies. Essentially, networking is about sharing and can help to build reciprocal professional relationships. Networking situations are full of learning opportunities, so if you don't engage in any, use this as a prompt to find a situation where you can begin to network with other like-minded people.

TIP **Peer learning as a framework for learning**

- Peer learning involves other people.
- Working with other people can provide many opportunities for learning.
- You can learn formally (such as on a course) or informally with and through other people.
- Communities of Practice provide many opportunities for the circulation of knowledge and learning.
- Learning and identity are inextricably linked.
- As you learn more about your own practice and identify more fully with the profession/position you are in/have, so you reach fuller participation in the process of legitimate peripheral participation.
- Your own behaviours may be influencing other people's learning.

Experience as a framework for learning

As a WB learner, you will inevitably be involved in a practice of some kind (for example, as a nurse, accountant, manager, designer and so on). Your experience of your own practice plays a critical role in affecting learning and change. Kolb is credited with the development of an experiential learning theory, which lays emphasis on learning as a process (see Kolb, 1984). Kolb draws upon the work of earlier theorists, especially, Dewey (1938) and Piaget (1970). Experiential learning theory advocates that learning is not the result of a behavioural or cognitive outcome, but is rather the process whereby knowledge is created through the transformation of experience. This means that you will learn from actually doing your job rather than reading about how to do it. According to Kolb (1984), learning is defined as the process of creating knowledge based on the transformation of experience. In this sense, you need to participate in something in order to learn; furthermore, participatory activities can act as a framework for learning.

There is much written on Kolb's experiential learning theory (ELT) and the learning styles model that is associated with it. Below we focus on the four-stage learning cycle within ELT in order to show you how you can use it in your own practice to develop your learning opportunities. ELT emphasises learning as a continuous cycle of developing new knowledge, altering existing perspectives, integrating old and new ideas and relearning. Exercise 9.11 below shows the four stages of ELT, which need to be followed sequentially in order to transform an experience effectively into learning (Kolb, 1984; Kolb and Kolb, 2005). Although Kolb proposes that one has to go through all four stages for successful learning to occur, the cycle can be entered at any point but all four stages must be followed.

1. Concrete experiences – The first stage of the cycle; Kolb recommends that to learn effectively, the individual (or team or organisation) must 'do', rather than just observe. The emphasis lies on personal involvement in everyday situations. Kolb links this stage of the cycle to feelings, that is, the learner is likely to rely on feeling more than on a systematic approach to a situation.
2. Reflective observation – The next stage is reflective observation; this means stepping back from the task and reviewing what has been experienced. People understand and experience situations differently with different points of view. It is important to reflect on our own experience and to gauge the opinions of others in order for learning to take place. Observation and vocabulary play a key role here, so you will be watching the situation, noticing how others experience it and talking to them to gather thoughts and opinions.
3. Abstract conceptualisation – this is the process of making sense of a situation or experience. It involves interpreting the events along with

understanding the relationships between them. This stage involves using theories, logic, previous observations and ideas in order to understand the experience. This stage is associated with thinking.

4. Active experimentation – This stage of the learning cycle is more active. The learner considers how they are going to put what they have learnt into practice. This stage is concerned with doing rather than watching, with the learner experimenting and making changes. For learning to be effective most people need to place it in a context that is relevant to them. If the learner cannot see how the learning is useful in his or her own context, then it is likely to be forgotten very quickly. Planning is important and enables taking the new understanding and applying it to a new situation where actions can be revised or planned.

Use Exercise 9.11 to test out the above theory.

Exercise 9.11   Identifying experiential learning

Use the template below to give an example and your observations for each stage of the cycle.

Stage of ELT	Example	Observations
Concrete experiences	*A concrete experience may arise from being in the classroom or at work. Try to be aware of the experiences you are involved in. Try something new. For example:* ● *Giving a presentation;* ● *Leading a discussion.*	*Note how you feel.*
Reflective observation	*Write down your reflections of your experiences and thoughts (get into the habit of adding to this regularly).* *Questions to answer include:* ● *What have I learnt today?* ● *What went well?* ● *What might I do differently as a result of that?* ● *What might I continue to do (remember that learning often comes from positive things we do)?*	*Note also how others experience the situation, and include their thoughts and opinions.*

Exercise 9.11 (continued)

Abstract conceptualisation	Planning to do something differently should (where possible) be informed by theory. Link a current situation of experience with a previous experience of a similar situation, for example – the last time that you gave a similar presentation. Link this to any theories or models you have learnt. Or can you search for models that make this applicable?	Make a note of the theories, logic, previous observations and ideas used to understand the experience.
Active experimentation	Plan how you will do something differently in the next situation you encounter (each situation will be unique to you). For example: • speaking up about something; • preparing some materials; • communicating with colleagues in advance.	Make a note of how you did something differently. For example: • How did you plan? • Did you have someone you used as a coach or mentor? • Did you talk to a friend/colleague about your plans and what you hoped to achieve by applying something different to the new situation?

You will find that experiential learning can be an incredibly personal thing, even as it takes place in a social context. You may wish to share your learning with others (and we encourage you to do this), but we appreciate this can be perceived as a daunting thing to do. Certainly, we encourage you to try to be reflective about your own practice and what you are learning. We urge you to be constructive in your reflections, looking at what learning you can take away and what you might do differently, or more of, if it is something you are proud of or has worked well.

Experience as a framework for learning

- Experiencing something can be a very powerful tool for learning.
- Knowledge is created through the transformation of experience.
- This involves a concrete experience, reflecting on it, making sense of it and actively trying to put the learning into practice.

Your own practice plus social learning

As noted already, experience of your own practice is crucial in the learning process. Of course, we need information and knowledge, which this tends to come from 'experts', but often we can place too much emphasis on expert knowledge. Exploiting your experience can be more valuable for learning than any amount of 'teaching', especially within a work-based learning context. While working for the National Coal Board in the 1940s Reg Revans created a learning tool called Action Learning that brought together small groups of peers to work on problems that were important to them. Rather than telling one another what to do, they worked according to an equation devised by Revans, $L = P + Q$, where:

- L refers to learning;
- P refers to 'programmed knowledge' or information we already know, have been taught, read or told;
- Q refers to insightful, open questions designed to make people think differently (see Figure 9.1).

So, learning happens when we use questions to look differently at things we already know. Of course, different kinds of issues require different approaches. Revans made a distinction between *puzzles* and *problems*, which is useful. A puzzle has a specific answer; for example, the following are puzzles:

- What is the latest version of Word?
- Who are the richest women in the UK?

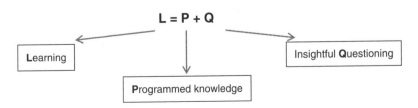

Figure 9.1   How action learning works

To answer these puzzles we do not need a new approach. They have one straightforward answer. Problems are more complex. They do not have one specific answer, and the outcome to a problem will be unique to the person who has asked it. For example, these are problems:

- What kind of software package do I need?
- What does success mean to me?

Problems are ripe for discussion and can only be resolved by asking insightful questions to explore the course of action that is right for the individual concerned.

Other kinds of issues might need a different approach again, but it pays to consider which approach is right for an issue. For example, see Table 9.1.

A complex problem that needs exploration and the asking of insightful questions might be best tackled using a problem-solving model to work through the problem in a logical way. Many exist but a simple one, easily remembered and followed is GROW (standing for Goal, Reality, Options, and Will). Each section of the model moves the questioning and problem-solving on and has certain kinds of questions that might help.

Table 9.1   Possible issues and solutions

Description of issue	Type of issue	How to solve it
How do I build a wall?	Puzzle	There is a way to build a wall. Follow or 'copy' what has been done before
I have built a wall before but now I have different bricks	Simple problem	The principles of wall-building remain the same. 'Bend' how you've built a wall before to accommodate the new materials
How do I build a house?	Complex problem	You must decide what kind of house, what it will look like, its size and so on. You must 'create' using your existing knowledge and experience by asking insightful questions

Box 9.1   The GROW model

	Purpose	Example questions
Goal	Agree on the topic and what the objectives are	What do you want to achieve?
		What does success look like?
		Where do you want to be?
		What is the key issue here?
Reality	Look at what has happened and what's happening now	What have you done so far?
		What assumptions are you making?
		What needs to change?
	Check assumptions	What's stopping you?
Options	Take a step back	What can you do differently?
		What *else* can you do differently?
	Think laterally	What would a different perspective be?
	Explore all the options	How would it look from someone else's eyes?
		If time/money were no object, how would it look?
		Who can help?
Wrap up or Will	Plan actions and time frame	How will you plan this?
		When will you start?
	Examine commitment	What needs to happen first?
		Who will you ask for support?
		How committed are you?

TIP Your own practice and social learning

- Experience of your own practice is crucial in the learning process.
- Engaging in a process of insightful, open questions can help you to gain a fresh perspective on something familiar.
- Place trust in your own knowledge and experience. You are the 'expert'.
- Learning opportunities are all around you.

Conclusions

Social learning theories are useful for understanding WB learning in practice. They provide a lens for thinking about learning as a social construct that involves other people and, importantly, activity or practice. Crucially, thinking about learning in this way can help you, as a work-based learner, to see and seek learning opportunities all around you. As learning becomes increasingly salient to you, so will you be able to filter what learning opportunities are relevant to your own context. The intention here is to help you become the best you can be in your own practice; positively exploiting the learning opportunities surrounding you – in the CoPs you participate in, in everyday work and family life – can aid your lifelong learning journey. The aim of this chapter has been to increase the salience of learning opportunities. We hope you enjoy being a work-based learner and can see the potential it offers. We wish you every success in harnessing the learning all around you. As Einstein recognises, 'Learning is not a product of schooling but the lifelong attempt to acquire it.'.

This chapter challenges the dominant view of education by presenting a social view of learning that applies to you as a work-based learner. Through this approach, we aim to help you create ongoing opportunities for learning and applying your learning to and from your own practice.

Summary

1   A social view of learning regards learning as taking place between people.

2   Increasing the salience of learning can help you learn from situations all around you.

3   Peer learning can provide a framework for learning.

4   Communities of Practice and networking provide valuable learning opportunities and are places where knowledge is constructed and circulated.

5   Identity and learning are inextricably linked.

6   Understanding experiential learning is beneficial for WB learners as you can use your everyday experiences to learn from.

7   Your own practice will enable learning opportunities and by stopping to reflect on them, you will create more learning.

References

Dewey, J. (1938/1991) 'Logic: The Theory of Inquiry'. In J. A. Boydston (ed.), *John Dewey: The Later Works, 1925–1953*, Vol. 12, pp. 1–5 (Carbondale, IL: SIU Press). [Originally published in 1938].

Gherardi, S. (1995) 'Organizational learning'. In H. Warner (ed.), *International Encyclopaedia of Business and Management* (London: Routledge & Kegan Paul).

Gherardi, S., Nicolini, D. and Odella, F. (1998) 'Towards a social understanding of how people learn in organizations: The notion of a situated curriculum', *Management Learning*, 29 (3), pp. 273–297.

Kolb, D. A. (1984) *Experiential Learning: Experience as the Source of Learning and Development* (Englewood Cliffs, NJ: Prentice Hall).

Kolb, A. Y. and Kolb, D. A. (2005) *The Kolb Learning Style Inventory – Version 3.1. Technical Specifications* (Philadelphia: HayGroup, Experience Based Learning Systems Inc.).

Lave, J. and Wenger, E. (1991) *Situated Learning: Legitimate Peripheral Participation* (Cambridge: Cambridge University Press).

Piaget, J. (1970) *Genetic Epistemology* (New York: Columbia University Press).

Raelin, J. A. (2007) 'Towards an epistemology of practice', *Academy of Management Learning & Education*, 6 (4), pp. 495–519.

Rogoff, B. and Lave, J. (eds) (1984) *Everyday Cognition: Its Development in Social Context* (Cambridge, MA: Harvard University Press).

Swan, J., Scarbrough, H. and Robertson, M. (2002) 'The construction of "communities of practice" in the management of innovation', *Management Learning*, 33 (4), pp. 477–496.

Wenger, E. (1998) *Communities of Practice: Learning, Meaning, and Identity* (Cambridge: Cambridge University Press).

Wenger, E. (2004) 'Knowledge management as a doughnut: shaping your knowledge strategy through communities of practice', *Ivey Business Journal*, January/February. Available at http://iveybusinessjournal.com/topics/leadership/knowledge-management-as-a-doughnut

Wenger, E., McDermott, R. and Snyder, W. M. (2002) *Cultivating Communities of Practice: A Guide to Managing Knowledge* (Boston, MA: Harvard Business School Press).

Websites

www.wenger-trayner.com (accessed 13 May 2014).

Suggested further reading

Arnell, R. (2014) Teacher Beliefs on Personal Learning, Collaboration, and Participation in Virtual Communities of Practice. Doctoral dissertation, Walden University.

Brown, J. S. and Duguid, P. (1991) 'Organizational learning and communities of practice: toward a unified view of working, learning and innovation', *Organization Science*, 2 (1), pp. 40–57.

Brown, J. S. and Duguid, P. (2001) 'Knowledge organization: a social-practice perspective', *Organization Science*, 12 (2), pp. 198–213.

Lankshear, C. and Knobel, M. (2011) *New Literacies: Everyday Practices And Social Learning* (3rd Edn) (Open University/McGraw-Hill International: Maidenhead).

Revans, R. (2011) *ABC of Action Learning* (Aldershot: Gower Publishing).

Sadler, T. D. (2014) 'Communities of Practice'. In R. Gunstone (Ed.), *Encyclopedia of Science Education* (pp. 1–6) (New York, NY: Springer).

Squires, S. and Van De Vanter, M. L. (2012) 'Communities of practice'. In D. D. Caulkins and A. T. Jordan (eds), *A Companion to Organizational Anthropology* (Chichester, UK: John Wiley & Sons, Ltd).

Wenger, E. (2011) *Communities of practice: A brief introduction.* Available online at http://www.scholarsbank.uoregon.edu.

Whitmore, J. (2009) *Coaching for Performance: Growing Human Potential and Purpose* (London: Nicholas Brealey Publishing).

Learning to be an international work-based learner

Tony Wall and Ly Tran

In this chapter you will learn:

► key success factors for work-based learning students across cultures;
► the importance of learning another way to think, write and act to be a successful work-based learning student in a multicultural context;
► how to build your own personal learning network and wider environment;
► ways to continually improve your academic performance through self-reflection and self-leadership;
► methods for planning and managing cultural factors when designing and implementing work-based learning projects.

Studying across cultures

Modern colleges and universities are now like multinational grocery store chains. If you walk around one of these stores in New York, London, Hong Kong, Lahore or Sydney, you will always find a wide variety of options to choose from. This is the same with work-based learning courses. Think about these options: Did your course require you to travel to a different country to study it, or did it allow you to study locally? Does your course involve some on-campus attendance, or is it entirely online? Are you in a group where you have contact with the same people over time, or are you on a totally negotiated course where you are the only student studying it? There are many combinations of these options.

But the features that put these courses in the same aisle in the store is that you will be *in work* alongside your studies, and that you will *learn through work* (see the Introduction and Chapter 1). Studying on a work-based learning course at a college or university *in a different cultural setting from your own*

Figure 10.1   Work-based learning student success in multicultural contexts

is challenging. But it can also fundamentally change the way you think and create life-changing, global opportunities for you – while also benefiting your employer in ways they have probably never seen education do before.

So how do you achieve academic success on a work-based learning course at a college or university in a different cultural setting from your own? The international research shared in this chapter teaches us that your academic success is largely determined by how much you learn how to 'think, write and act' for your course, and how much you integrate study into your daily life. The next three sections give your more detailed advice on how to do this: learning additional cultures, building your own transcultural study environment, and doing work-based learning projects across cultures (see Figure 10.1).

Learning additional cultures

Not including normal bodily functioning, there are very few things that we are born knowing how to do well. For example, we are not born knowing how to cross the road safely; we learn it over time with help from older and wiser people. You learn where to cross the road, and how to do so. This does not mean, however, that there is only one way to cross the road. Imagine you are standing next to a road and you are waiting to cross. Where do you look *first*: left or right? The answer is: it depends where you are. You might, if you are in Sydney, look *right* first, as people drive on the left of the road. But if you are in Chicago, you might look *left* first, as people drive on the right of the road. And if you are next to one of the busiest roads in India, you may need to continually look in all directions while you walk through stationary traffic.

This teaches us that we need to learn different ways of doing even very simple tasks that we think we already know how to do, and that we need to keep learning. It is useful to expect that you will need to invest time and energy in learning how to be a successful work-based learning student in a cultural setting different from our own. If your course involves you interacting with others, it is useful to expect to learn about the culture of the country in which your college or university is located. But this is just one aspect.

It is useful for *all* work-based learning students to expect to learn about the *culture of the course* they are studying. This includes learning *additional* ways of thinking, writing and acting while studying. Sometimes, aspects of the additional culture will be similar to what you already know, and so will be easy for you to do. But often you will need to find your own *creative way* to study, which both:

- positively uses your own cultural background, knowledge and values;
- and which also meets the requirements of your course.

The research teaches us that learning the culture of your course partly determines the success in your studies (Baxter, 2012; Gebhard, 2012; Subotzky and Prinsloo, 2011).

Exercise 10.1   Finding out what your course requires of you

1. Think about your previous studies.
2. Think about the ways you *found out* how to 'do well' (or succeed) in these previous studies. Write them down.
3. Compare what is similar in your list to the list of tips below. These are the things to continue doing.
4. Compare what is different in your list from the list of tips below. These are the things to consider doing.

TIP   Finding out the requirements of your course

In her research, Tran (2008) concluded that students use a number of ways to find out the requirements of their course. You can consider:

- Reading the guidance on your course website.
- Asking for advice and guidance from your tutors

TIP
- Getting advice from your student skills development tutors.
- Getting advice from your English as a Second Language tutors.
- Reading 'example' essays, portfolios or presentations from your course.
- Getting to know your tutors and their preferences for how you should 'think, write and act'.

Also see Chapters 1, 2 and 6, about developing your academic skills and learning to learn on a work-based learning course.

Learning another way to 'think'

In some educational cultures showing that you have read the core text of your course is good and highly valued. In those cultures, you are being assessed on how well you can recall or repeat what respected writers have written in academic textbooks. However, in other educational cultures, this can be seen as unacceptable or bad. Within work-based learning, reading theory and textbooks is very important. But it is only one aspect of your learning. In addition, you are expected to do these additional six things:

1. Use the theory to think about the way you or others act in the reality of your workplace. This can also be called 'applying' or 'using' the theory to analyse practice.
2. Use multiple texts or perspectives so that you can think about different and multiple aspects of a situation. See the example below.
3. Compare the *similarities* of various texts so you know the most important elements to think about as you analyse your situation.
4. Contrast the *differences* of various texts so you know which additional features you need to think about in your analysis of a situation. This might teach you something different than the similarities.
5. Evaluate the theory so you can make a decision about how useful the theory was in understanding your situation.
6. Evaluate your (or other people's) thinking and behaviour so that you can make a decision about how useful they are in understanding your situation, or in changing the situation.

However, it is important to find your own style in achieving these features. Read Case study 10.1 to learn more about finding your own style of critical reflection.

Case Study 10.1   Using various texts

Shui is an international student from China, enrolled on a work-based Master's degree in the UK. She wanted to design a marketing plan for her business in Beijing. She read five textbooks on marketing from different authors. She was surprised: one textbook said there was only three stages in marketing planning, and the other textbooks said there were between 10 and 20 stages in marketing planning.

After comparing the similarities and contrasting the differences, she realised that many were the same 'stages' but used different words to describe the same stage. However, there were some texts that included a stage related to calculating how much all the planning would cost (cost of planning).

This was an important stage to a small business that had limited money to spend on planning (she evaluated the theory, in terms of how useful it was *in her context*).

Within your course, these skills might be referred to as 'critical analysis' or 'critical reflection'. A useful way of thinking about them might be that 'critical analysis' is where you compare, contrast and evaluate the theory and texts you use, and 'critical reflection' is where you examine your own thoughts and behaviours, and the reasons for them.

Chapter 1 above teaches you more about the kind of academic skills (such as critical thinking) you will be expected to develop during your course. It is important that you spend time and effort finding out what is required from you on your HE-level work-based learning course (see Exercise 10.1).

Case Study 10.2   Displaying critical thinking in Australia

Xuân was a Vietnamese international student who did an undergraduate degree in South West Vietnam and then enrolled on an education course in Australia. Xuân enjoys free writing and inspirational writing, and found it most challenging to understand the 'Western' concept of critical thinking. In her Vietnamese culture, comments on others' work should focus on 'good thing, not bad thing' to preserve harmony in communication and in life. Xuân explained:

It's some kind of comparing or contrasting. That's because Vietnamese culture, in our educational background, we don't have

Case Study 10.2 (continued)

critical thinking. It's very difficult for me to know about that, to evaluate an author when you always think that that person is high above you, that person is very knowledgeable, that's the person who can write the book. That person is so right, so good … Actually, I am starting with comparing and contrasting, I read that author and the other authors and then I think okay, they have their good point of views and how they argue that and then I think that okay that person is more convincing.

In the above comment, Xuân stressed the significance of finding the mismatches among different research as her strategy for critical thinking. She highlighted the need to focus on identifying the strong points of each author's work. Xuân is influenced by her Vietnamese values, and brought her voice of being a Vietnamese into her academic writing in Australia.

She believed that it did not seem sensible to be 'critical' of the person who had the authority of a writer of the book and was thus more knowledgeable than her. This aspect appears to link to the Vietnamese tendency to respect authority and value harmony in knowledge building.

Xuân used her strategy of comparing and contrasting but focused on the good points of the author's work. While finding it difficult to evaluate the author's work, the above strategy seemed to place her in a safe position and gave her more confidence in writing.

It seemed that by using this strategy, Xuân reached a compromise of her voice as Vietnamese and her wish to engage in thinking and writing for her course. This enabled her to avoid pointing out the weaknesses of the author's work and preserve her own view of critical writing while allowing her to engage the particular form of academic writing valued on her course.

So, in summary, Xuân found her own way to show critical thinking by mixing together what was expected from her with her Vietnamese cultural values.

Learning another way to 'write'

You show your thinking through writing, and this is the main way your study efforts will be assessed. So it is crucial to write in ways that are expected by your course. You might be familiar with (and very good at) copying or repeating the words of one author, from one textbook, but this will not allow you to meet the expectations of a HE-level work-based learning course, and it is not what is valued in work-based learning. It's useful to take time to think about how you have written previously in your educational studies. Becoming aware of what you currently do will be very helpful for you when learning additional study skills.

Exercise 10.2   How have you written before?

First, think about your previous educational studies.

Describe how you write an academic piece of work, from start to finish (if you have never written an academic piece of work, think about a professional piece of writing you have done for your workplace). Use these questions to give you some ideas:

- how did you decide what to focus on?
- how did you decide what to read?
- how many published sources did you read?
- what did you read that was given to you by your teachers?
- how did you plan your writing?
- how did you decide what to comment upon?

Now, for each of your replies to the above, think about what you might need to do differently to achieve the 'additional six things' expected of you, below:

1. You use the theory (rather than repeat or copy it).
2. You read multiple texts or perspectives.
3. You compare the similarities of various texts.
4. You contrast the differences of various texts.
5. You evaluate the theory.
6. You evaluate your (or others peoples') thinking and behaviour.

TIP   Building on your writing

- Become clear about the core focus of the assignment (is it focused on theory, reflection or both?).
- Identify texts with multiple perspectives. This might be given in your learning materials or course materials. Your tutor might also give you advice.
- Build time in to read more than one text.
- Read selectively (choose books carefully, read cover details and brief introduction or 'abstract' sections before reading chapters).

TIP

- Use a note-taking method such as 'mind-mapping' to compare the similarities of various texts and contrast the differences of various texts (search Google for 'note-taking strategies').
- Use a theory to help you create logical headings for your writing.
- Use your note-taking method to help you plan comments for each heading.
- Use reflective models to help your critical reflections. See Chapter 2 about the learning skills needed on a work-based course.
- Write in your words, and do not copy or repeat the words from the texts you read (you can occasionally copy short sentences or paragraphs, but you must include where the sentence or paragraph was originally written – see the guidelines on 'referencing' or 'citations' in your course materials).
- Make comments about the theory you have used: in what ways did it help you? In what ways was it limiting?

Also see Chapters 1 and 2 about developing your academic and transferable skills on a work-based learning course. Chapter 11 also offers very useful advice about preparing for assessments on a work-based learning course.

Case Study 10.3   Writing to help you learn, or, copying the texts of others?

Alayah is an international student in Pakistan enrolled on a work-based degree course in the UK. She was designing a work-based project to encourage more customers to return and buy more from her business. She had read lots of journal articles about customer retention and had written a summary of what she had learnt from the journals.

She sent this to her tutor, but was surprised when the tutor said it was unacceptable. Alayah then realised that she had used text (repeated the text) directly from articles without referencing the original author. This was acceptable in her previous studies, but was not acceptable in her degree studies in the UK.

Her way of learning the theory was to copy the text from the articles; the rewriting helped her understand. She learnt she could still use the text from books, but that she would need to change the text into 'her words' before giving her work to the tutor, and reference the author's ideas.

Learning another way to 'act' on your course

How you 'act' on your course includes 'thinking' and 'writing'. But it is also wider. You may be familiar with the teacher teaching you about theory, telling you what to learn, what to read and when to study. You are probably familiar with sitting in a classroom with others, with a teacher standing at the front of the room. Within a work-based learning course, having a tutor is possibly different from what you have experienced before. This means it is useful to expect to learn about their role and how to interact with them. They might be different from a traditional teacher in the following ways. A work-based learning tutor will guide you:

- around what to focus on – but you have to decide what precise reading to follow up, because only you have detailed knowledge of what is important in your workplace;
- around what to read – but you have to choose which books, articles and websites to read, which involves you deciding how credible or trustworthy the source is;
- in your reflections – but only you know how you feel and think about your situation (the teacher cannot know your own thoughts).
- in your writing – but only you can plan and write all of the work.

Exercise 10.3   Interacting with your tutors

Questions/observations	Answers
Think about your favourite teacher in your previous studies	
What did they do differently from other teachers?	
How did you interact with them?	
How do you think your interactions with tutors might be different on your work-based learning course?	
Now, think about what you might do to manage these differences: • What might you need to do, to adapt to these differences? • What might you do to help your own tutor learn about *your history and cultural values*?	

In addition to a tutor, you will also have access to a course website. Your course website is probably more important than you think: research teaches us that whether or not you find your course relevant, useful and motivational relates to how much *you believe* you can use the course site and other technologies used in your course (Sun and Rueda, 2012). Therefore, to maximise the value of your course, you should spend time learning how to use the online course materials and technologies for your course. See Chapter 8 to learn more about learning technologies in work-based learning.

International research suggests that learning how to interact with your tutor and how to use the online materials influences how successful you can be on your course (Baxter, 2012; Gebhard, 2012; Subotzky and Prinsloo, 2011; Sun and Rueda, 2012).

Case Study 10.4 Improving English language and developing cultural knowledge

Ajani is an international Mexican student on a work-based horticultural course in Australia. Ajani struggled with communicating in English and felt a lack confidence in approaching his teachers to ask questions during his first months of studying. He used a variety of ways to improve his English and developed trans-national knowledge in his professional field, which included:

- Using a variety of learning strategies to improve English, including any opportunities to interact with and ask English-native students for help in clarifying the learning content whenever he did not fully understand.
- Sharing his knowledge of the professional practices from his home country with teachers and others on his course – and learning about trans-national practices from others on his course.
- Bringing photos of different gardens and plants from Mexico to show to his class members.
- Preparing presentations on topics based on his perspective as a Mexican landscape designer.
- Talking about the Mexican professional associations related to course topics.
- Actively asking questions about different trans-national professional practices.
- Seeking help from the international student co-ordinator when needed.

Case Study 10.5   Achieving higher grades

By Sandra Hopkins, Lecturer in Management, Henan Province, China

Yufang is a hard-working Chinese learner studying international management in China. In her previous studies, she would often achieve high grades, but on her degree she achieved much lower grades. Yufang realised that her teacher wanted her to think differently from before; now, Yufang needed to question what the teacher said and needed to find the similarities and differences in management theories. Yufang improved her grades and her understanding of management by:

- observing what other students did in and outside of class;
- joining in with class discussions and trying out new ways of learning;
- accepting that she would make mistakes in group discussions, and that she would also learn from these mistakes;
- reflecting on how these things affected her time management, her perceptions and her feelings towards her study.

Case Study 10.6   Being aware of your cultural expectations

By Yoshimoto Oikawa, Executive HR Advisor, Yamato Holding Co. Ltd (Japan's leading logistics company)

Kaito is an international student from Japan on a work-based learning course. Before he started his course, he undertook a 'PICO' questionnaire. PICO stands for *Personal Intercultural Change Orientation*, which identifies a person's expectations related to living and working in an environment with multiple cultures. In the questionnaire, Kaito had to choose between two statements, such as (a) Fairness requires that everyone follows the same rules or (b) Fairness requires that we make exceptions to the rules. Whichever statement a person chooses shows that person's cultural assumptions. Using PICO, Kaito found various cultural expectations that were different from others in a multicultural environment, but he was not aware of them. This learning helped him adjust to his learning and business context, and helped him realise how people in different cultures think and act differently.

Building your own multicultural study environment

Making enough regular study time available

International research also suggests that the amount of time you spend on your studies can predict your academic grade (Mo and Zhao, 2011; Ren and Hagedorn, 2012). Even the amount of time you spend on your course website has been linked to your academic grade (Sun and Rueda, 2012). But as a person who needs to balance work, home and study, research further suggests that you need to:

- make *regular* time available for your studies, so that it becomes part of your life;
- ensure that that this is *enough* time (Baxter, 2012; Selwyn, 2011; Sun and Rueda, 2012).

Scheduling *regular* time in your diary is different from scheduling *enough* time. Scheduling regular time enables you to keep your learning connected across time, which means that you can build on what you thought last week. But *enough* time is about whether you personally need more time to access, read, digest and reflect on the texts you read. Exercise 10.4 will help you to schedule enough regular time for your studies.

Exercise 10.4　Scheduling enough, regular time?

Reflect on the statements below and consider how often the statements apply to you. This exercise will help you decide whether you need to spend more time and/or more regular time in your studies. Tick (✓) for how often a statement applies to you: never, sometimes or often.

	Never	Some-times	Often
Indicators of not scheduling *enough* time:			
Your tutor gives you advice about:			
your essay or portfolio structure;			
your English language;			
how much reading you are doing.			
You do not submit on time, or miss elements of your assessments.			
Your tutor comments (or grades) are not improving over time.			

Exercise 10.4 (continued)

	Never	Some-times	Often
Indicators of not scheduling *regular* time:			
When you study, you forget about:			
what the assessment is;			
where you have put your notes;			
what you have read, or have not read;			
what you have already written.			
You ask tutors or other college or university staff the same questions again, and again.			
You respond late to college/university emails.			

Now reflect on how your results: where do you have most of your 'sometimes' or 'often' statements? The more ticks you have, the more evidence there is for you to change your study patterns: Are you spending enough time? Are you building that time in regularly enough?

Case Study 10.7   Scheduling time

Usmani is an international student from India, enrolled on a Master's degree in the UK. He worked in a family business and was studying for a work-based degree part time. He was a very busy manager within the business and wanted also to watch his young children grow up. He found studying difficult to fit in until he realised he needed to schedule weekly time for his personal studies, but also to ensure others in the business and at home understood how important education was to him. He scheduled study time in, which was to be prioritised in the same way as important business and family events.

Building your own multicultural, personal learning network

Scheduling enough, regular time for your studies tells you how much you are integrating your studies into your life. International research teaches us that this is important to your success (Baxter, 2012; Gebhard, 2012; Park and Choi, 2009; Subotzky and Prinsloo, 2011).

But making enough, regular time can mean asking for time and emotional support from people at home and at work. These people are therefore an important part of your personal learning network, but you must carefully respect their time and offer of support (see the tip below).

TIP Building your multicultural network

- Assume that each of your connections is not required or obliged to offer you anything – carefully request time and explain the benefits to them, of them helping and supporting you.
- Connect with people across cultures who you are familiar with, and who you are not familiar with – this helps when you need to understand why something has happened a particular way.
- Over time, reflect on where you are getting the most help and motivation from – see the next part of this section.

Figure 10.2   Your personal learning network

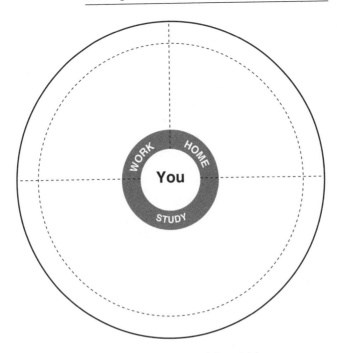

Figure 10.3   Identifying your personal learning network (template)

Learning which of your connections in your network can help you and motivate you is crucial to study success. See Chapters 7 and 9 to learn more about how the people around you can help you in your studies.

Exercise 10.5   Knowing and using your 'personal learning network'

For this task, either use the empty diagram (Figure 10.3), or draw your own which looks the same.

- In the empty spaces, write the names of people who have helped you or who have motivated you in your studies so far. It is important to write names for each of the categories listed (for example, managers, friends, family and so on). For example, you might write Alaya (your sister) and Jacob (your uncle).
- If you cannot find a name for a category, look at the next category and continue writing names in the spaces.

Exercise 10.5 (continued)

- Now look over what you have written and identify the categories that do not have any names listed. Write down these missing categories.
- Now, for each category, identify additional names to ensure you have at least one name for each. This might involve you thinking about who you already know that can help or motivate you, or it might mean asking your manager who else is studying at work. It may also mean searching your university website to identify what services are available to you. List the additional names in the space below.
- Once you have identified at least one name for each category, create a 'personal contact sheet', with names, area of help and contact details. This is your personal learning network, which is a source of significant power for you, so make this as easy as possible for you to access at any point.

Doing work-based projects across cultures

Personal reflection and leadership

So far in this chapter, you will know the importance of learning how to think, write and act for your course, and know how to build a powerful network of people around you. Now, the final aspect of your success in your work-based studies is about being reflective in your role as a work-based learning student (Gebhard, 2012; Subotzky and Prinsloo, 2011).

Reflecting on how to do things better is not just a key tool for improving your performance in the workplace (see Chapter 2). It is also crucial to learning how to maximise the learning and value from your studies, and your performance as a student. According to international research, reflection is particularly important to your success in two ways:

- To be able to motivate yourself through your studies (Baxter, 2012; Masjuan and Troiano, 2009). So be clear about the strongest reasons for why you are studying – and remind yourself of these regularly.
- To help you believe you can succeed (Subotzky and Prinsloo, 2011; Sun and Rueda, 2012). Monitor and find examples of when you are doing the right things (see Exercise 10.6). The good news is that even if you have low confidence (or do not believe you can succeed), you still can! Using the exercises in this book can overpower any lack of self-belief and boost your success.

Case Study 10.8   Self-leadership to overcome culture shock and maximise learning

Kim is an international student from the Republic of Korea, who enrolled on a work-based hospitality course in Australia. For Kim, culture shock and learning how to adapt to the Australian academic and social environments were the most challenging things. She overcame the cultural barriers by stepping out of her own comfort zone and actively seeking the opportunity to engage with cultural diversity by:

- widening her social networks by not only socialising with Korean friends as she used to, but also with international students from different countries and domestic students;
- enhancing her understanding of the Australian culture and learning how to mediate between different values through her engagement with different groups of friends;
- reflecting on what she often took for granted as being unique Korean values and 'Asian' values;
- learning to be mindful of stereotypical views of international students that may emerge from the workplace or classrooms;
- actively looking for a hospitality job to refine her occupational and improve her communication skills;
- taking the opportunity to participate in class discussions.

Exercise 10.6   Record your achievements (whether small, tiny or minuscule)

Buy or create a small notebook (you choose the design), and each time you do an academic task that you think is good, or somebody tells you is good, record it. Draw a picture or make a written note of what it was. Record small comments or feelings, or, even better, record each tiny moment in the book.

Planning for multicultural features of work-based projects

It is crucial to consider cultural factors in designing your work-based projects (also see Chapter 12 about designing work-based projects as part of your studies). Not planning for these factors can mean that your project will not be supported by managers, make no impact within your organisation, or worse, create problems for you or other staff in your organisation. One way of thinking about your organisation's cultural factors is to consider them against the four cultural variables highlighted by Flores et al. (2012). I have expanded on these headings in Box 10.1 and Exercise 10.7 below.

Box 10.1   Features of culture

Participative decision-making

Does the team, department or organisation you are trying to influence, allow staff to:

- Share their views on what the problems are?
- Share information and ideas about solutions?
- Share the implementation of solutions?
- Share the evaluation of results?
- ... or do a specific individual or small group of individuals do these tasks?

Openness

How easy it is to consult with others and share information within and outside the organisation?

Learning orientation

Does the team, department or organisation you are trying to influence:

- Encourage people to learn new things at work?
- Encourage people to learn without fear of mistakes?
- Have processes to evaluate and improve results at work?

Transformational leadership

Does the team, department or organisation you are trying to influence have leaders who:

- Communicate a clear sense of strategic direction of where the team/department or organisation is going?
- Encourage people to learn and develop new skills?
- Encourage new ideas and innovative problem solving?

In some cultures, there is only one person who makes the decisions about which problems are worth solving, and it might be this person who works out a solution (this is low participative decision-making). This person might collect the information they need to solve the problem themselves, because they are the only person with access to it (low openness). This person might prefer not to change processes within the business, so does not encourage staff to learn new things or change established processes (low learning orientation, low transformational leadership). This sounds like a bad place to work, but staff can still respect and enjoy working for their leader even in these circumstances.

Within this workplace context, it is still possible to do a work-based project, but you must plan it carefully. The cultural factors will give you ideas about how to plan your work-based project, for example:

- Deciding who to involve in your project – within this culture, the leader is the key decision-maker within the business. You will probably need to involve them in many stages of the design and probably implementation. They will also know who else has the information you need.
- Deciding the focus of your project – you will need to get agreement from the leader in this example. If not, the leader may reject the focus at the start of the project, during its implementation or at the end (when you have done all of the work!).
- Deciding the methods involved in your project – you will need to involve the leader in setting the methods for your project, otherwise they may not trust the results. This may therefore mean no changes are made.
- Deciding who will have access to the results of your project – because of a 'low' openness culture, you will need to get agreement about who will be able to access the information created by your project.
- Planning how to manage conflict in your project – if there is potential for conflict as a result of your project, it would be useful to ensure that the leader is aware of all stages. In this way, they will feel better able to manage any unpredictable surprises.

Exercise 10.7 Thinking about culture when designing work-based projects

- Think about your team, department or organisation.
- How would you describe the culture, in terms of the following statements (please tick one column for each statement)

Participative decision-making Staff are allowed to:	Never	Some-times	Always
Share their views on what the problems are.			
Share information and ideas about solutions.			
Share the implementation of solutions.			
Share the evaluation of results.			
Openness It is easy to consult with others and share information within and outside the organisation.			

Exercise 10.7 (continued)

Participative decision-making Staff are allowed to:	Never	Some- times	Always
Learning orientation Staff are encouraged to learn new things at work.			
Staff are encouraged to learn without fear of mistakes.			
Processes are used to evaluate and improve results at work.			
Transformational leadership Leaders:			
Communicate a clear sense of strategic direction of where the team/department or organisation is going.			
Encourage people to learn and develop new skills.			
Encourage new ideas and innovative problem-solving.			

- Now reflect on how these results might affect how you design a work-based project (see Chapter 12 for further details on work-based projects).

Summary

1 Expect to learn new ways of doing very simple academic tasks.

2 Spend time and effort finding out how you should 'think, write and act' as a work-based learning student.

3 Learn how to write for your course: use multiple theories and texts in your writing, evaluate them and also evaluate your own thinking and behaviours.

4 The work-based learning tutor might be different from a traditional teacher: they act more like a guide than your own 'personal professor' or 'personal Google search engine'.

5 Find ways to build regular study into your life, and build your personal learning network (PLN) – see also Chapter 8 to help you to do this.

6 Spend time building your multicultural personal learning network, and reflecting on your performance as a student (not as a worker).

7 Use feedback to give you ideas about where to enhance your study time and technique.

References

Baxter, J. (2012) 'Who am I and what keeps me going? Profiling the distance learning student in higher education', *The International Review of Research in Open and Distance Learning*, 13 (4), 107–129.

Flores, L. G., Zheng, W., Rau, D. and Thomas, C. H. (2012) 'Organizational learning: subprocess identification, construct validation, and an empirical test of cultural antecedents', *Journal of Management*, 38 (2), 640–667.

Gebhard, J. G. (2012) 'International students' adjustment problems and behaviours', *Journal of International Students*, 2 (2), 184–193.

Masjuan, J. M. and Troiano, H. (2009) 'University students' success: a psycho-sociological approach', *Higher Education*, 58, 15–28.

Mo, S. and Zhao, L. (2011) 'An analysis of student activities and performance in management distance education courses', *International Journal of Education Research*, 6 (1), 86–96.

Park, J.-H. and Choi, H. J. (2009) 'Factors influencing adult learners' decision to drop out or persist in online learning', *Educational Technology & Society*, 12 (4), 207–217.

Ren, J. and Hagedorn, L.S. (2012) 'International graduate students' academic performance: what are the influencing factors?', *Journal of International Students*, 2 (2), 135–143.

Selwyn, N. (2011) 'Digitally distanced learning: a study of international distance learners' (non) use of technology', *Distance Education*, 32 (1), 85–99.

Subotzky, G. and Prinsloo, P. (2011) 'Turning the tide: a socio-critical model and framework for improving student success in open distance learning at the University of South Africa', *Distance Education*, 32 (2), 177–193.

Sun, J. C-Y. and Rueda, R. (2012) 'Situational interest, computer self-efficacy and self-regulation: their impact on student engagement in distance education', *British Journal of Educational Technology*, 43 (2), 191–204.

Tran, L. (2008) 'Unpacking academic requirements: international students in Management and Education disciplines', *Higher Education Research & Development*, 27 (3), 245–256.

Suggested further reading

Copus, J. (2009) *Brilliant Writing Tips for Students*, Pocket Study Skills Series (Basingstoke: Palgrave Macmillan).

Cottrell, S. (2013) *The Study Skills Handbook – Simplified Chinese Language Edition* (Basingstoke: Palgrave Macmillan).

Godfrey, J. (2014) *Reading and Making Notes*, 2nd edn, Pocket Study Skills Series (Basingstoke: Palgrave Macmillan).

Lipson, C. (2008a) *Doing Honest Work in College: How to Prepare Citations, Avoid Plagiarism, and Achieve Real Academic Success*, 2nd edn (Chicago: Chicago Guides to Academic Life) [for students in the US, Canada and similar systems].

Lipson, C. (2008b) *Succeeding as an International Student in the United States and Canada* (Chicago: Chicago Guides to Academic Life) [for students in the US, Canada and similar systems].

Macmillan Publishers (2014) *International Student Study Skills Useful Resources*. Available at http://www.palgrave.com/skills4study/studentlife/international/useful.asp.

Williams, K. (2014) *Getting Critical*, 2nd edn, Pocket Study Skills Series (Basingstoke: Palgrave Macmillan).

Williams, K. and Reid, M. (2011) *Time Management*, Pocket Study Skills Series (Basingstoke: Palgrave Macmillan).

Making the most of your assessment opportunities

Sue Graham and Garth Rhodes

In this chapter you will learn:

► why WBL needs to be assessed;
► the different types of WBL assessments;
► how you will be assessed; the methods, processes and procedures;
► the rules and regulations;
► your roles and responsibilities.

Introduction

If you asked the majority of students what was the most worrying aspect of their learning experience, the answer would probably be 'assessment'. Similarly, if you asked tutors what they thought concerned their learners most, the likely answer would be 'assessment'. Why is this? It is probably that assessment is used to judge our performance, telling us how well, or badly, we have done, so it is natural to worry about it, as nobody wants to do badly.

Adult learners often recount unhappy experiences of assessment at school as having turned them off learning. At some point you may have worked incredibly hard on your work, only to have your enthusiasm dashed because you did not receive a good grade. There are a number of reasons for this, including:

• lack of clarity in the teaching, or the instructions given for the task;
• use of assessments incapable of measuring what you have learned.

Negative attitudes to assessment can also be self-induced; try not to let assessment undermine the enjoyment of your learning experience. Avoidance strategies, such as leaving the work until the night before, very occasionally produces inspirational work, but usually only poor marks. Everyone is different, but when it comes to assessment there are some clear personality differences. We have identified five broad categories. You want to be:

a. the best, above everything else, no matter what;
b. 'your best' and get the most out of your learning;
c. doing as little as possible and scraping by;
d. average, doing as well as you can in the circumstances;

and unfortunately some are:

e. so consumed by worry that they feel doomed to fail.

Case Study 11.1   John

John is extremely nervous about his assessment after a bad experience of learning at school, and expends all his energy on worrying about whether or not he will pass. He is classic category (e), and has been considering what he needs to do to move towards category (b) above. His action plan involves him:

- using the university support mechanisms, for example, Study Skills;
- talking about his concerns with his tutor, supportive colleagues and fellow students;
- making sure he understands what is expected by breaking down assessment tasks and criteria, to remove trepidation;
- planning and prioritising;
- using all opportunities to learn rather than being end-focused;
- submitting drafts of work for early feedback to build up his confidence.

Exercise 11.1   How do I view assessment?

Consider your own attitudes towards assessment:

- Into which of the above categories do you fall?

_____

_____

- To which category do you aspire?

_____

_____

Exercise 11.1 (continued)

- How will you need to change, and what will you have to do to achieve this?

_____

_____

_____

We have all experienced some form of assessment; you will have completed homework, written essays and taken tests or 'exams' at school. HE students were traditionally assessed through examination, essay, dissertation and thesis, but more recently newer, more innovative methods of assessment have become popular such as making presentations, developing a portfolio of work and evidence, or even developing work in groups of peers, some of which may be assessed by those peers. If you joined the workforce straight from school perhaps through an apprenticeship, trade tests and professional body qualifications were used. So, how does WBL assessment differ from what you have experienced already?

Purposes of WBL assessment – the 'why'

WBL assessment enables you to:

- gain qualifications and let the university judge your performance;
- demonstrate your learning;
- develop yourself;
- improve your career opportunities;
- improve your workplace performance.

Assessment is not only concerned with the standards of qualifications and judging your performance; it is also a key vehicle to enable you to get the most out of your learning experience and to perform to the best of your ability. Viewing your assessments as learning strategies will enhance your enjoyment of your learning experience while helping you to achieve.

Race (2007: 27–32) suggests that good assessment should:

- motivate you;
- enable your progression to further learning;
- diagnose your faults and help you rectify mistakes; .
- offer you a variety of learning experiences;
- help you 'get down to serious learning'.

WBL assessment – the 'what'

When tutors assess WBL on a university course, they look for more than just the demonstration of workplace skills and competencies. They want to see evidence of your academic ability delivering a real and positive impact upon you and your working environment. You will be assessed upon your ability to articulate and apply high-level critical thinking (which is methodical, analytical, clear, rational, open-minded and informed by evidence) and reflection (which examines learning experience to develop, and build upon or even change behaviour and practice – see Chapter 2) within complex situations in your work, organisation or your wider profession. The learning for which you will be assessed will, to a great extent, be unique to you. This requires a high degree of autonomy on your part (Chapter 6), as well as negotiation of what you will be learning and how you will evidence this for assessment purposes.

As a work-based learner you are likely to have:

- considerable professional/occupational knowledge and experience;
- opportunity to engage in active learning through reflecting upon everyday work tasks;
- confidence in your own competence, already proven through your ongoing ability to do your job;
- a sense of motivation and expectation of success;
- a predisposition to engage in a meaningful learning experience (Walsh, 2007: 79–87).

These characteristics will help you to get the most from assessment.

Your tutor will expect you to show that you have undertaken significant investigation and enquiry around key issues affecting your workplace, and drawn upon relevant theories, concepts, new research and policies to support your thinking.

Negotiating assessment in work-based learning

Boud and Solomon (2001: 47) identify that WBL not only focuses on the needs of the workplace, where the learning is both purposeful for both you and your organisation, but also provides 'an excellent example of a learner-centred approach'. Traditionally interaction revolves around the 'teacher' determining and disseminating the content of the course (syllabus) on which you are tested. In work-based learning there is a shift with you, as learner, taking a much more proactive role. Key to this is your responsibility for the negotiation of your learning and how it is assessed. Your tutor will expect that the learning agreed should challenge you, extend you and encourage you to explore new boundaries. The idea that you have the power to negotiate much of your learning and assessment might feel daunting at first, but it gives you increased ownership, which can make the assessment process far less intimidating.

At the beginning of your programme you will negotiate with your tutor and your workplace some or all of the following:

- *Specific aims and outcomes* of your intended programme of study – unique to you.
- *Assessment design* – you may have considerable freedom to negotiate the way your learning is assessed; for example, agree a suitable title and scope for your assessed piece(s) of work with your tutor.
- *Method of assessment* – see the section 'Different types of WBL assessment – the variety (and the diversity)' below, for many examples.
- *Hand-in dates* (particularly with regard to drafts).
- *Your learning agreement* (Chapter 6), which might be assessed.

Areas that are likely to be non-negotiable:

- university regulations and academic requirements (for example, presentation of work, referencing, confidentiality and ethics);
- learning outcomes (the overarching aims and learning outcomes of the programme);
- final submission dates;
- word count.

Linking learning and assessment

The vital link between the learning process and its assessment is at the forefront of designing assessment, and it is sometimes referred to as constructive alignment (Biggs and Tang, 2011: 50–63, Walsh, 2007: 79, Workman, 2009: 193–201). There should be a clear link between the objectives of the course or module, the teaching and learning activities undertaken during the course and how and when these are assessed (see Figure 11.1).

Learning Activities	Learning Outcomes	Assessment
• Attend seminars on project management research and enquiry skills • Planning & Development workshops with fellow students (for example through Action Learning Sets) • Tutorials with tutor and/or workplace adviser to discuss project proposal and development	• Identify and negotiate a project • Select, develop and apply sound research skills and techniques • Identify and apply appropriate theories, frameworks and principles • Plan and manage a project • Evaluate a project • Make recommendations	**Formative*** • Produce a project proposal with action plan and timeline • Short presentation to tutor and fellow students **Summative*** • Written report including recommendations for own practice and the workplace *See below

Figure 11.1   An example of constructive alignment in a work-based project

Level and volume of learning

Referring at regular intervals to information on 'level' and 'volume' within your course descriptors (for example, programme and module handbooks) will help you to ensure that you are working at the correct level and doing enough (see Chapters 1, 4 and 5). The level of work at which you are expected to perform for your course will be determined by a number of factors such as:

- Context in which you are expected to apply the learning (for example, your day-to-day work, your wider organisation, your profession or sector).
- Complexity of the study and your responsibility within it (for example, a small scale, short-term study or a broad-ranging longitudinal approach).
- Depth and extent of thinking and understanding (for example, using different theories and approaches and applying these in an analytical way).
- Degree of investigation and evaluation you are required to demonstrate.
- Amount of innovation and originality you exhibit.

The amount of credit attached to the assessment will vary, depending on how much work is undertaken, but as a general rule, in UK Higher Education, 10 credits equates to approximately 100 hours of study (including attending classes, reading, independent study and assessment).

Methods, process and procedures – the 'how'

Formative and summative assessment and feedback

You may come across the terms *formative* and *summative assessment*. The key to understanding the difference between them is to think about the purpose of the assessment. Assessment undertaken at the end of the learning process (such as exams or tests) is known as *summative assessment*.

By contrast, *formative assessment* is where feedback is given on work-in-progress (and usually not given a mark). This type of assessment is much more common in WBL, and is a more useful tool for assessing learning because you learn from assessment as you progress and hopefully improve your performance. This term may also be referred to as 'feed-forward', conveying the idea that the comments you receive will help you to progress through the module, and then further modules, successfully. Key to successful formative assessment is the feedback you receive from your tutor, your fellow learners and your workplace supervisor or mentor. Formative assessment can also be helpful to your tutor, for example, if everyone is clearly struggling with the same part of the formative assignment it might signal to the tutor that they need to cover a certain point again or approach it in a different way.

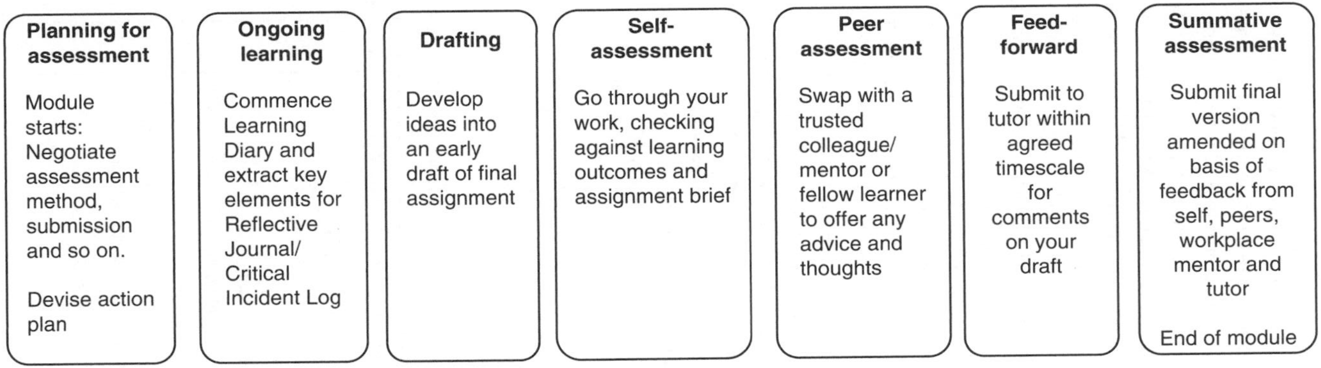

Planning for assessment	Ongoing learning	Drafting	Self-assessment	Peer assessment	Feed-forward	Summative assessment
Module starts: Negotiate assessment method, submission and so on. Devise action plan	Commence Learning Diary and extract key elements for Reflective Journal/ Critical Incident Log	Develop ideas into an early draft of final assignment	Go through your work, checking against learning outcomes and assignment brief	Swap with a trusted colleague/ mentor or fellow learner to offer any advice and thoughts	Submit to tutor within agreed timescale for comments on your draft	Submit final version amended on basis of feedback from self, peers, workplace mentor and tutor End of module

Figure 11.2 A formative assessment flowchart for work-based learning

Self and peer assessment

There will be opportunities to undertake self-assessments on your progress. To do this you need to look at the aims, learning outcomes and assessment criteria of your work-based programme and reflect upon what you have produced so far. Even if this is not a formal process, you should do it for yourself; perhaps this is a process you're familiar with at work? It helps you to become more critical about your practice and keeps you on course towards attaining a respectable mark/grade. The formative assessment flowchart (Figure 11.2) shows how you might build in self-assessment to get the best possible outcome, while Exercise 11.2 provides an assessment checklist to enable you to achieve the best outcome.

Peer assessment, where students on the same programme assess each other's work and provide constructive feedback to each other, is also useful and a well-established process in workplaces. On some programmes peer assessment can go towards the final mark. As a WBL student you are encouraged to develop informal peer-assessment arrangements with fellow learners, and possibly with trusted colleagues who will be able to comment on specific aspects relating to the workplace. Peer assessment is very much a reciprocal process, and the more you contribute to others' work the more they will be likely to support you. Nowadays WBL learners often communicate and comment on each other's work in order to support each other through online communities of practice (see Chapter 9).

Exercise 11.2   How do you measure up?

Self-assessment checklist for planning and carrying out assessed work

Planning for assessment	✓	Notes/Questions
Have you read and do you understand the: • Student handbook; • Module/unit/programme handbook(s); • University assessment regulations?		*For example, clarify with submission arrangements with tutor*
Have you identified what help you need and accessed information on Student Study Skills and read about assessment and assignment issues?		*For example, find out when Study Skills sessions are offered by the University Library*

Exercise 11.2 (continued)

Planning for assessment	✓	Notes/Questions
Have you read and do you understand the assessment brief/instructions: • Aims and learning outcomes; • Marking criteria and how marks will be awarded; • What the learning outcomes require you to demonstrate; • Word count/portfolio size/presentation length; • Presentational style; • Hand-in dates and submission arrangements?		
At the planning stage Have you negotiated with your tutor and/or workplace mentor regarding the assignment task/brief?		*For example, send first draft of proposed assessment brief to tutor and workplace mentor by set dates*
Are you clear about what your tutor is wanting from your assessed work? Do you know what you have to: • do; • know; • apply; • reflect upon; • present?		
Have you produced a Plan of Action with realistic timescales?		*For example, use a Gantt chart*
Have you clarified any outstanding issues with your tutor? Do you now feel ready to proceed with your assessed work? If not, what do you need to do?		
Doing the assessed work Are you doing all the necessary reading and enquiry in order to proceed?		

Exercise 11.2 (continued)

Planning for assessment	✓	Notes/Questions
Are you keeping to your plan? If not, have you rescheduled your work, negotiated changes in focus/timescale/submission with your tutor?		
Are you regularly checking what you are doing against the assessment brief and criteria to ensure you are on track?		
Are you attending tutorials, seminars and keeping in contact with your tutor?		
Have you spoken to peers about the assessment and shared ideas and concerns?		*For example, log in to online programme discussion group to discuss assessment task once a week*
Preparing for submission Have you carefully proofread your submission? Have you got someone else to read it? Have you made the necessary revisions?		*For example, meet with colleague to proofread each other's work*
Have you met the requirements for presentational style? These include: • Front cover, including title, your name, name of the module/programme and reference number – *you can be penalised for this if not done correctly: it frustrates the marker, and it could get lost*;		
Have you included all the elements? Such as: • Contents list; • Structure – *often you will be provided with a recommended format*;		

Exercise 11.2 (continued)

Planning for assessment	✓	Notes/Questions
• Ethics and confidentiality; • Headings/sub-headings/numbering/figures/tables – *good navigation is essential;* • Appendices.		
If you are doing a presentation, have you practised and ensured it meets the requirements for time and structure?		*For example, practise presentation – arrange a lunch-time session at work*
Have you undertaken a final self-assessment matching your work against the module/programme aims, learning outcomes and marking criteria?		
If you need more time or have a personal circumstance that's preventing you completing your work, have you: • checked the submission regulations; • negotiated an extension with your tutor; • completed the necessary forms, got them signed and submitted them on time?		
Submission Have you completed the necessary assessment submission form, and do you know where to submit in order to submit on time?		

Different types of WBL assessment – the variety (and diversity)

University assessment brings exams to mind; a large hall with desks neatly spaced out and three hours in which to write four essays. However, exams are rarely, if ever, used in the assessment of WBL. Other assessments to evaluate academic knowledge such as essays and reports, multiple choice tests, dissertations and oral presentations may also be used. However, because we assess 'tacit' knowledge (gained through experience of work and often not written down anywhere) as well as traditional learning, innovative forms of assessment are required. This section describes some of the most commonly used WBL assessment methods.

Box 11.1   Typical work-based assessments (see below for explanations)

1. Learning contracts.
2. RPL/APEL.
3. Work-based projects.
4. Portfolios.
5. Reflective diaries, learning journals and critical incident logs.
6. Collaborative assignments and group assessments.
7. Case studies.
8. Reports.

Learning contracts (also known as learning agreements and learning plans)

A learning contract (see Chapter 6) is a written critical account of where you are now, your aims and objectives and how you intend to achieve them. The contract is often submitted for assessment, and provides the 'map' for the rest of your learning journey. For example, your learning contract, which may itself be worth 20 credits at level 5, might set out that you will undertake an Independent Study into 'Approaches to Management of Change in the Workplace' that will be worth 20 credits at level 5, and then a work-based project into 'Implementing a Change project in My Organisation' (worth 30 credits at level 5), so also mapping connections and progression.

Recognition of Prior Learning (RPL) and Accreditation of Prior Experiential Learning (APEL)

While your learning contract lets you plan ahead, the RPL/APEL process (Chapter 5) looks back and facilitates your reflection on your previous learning from experience. Many universities include assessment of RPL/APEL in modules such as 'Recognising and Assessing Learning'; 'Making your Learning Count'; or 'Evidencing Prior Professional Learning'. Here you will be assessed on the quality of the evidence you use to demonstrate what you have learnt, and how you have reflected and acted upon this. Evidence can be presented in a variety of ways, including a portfolio of evidence with commentary (electronic or hard copy) or by oral presentation.

Work-based projects

One of the most popular ways that WBL is assessed by universities is through a work-based project, which is a piece of real work that you are required to do, as part of your job. Reflecting on this work to show what you have learnt and how you will apply this is the key element of assessment. Chapter 12 provides more detailed information about work-based projects.

Portfolios

'Portfolio' literally means a 'folder' in which papers are carried; in assessment terms the portfolio brings together evidence (including paper-based documents, artefacts and audio-visual) acquired and matched against the assessment criteria, to demonstrate the learning achieved. Your portfolio's contents must illustrate clear links between your learning activities and the evidence presented. It is important that your tutor can clearly see what you have learnt. Portfolios (and increasingly electronic portfolios) are widely used in WBL assessment because of their versatility, but please don't confuse versatility with randomness – a file full of mismatched unexplained bits and pieces will never get you a good mark!

Reflective diaries, learning journals and critical incident logs

Writing about your progress on your course or programme each week will help with your formal assessment opportunities. Writing things down helps to clarify your thoughts, and in this instance will capture what you are learning. This forms the basis for you to reflect upon your learning process (Chapter 2), and will enhance your final assignment immeasurably. This more informal approach to learning and assessment has the potential to liberate you if you feel self-conscious or inexperienced about the more academic style of writing. It allows you to show your tutor how your ideas have developed over time as you become increasingly confident and more aware of underlying theories and principles (Dunn et al., 2004: 164; Ramage, 2005: 102).

- Reflective diaries – These are used to note your key work activities and allow you to reflect on what has been learnt in order to perform better in the future. Used mostly for formative or ongoing self-assessment, these diaries are initially private to you, but will provide you with useful material to develop for formal assessment.
- Learning journals – Sometimes appropriate extracts from your reflective diary, which clearly demonstrate your learning and reflection upon it, can be included for assessment as evidence within a public document called a learning journal.
- Critical incident logs – Critical incident logs encourage a move away from a descriptive approach to learning towards a more reflective approach. Logs require you to focus on a key event, often one that took you out of

your comfort zone – for example, a tricky meeting, a complex report or a difficult case – and to comment on:

- a brief description of what happened with a particular focus on your actions;
- relevant theories or concepts drawn upon;
- courses of action you did/did not take and why;
- how you would tackle a similar situation in another circumstance;
- what learning you took from the incident;
- implications for future practice.

(Brown, 1999: 97–98)

Collaborative assignments and group assessments

You may be asked to work in groups to identify, address and write up a shared idea/project. This could be based on a real-life piece of work, or a hypothetical scenario – but both will require you to use many of your workplace skills. Your tutor will be looking for evidence that each individual has addressed and met the learning outcomes. Sometimes there will be a group assessment task, for example, a joint presentation, but you will often be required to submit an individual piece of work for grading purposes, demonstrating your personal contribution. Remember, the more you put in collectively, the more you will each draw from it in the longer term as this enables you to benefit from the strengths and knowledge of others, just as real-life teamwork does. There may be an expectation to use technology to undertake and deliver this collaborative work, for example, through blogs, wikis and social networking (Chapter 8).

Case studies

These can be presented as 'typical' work-based scenarios that demonstrate your ability to analyse and make critical recommendations for improvement in the workplace practice being described. Alternatively, you might be asked to develop your own case study based on your 'real-life' professional settings and experiences.

Reports

Many WBL programmes ask you to present your substantive assessed work through a professional report. You may well be comfortable with this approach, as it is probably more familiar to you than academic-style essays. Report writing is an incredibly useful skill for you to hone and develop, as most workplace roles require some level of this. There are many excellent guides (online and in print) that will help you structure and focus your reports (also search your university's 'Study Skills' pages). Some key points to bear in mind:

- ensure you have a clearly defined objective/purpose;
- know what type of report you are writing (management report, feasibility study, laboratory/scientific report and so on);

- be concise and specific;
- know your audience and use language accordingly;
- always explain any abbreviations in full the first time you use them;
- aim to have a set of recommendations at the end of the report and a clear conclusion;
- avoid including material that is extra to requirements;
- use tables and figures where appropriate;
- provide clear evidence for any arguments you put forward;
- make your sources as relevant and up to date as possible;
- check your own research data for accuracy, objectivity (not skewed or biased towards a particular viewpoint), validity (authentic) and robustness (would you get the same or similar outcome if it were repeated?);
- ensure that sections and subsections follow a logical sequence (see Chapter 12).

Case Study 11.2   Innovative practice in negotiated assessment of WBL

Fiona, a supervisor in a small engineering company supplying electrical components for larger national companies (and keen to expand into European markets), was undertaking her work-based learning module as part of her university management course. It was agreed that assessment for the module should be to write a proposal and prepare a presentation for the Board of Directors on developing their international client base; this would both meet the assessment brief and be of direct benefit to the business.

Fiona carefully went through the assessment brief, highlighting key requirements and criteria. She also reread the module handbook to ensure she was clear on rules and regulations. Having done this, she was then able to identify her strengths (knowledge of international marketing and export regulatory environments, project management and presentation skills), as well as her weaknesses (academic and reflective writing and referencing skills).

To address these weaknesses Fiona accessed the university online Study Skills programme, which explained how to find and extract information from academic texts and key business reports. It also helped her identify some useful tools and techniques to ensure that all sources were robust and correctly referenced.

In order to improve her analytical and reflective skills Fiona undertook some online exercises, which enabled her to complete an outline and action plan of her project to submit to her tutor. Feedback from

Case Study 11.2 (continued)

her tutor was positive; it also suggested that both the report for the Directors and the accompanying work-based report could be improved by being less descriptive and providing more analysis and reflection, backed up by correctly sourced data to support her arguments.

Fiona met with her workplace learning mentor to reflect on the feedback from her tutor and agree on how to progress from there. Using and refining her action plan, she was able to undertake the necessary reading to provide some theory to underpin her report.

Fiona found it helpful to attend a mid-point review session with her tutor group where she was able to discuss her progress to date with her fellow students, identify some key issues to address and run through her presentation. Towards the end of her assignment she was required to submit a draft of her report to her tutor, and again feedback was received, highlighting areas where she could strengthen and develop her ideas.

Before writing up her final report Fiona revisited the brief and assessment criteria to ensure that she was still on the right track. A week before the final deadline she asked a trusted colleague and fellow learner to proofread her work. This identified some spelling and punctuation errors, as well as a small number of points that required further clarification, which she was able to address.

Finally, before submitting her assessment, Fiona read through her assignment, ensuring that it met all the criteria and incorporated all the feedback provided. Fiona received an excellent mark for her assignment and was commended by the Board of Directors on her report and presentation, in particular the high level of analysis included.

Rules and regulations – the nuts and bolts

Universities adhere to standard codes of practice; these will be issued to you as university regulations. Although your programme might be partly, or entirely, based in the workplace, and perhaps not feel or look much like a traditional university course, it will still have been rigorously checked against the guidelines set out by the Quality Assurance Agency (2008).

Handbooks

When you enrol you will receive several key documents (hard copy and/ or electronic), including a handbook, which will provide information on university assessment regulations, your WBL programme and modules as well as student study support provision offered. The handbook will also include:

- aims;
- learning outcomes;
- assessment brief;
- assessment criteria;
- marking criteria.

Familiarise yourself with these documents as they offer you useful ways to maximise your assessment performance. In more detail:

Aims

The module 'aims' set out what the module is attempting to achieve. Box 11.2 gives an example of a typical work-based learning module's aims.

Box 11.2   Typical work-based learning module aims

The aims of this module are to:
- Enhance the learner's individual effectiveness; employability and/or business competitiveness by locating the learning and development in his/her own organisation.
- Extend the learner's capability, promote personal development and a range of interpersonal, intellectual and practical (functional) skills and knowledge based around and demonstrated through an individually negotiated real-time work-based project that will be of benefit to their organisation.

Source: Adapted from 'Northumbria University – Work-based Project Module Descriptor Level 6'.

Learning outcomes

These provide a breakdown of what you are expected to achieve (and demonstrate) by the end of the module (Box 11.3). The learning outcomes will be closely aligned to your assessment brief, so it is vitally important that you address these.

Box 11.3   Typical work-based learning module outcomes

By the end of the module *(WBL project, in this case)* the learner will be able to:

- Identify and negotiate a project that addresses own personal goals and organisational/professional requirements
- Select, develop and apply appropriate practical, methodologically sound research skills and techniques.

Box 11.3 (continued)

- Draw on, apply and review considerable prior knowledge and new learning to changing situations.
- Extend a wide range of specialised technical, creative and/or conceptual skills that apply to his/her work in order to make informed judgements.
- Identify and apply appropriate theories, frameworks and principles relevant to the issues/situations addressed in the project in order to consolidate and extend a systematic and coherent body of knowledge that applies to his/her discipline.
- Plan and manage a project within an agreed framework, dealing with unpredictable situations, making informed judgements and managing dilemmas, which include those that impact outside the immediate work area.
- Evaluate a project, drawing upon concepts, models and theories to support own ideas and innovative responses through oral presentation and written report.
- Make recommendations for own professional development and that of the organisation, and propose a strategy for implementation.

Source: Adapted from: 'Northumbria University – Work-based Project Module Descriptor Level 6'.

Assessment brief

As a learner you want (and need) to know what is expected of you:

- 'How many words are expected in this assignment?'
- 'Do I have to reference theory?'
- 'What happens if I miss the deadline?'
- 'Does it have to be word processed?'
- 'How much time do I have?'

The assessment brief (Box 11.4) is your best friend in the entire assessment process (in conjunction with the learning outcomes mentioned above); ignore it at your peril! This is what you are being asked to do.

Box 11.4   Typical work-based learning assessment brief

The summative assessment for the module will be through the submission of a work-based project report, which should demonstrate how the stated assessment criteria have been met (see Box 4.5). This module offers 20 credit points. In order to achieve the 20 points you must successfully achieve a pass mark of 40% at undergraduate or 50% at postgraduate for the report.

You are required to submit for assessment a report, which will comprise a study report (for example, 4000 words for 20 credits) incorporating the proposal, presentation and supporting evidence.

Assessment criteria

The assessment criteria set out the requirements of the assessment brief (as described above) and identify what your tutors are looking for in your submitted work. It is really important that you take the time early on to understand the criteria and to keep checking your work against them. You will need to consider them in conjunction with the learning outcomes and marking criteria for your module.

Box 11.5   Example of assessment criteria for a Level 6 work-based project

- Demonstrate the relevance of your work-based project to your work role, academic level and learning and development needs.
- Demonstrate use of principles relevant to the issues/situations addressed in the project.
- Negotiate a project proposal (500 words, formatively assessed).
- Manage, record, analyse and reflect upon the work-based project.
- Demonstrate an in-depth knowledge and understanding of your immediate area of work and its relevance to the project.
- the appropriateness of different options, taking into consideration relevant ethical, commercial, confidential and data protection issues.
- Carry out small-scale practical investigation/s.
- Apply knowledge, experience and new learning to a range of workplace problems.
- Make clear, concise and realistic recommendations for further development of the project.
- Present the projects findings through the use of oral presentation (15 minutes, formatively assessed, that is feedback- and feed forward-given but not marked).
- Write a report (4000 words, summatively assessed) in an appropriate academic format, typically for an academic assessor and line manager.

Marking criteria

Marking criteria sets out the areas for assessment (academic rigour, academic referencing, presentation and structure (Box 11.6), and describes what you need to do to achieve a high mark, an average mark or a fail. This can be a very useful self-assessment tool.

Box 11.6   Example of marking criteria for work-based assessment (for presentation and structure of work)

% marks used as guide by assessor in determining final mark	For example, Presentation and Structure
Outstanding work. Logical, analytical, well-structured 80–100% (Distinction)	Logical development. Fluent and engages reader. No flaws in language, grammar and spelling. Accurate academic style
Excellent work with detailed analysis 70–79% (Distinction)	Well-structured, clear development of ideas. Majority of work is expressed clearly. Grammar and spelling accurate
Good work, sound knowledge and understanding 60–69% (Merit)	Clear and appropriate structure has been adopted. Most ideas expressed clearly. Only minor errors in grammar and spelling
Clear pass, knowledge and understanding could be developed 50–59% (Pass)	Structure apparent but has some limitations. Language mainly fluent. Grammar and spelling mainly accurate
Pass, content limited 40–49% (Pass)	Basic structure provided. Use of language not always fluent. Meaning apparent although there are grammatical and spelling errors
Poor, clearly inadequate 30–39% (Fail)	Poor structure. Language, grammar and/or spelling poor. Errors affect meaning of work
Unacceptable, clearly lack of knowledge and/or understanding 0–29% (Fail)	Little care evident in relation to structure, use of language, grammar, and spelling. Badly affects meaning of work

Assessment success is often about going back to basics and following simple steps.

TIP **Meeting the assessment requirements – six steps to success!**

- Read the module learning outcomes, assessment brief, assessment criteria and marking criteria carefully.
- Read them again ... Make sure you understand what is being asked of you. If not, seek advice.

- Break the assessment brief and criteria down to identify key words and phrases to ensure that you understand *what* are you being asked to *do*.
- Use this to plan out your assessment/break it down into sections.
- Prioritise the sections based on the marks allocated to them – allocate your word count on this basis (for example, don't use 30% of your word count in a section that carries only 5% of the marks).
- Keep referring back to your plan while you are writing.

Academic misconduct

As in the workplace, trust and integrity are vital elements of any university programme, and there are strict rules governing what is known as academic misconduct (cheating). You should ensure that you adhere to these. Consequences can range from marking your work down or failing that particular module to expulsion from your course. Institutions find it much more straightforward to pinpoint cheating now with the widespread use of electronic detection methods.

Avoid these common types of academic misconduct

- Cheating, for example, during a formal examination.
- Plagiarism, that is, *unacknowledged* incorporation into your work of material derived from the work (published or unpublished) of another.
- Collusion, for example, collaborating with another student/person in the completion of work with the intention of one of you submitting that work as the work of one person.
- Falsification, for example, making up data or references.
- Impersonation of another to gain benefit in assessment.
- Ghosting, for example, submitting as your own, work that has been produced by another person on your behalf.

Submission arrangements

Follow to the letter any instructions you are given relating to the submission of your work. Failure to do so could severely jeopardise your position.

TIP **Before submitting your work, check the following:**

- Deadline – date/time? – Aim to get it in well before the final cut-off point.
- Where do you hand it in?
- Electronic submission – is it allowed? And if so, what are the instructions? Are you able to use a tablet or your work computer, for example?
- Posting your work – have you allowed time for it to arrive?
- Coversheet – do you need one? Have you completed it?
- Key identifying information – module code, student ID number and so on?
- Name/student number on every page or artefact?
- Page numbers (usually in footers)?
- Multiple copies – how many required?
- Receipt for your work – make sure you get one.
- Your copy – always keep a back-up copy of your work.

If things go wrong – don't panic!

Things sometimes go wrong, and this can feel like the last straw if you are already trying to juggle the demands of a job, a family and study. If you do encounter a problem (personal, health or work-related), you must communicate this to your tutor as soon as possible; don't leave it until you have a crisis on your hands. Universities will be as accommodating as possible, and depending on the circumstances will work to try and find a way to help you to carry on with your studies. This might involve requesting that a deadline be extended or a more formal process, known as personal extenuating circumstances. It is worth finding out who your point of contact would be in such circumstances.

Marking and moderation

Imagine you've finished your assessment, having followed all the advice above, and handed it in on time. You probably want to know what happens to your hard work once you have submitted it.

Normally your tutor will mark your work and complete some form of summary sheet that will give you overall comments and a percentage mark, grade or pass/fail – depending on the grading structure of the module in question.

A sample of your assignments will also be sent to an academic colleague, who will second-mark this work. Any disagreement between the two markers will be resolved by a third marker, or moderator, who is asked to give an overall opinion. Following this you may get your work returned to you with a 'provisional' mark; alternatively, you may not hear anything until there has been an assessment board meeting held.

External examination

Universities rely on a system of self-regulation, whereby they undertake to maintain standards between themselves, using, among other things, a system of external examining. Each university award has an external examiner, a subject expert from another university, who provides a neutral, unbiased but expert point of view. A sample of work will be sent to the external examiner, who will again check that it is of a correct level and standard to merit the mark or grade that it has been awarded.

Examination boards (modular and progression/award)

The final piece of the jigsaw is the examination board. At the module exam board all marks for people on your module or course are considered and confirmed. This is followed by the progression and award board, which will look at your individual profile and determine whether you continue on to the next stage of your course or, if at the end of the course, whether you are awarded the qualification. Once these exam boards have met, the results will normally be posted up in a public place. You will be sent, or given access to an electronic version of, a transcript detailing your marks and/or final award.

Fails and appeals

If you fail a module or any part of your award, you may, depending upon your marks, be allowed to resit the assessment. If you have a complaint against the university or wish to appeal against a decision, there are set procedures to enable you to do this.

Your roles and responsibilities – the bottom line

You are in the driving seat. Much of the responsibility for your learning and for ensuring you meet assessment requirements rests with you. While you will be provided with a great deal of information and support, don't expect to be spoon-fed. *'I wasn't told about this'* is rarely accepted as an excuse about assessed work. If you don't know something then it's up to you to find out, and your module and programme handbooks are always a good starting point.

Summary

1   There are different types of assessments – some are formative (assessed on work-in-progress) and others are summative (assessed at the end).

2   WBL assessment will test your ability to articulate and apply high-level critical thinking and reflection to workplace situations.

3   Assessment will help you to demonstrate your learning, develop yourself and improve your performance at work and career opportunities.

4   You can (within parameters) negotiate your learning and assessment with your tutor – choose an area that interests you, making sure it is realistic and feasible.

5   Make sure you understand the assessment brief and criteria, as well as the marking criteria and submission details.

6   Consult with your peers (including fellow students and work colleagues), share your ideas about your assessment, ask for their comments.

7   Don't cheat or plagiarise.

8. Maintain an ethical and confidential stance in your work (that is, ensure that you respect the rights and anonymity of any participants in any workplace study and that you have received their informed consent to participate).

9. Proofread your work thoroughly and get someone you can trust to be honest with you to read it too.

References

Biggs, J. and Tang C. (2011) *Teaching for Quality Learning at University* (Maidenhead: McGraw-Hill and Open University Press).

Boud, D. and Solomon, N. (2001) *Work-based Learning: A New Higher Education?* (Buckingham: Society for Research into Higher Education and Open University Press).

Brown, S. (1999) Assessing Practice. In S. Brown and A. Glasner, *Assessment Matters in Higher Education: Choosing and Using Diverse Approaches* (Buckingham: Society for Research into Higher Education and Open University Press)

Dunn, L., Morgan. C., O'Reilly, M. and Parry, S. (2004) *The Student Assessment Handbook: New Directions in Traditional and Online Assessment* (London: Routledge Falmer).

Quality Assurance Agency (2008) *The Framework for Higher Education Qualifications in England, Wales and Northern Ireland.* Available at: http://www.qaa.ac.uk/Publications/InformationAndGuidance/Documents/FHEQ08.pdf (accessed 28 February 2014).

Race, P. (2007) *The Lecturer's Toolkit – A Practical Guide to Assessment, Learning and Teaching* (Abingdon: Routledge).

Ramage, C. (2005) '"It's Hard Work!" An Analysis of the Concept of "Hard Work" as an Experience of Engaging in Work Based Learning'. In K. Rounce and B. Workman (eds), *Work-based Learning in Healthcare: Applications and Innovations* (Chichester: Kingsham Press).

Walsh, A. (2007) 'An exploration of Biggs: constructive alignment in the context of work-based learning', *Assessment & Evaluation in Higher Education,* 32 (1), pp. 79–87.

Workman, B. (2009) 'The Core Components: Teaching, Learning, and Assessing'. In J. Garnett, C. Costley and B. Workman (eds), *Work-based Learning – Journeys to the Core of Higher Education* (London: Middlesex University Press).

Suggested further reading

Assessment Standards Knowledge Exchange (2009) *Feedback: Make it Work for You!.* Available at http://www.brookes.ac.uk/aske/documents/2482_123–MakeFeedbackWork.pdf (accessed 28 February 2014).

Boud, D. and Falchikov, N. (2007) *Rethinking Assessment in Higher Education – Learning for the Longer Term* (London: Routledge).

Bowden, J. (2008) *Writing a Report: How to Prepare, Write and Present Really Effective Reports,* 8th edn (Oxford: How to Books).

Falchikov, N. (2013) *Improving Assessment through Student Involvement: Practical Solutions for Aiding Learning in Higher and Further Education* (Abingdon: Routledge Falmer).

Ghaye, T. and Lillyman, S. (2006) *Learning Journals and Critical Incidents: Reflective Practice for Health Care Professionals,* 2nd edn (Dinton: Quay Publishing).

Knight, P. (2014) *Assessment for Learning in Higher Education* (Abingdon: Routledge Falmer).

Miller, A. H., Imrie, B. W. and Cox, K. (2014) *Student Assessment in Higher Education: A Handbook for Assessing Performance* (Abingdon: Routledge).

Moon, J. (2006) *Learning Journals: A Handbook for Reflective Practice and Professional Development*, 2nd edn (London: Routledge).

SEEC (2010) *SEEC Credit Level Descriptors*. Available at http://www.seec.org.uk/wp-content/uploads/2013/seec-files/SEEC%20Level%20Descriptors%202010.pdf (accessed 28 February 2014).

Zubizarreta, J. (2009) *The Learning Portfolio: Reflective Practice for Improving Student Learning*, 2nd edn (San Francisco, CA: Jossey-Bass).

Work-based projects

Barbara Workman and Paula Nottingham

In this chapter you will learn:

► the characteristics of a work-based project;
► how to plan, design and structure a project proposal;
► about the ethical issues to be considered;
► key points on how to implement a work-based project;
► ways to establish evidence and outcomes;
► how to evaluate a work-based project.

What is a work-based project?

Work-based (WB) projects are at the core of most WB programmes, and although they take many forms, they will all provide you with the opportunity to learn from your work activities in a structured way, while also bringing a rigorous academic approach to meeting the needs of the workplace. WB projects are usually focused upon the real-time work demands of your job and will contribute new knowledge and learning that reflect work developments. You can undertake WB projects at any academic level in your higher education studies, but they usually consolidate learning at academic milestones within, or at the end of, a programme, in much the same way that more traditional degrees culminate in a dissertation.

WB projects offer you a great opportunity to transform a workplace activity into a meaningful learning experience, which will benefit: you as a learner, your workplace and the university where you are studying. WB project work reflects a project cycle of activity – planning, implementation, outcomes and evaluation – while meeting academic research requirements. The process of a WB project maximises the time spent on these activities, providing genuine capacity-building and knowledge management skills, both of which are valued highly in professional settings.

A WB programme may include several projects at different stages, or various academic levels of achievement, building up towards a final large WB project to complete an award. For example, you might start with a project entitled; 'Designing an Action Plan', which is your preparation for a bigger piece of work. This smaller, initial project will involve reading around a subject to gain understanding of factors influencing the larger project. Another interim project might be 'Implementing the Action Plan', which is finally revisited later to evaluate the effectiveness of the total project.

A WB project will include data collection, usually as part of your research methodology framework; this is a formal structured method for collecting information together via appropriate inquiry activities. Practitioner research is incorporated into the project process to enable you to unpack and develop particular aspects of your project. This chapter does not discuss specific research methodologies as these can be found in many general research texts, some of which are listed at the end of the chapter. Most WB programmes include a research methods module (sometimes called practitioner enquiry) or will refer you to research texts that will help you to understand appropriate workplace research approaches for your programme.

This chapter will guide you through the project process. Studying at university involves learning to use appropriate evidence, such as academic research literature, or, in the case of WB projects, evidence from work-related policies or practice, or a combination of sources to inform your thinking. Practice evidence may include local, national and possibly international documents, policies, guidelines and directives. For example, your professional organisation might have commissioned some large-scale research that you can access. While a great deal of literature can be found within disciplinary frameworks, the workplace also has transdisciplinary elements (McGregor and Volckmann, 2011) that reflect its multifaceted nature and present a broader understanding of the topic area. WB projects help you to become a 'scholarly practitioner' who is able to structure a case for your actions and decisions.

Do not be daunted by the term 'research'; you are probably happy to research a holiday destination or investigate a major expenditure. These inquiry and planning skills are very similar to those needed to investigate your WB project and can be transferred. The 'research and development' stage in a project might be more familiar to you as consultancy activity, which provides guidance and expertise for specific work-related issues. Once you have undertaken the first project, subsequent ones become easier as your repertoire of information sources, helpful people, critical reading, writing and project management skills grows and develops. With academic support from your tutor you will learn tools and techniques to investigate your work, both now and for the future.

Armsby and Costley (2000) provide a useful summary about undertaking a work-based project, and what it does for you:

1. Develops your critical awareness of research and inquiry.
2. Monopolises this to enhance practical competence.
3. Facilitates collaboration with an expert tutor and/or work colleagues, and stakeholders.
4. Differs from a dissertation – practice-focused, leading to a product.
5. Develops your personal and professional knowledge.
6. Uncovers and shares 'tacit' knowledge (Eraut, 2001), which is intuitive and embedded in practice.
7. Contributes to the organisation's knowledge and intellectual and human capital (Garnett, 2005).
8. Usually explores some degree of 'change'.
9. Enhances communication, negotiation and dissemination skills.
10. Contributes to career development.
11. Provides academic recognition and facilitates different audience engagement.

Case Study 12.1   Roland – problem-based project work

Roland worked for an engineering firm and wanted to introduce processes to his company that would reduce development time in order to get the design products out more quickly to clients. This was a new way of working for the company, but research about the success of using similar processes and procedures provided Roland's manager with the evidence needed to allow Roland to create a new systems framework for himself and to train other staff to work in this way. The WB project led to the company adopting Roland's ideas to increase productivity and provided a strategic direction for the company to adopt for future work practice.

This example shows how WB projects are focused on daily work activities, are relevant to work practices and update knowledge by solving problems and providing solutions. Looking for solutions might mean identifying practice that is working well in order to plan for positive change (Cooperrider and Whitney, 2005).

How do WB projects differ from dissertations?

Degrees usually incorporate the idea of a capstone project in the final year of study, most often in the form of a dissertation. WB projects differ from dissertations in that:

- dissertations are theory-orientated rather than practice;
- dissertations often are purely desk-based with no field work;
- workplace ethical issues are less prevalent in dissertations;
- personal and reflective learning is not explicitly included in a dissertation;
- it is customary for a dissertation to reflect the conventions of its subject discipline, while WB projects consider the transdisciplinary aspects of a workplace;
- a dissertation format is usually an extended piece of narrative, unsuitable for a WB project, which involves a report with critical reflection;
- a dissertation is unlikely to include change strategies – although it will be original, provoking thought and challenging opinions;
- a dissertation may have little relevance to actual work practices because it investigates theory into practice rather than practice into theory.

Planning a project

A successful project requires careful consideration of these four stages (see Figure 12.1):

1. Plan: what is it about? Why is it necessary, and why should you do it?
2. Implement: project actions as described in the section 'Writing your project proposal' (see later in chapter).

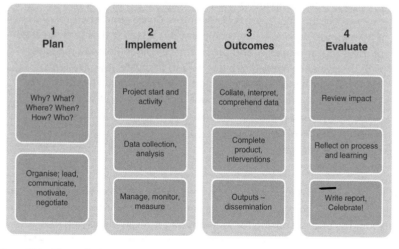

Figure 12.1   The project process

3. Outcomes: what are the products, services and/or results?
4. Evaluate: review the outcomes, implications and impact.

Planning: the starting point

The choice of project will be directed, to some extent, by the programme requirements and your learning needs. Factors concerning size, academic level, content and inquiry focus are usually discussed with your tutor, and formalised in a learning plan, determined by your programme requirements (see learning contracts in Chapter 6). The final WB project in an award is usually the most significant unit of study and often carries the most academic credit because it draws together key aspects of learning and application from the overall programme. Ideally your employer or manager will be involved throughout as WB projects should be explicitly relevant to your workplace, and permission to undertake them is agreed in advance. Your manager or employer's role is to give permission and access as 'gatekeeper' who ensures the health and well-being of people for whom they are responsible (see Figure 12.2).

Different types of projects that can come from work may include, for example: projects triggered by asking a question about practices; trying to solve a problem; needing to improve practice; or an area of interest that you have always wanted to investigate to develop your professional role. Your employer, manager or team leader may direct you to a project, particularly if sponsoring you on the programme. The project may relate to an existing area of practice, or an area of new development.

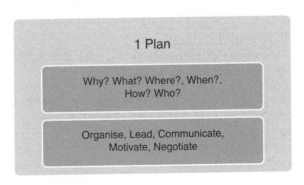

Figure 12.2 Planning the project

Exercise 12.1   Reflecting on your work-based project options

Use the table below to ask yourself whether the proposed work-based project:

Questions	Answer
Relates to my current work practice?	
Arises from a work issue?	
Develops my personal interest and expertise?	
Has got clear outcomes? (for example, a report, a new way of working or specific skills)	
Is part of a larger work project that is relevant to my role?	
Requires any preparatory work? (for example, learning requirements)	
Will inform bigger, more complex projects in the future?	
Will contribute to the organisation?	
Involves change management?	
Requires higher authority to implement? (both the project itself and future resulting changes)	

You do not necessarily need to respond positively to all of the above questions in order for a project to be viable or successful.

Case Study 12.2   Peter – career development and change

Peter had reached a crossroads in his career. He had been a manager for over ten years, with a second career in business training for private clients. He was interested in a full-time teaching job in the state sector but needed to complete his undergraduate degree before he was able to gain his qualified teaching status. Peter's WB project contained two main elements: (a) research into how business was framed in the secondary school curriculum, and (b) building his disciplinary resources in order to teach business more effectively. His project research relied on his own experience as a manager and his analysis of supporting literature to develop his teaching of business studies. This WB project meant that Peter acquired academic skills to complete the degree and the resources to apply for teacher training. Peter later successfully became a full-time teacher.

How, who and when?

Choosing a suitable project will depend on your work-role and opportunities within your workplace. The best-planned project may not be straightforward; consider the difficulties as challenges or solutions rather than problems. Remember, you will learn more from dealing with the complexities of the project than if everything was 'plain sailing'. Small is beautiful when it comes to scoping your project: too big and it will overwhelm you and become unmanageable, yet it must be 'big enough' to extend your learning and meet organisational and academic requirements (Raelin, 2008).

Not everything you do at work will automatically provide a suitable subject for a WB project within your work-based qualification. If the project only requires some desk/internet research it is probably not substantial enough to sustain an entire academic project. However, it may be suitable as a small starter project, if your course allows, to prepare you for a more substantial project later.

Exercise 12.2   Know your boundaries

To help you define the boundaries of your project consider these questions and make some notes for your answers:

Questions	Answer
Why are you undertaking this project?	
Why is it relevant to you, your work and study?	
What are you going to achieve?	
What are the likely outcomes? (for example, a machine, a policy, improved practice)	
What kind of evidence would you generate as an effective outcome?	
What are your aims, and how will you achieve them?	
Who should be involved?	
What is the timescale of the project and the completion date?	
Will there be any cost involved?	
What boundaries or limitations are there?	
What constraints will there be in relation to: data access, confidentiality, limited time frame, current safe practice and available finance?	

Some common problems – a quick reality check

To follow on from Exercise 12.2, reflect on ways to avoid some common problems:

- *'Is it do-able?'* Realistically, is there time, authority, resources, access to knowledge and skills for this or should you scale it down?
- *Will resources be wasted because it is too complex or fraught with internal problems?* Internal politics, lack of support from key individuals, late consent from managers or ethics committees or lack of understanding from colleagues could sabotage your plan!
- *Does the project lack definition? For example, is it too broad to be achieved within the timeframe?* Discuss this with your tutor/colleagues/yourself! Do the written aims explain what you have in mind and have discussed with others? Have you captured your ideas accurately?
- *Have you chosen an area with insufficient resources, for example, lack of expertise, insufficient funds?* Investigate who might assist you.
- *Have you negotiated the topic with your line manager? If not, then you may encounter resistance when local support or access is needed.* Ensure you have your manager's permission before you plan too far; include this in your learning plan (Chapter 6).
- *Have you chosen to collect appropriate and accessible data?* Inappropriate and unnecessary data will not fulfil the project requirements, could mislead the results and distract you from the main project. Typically if the research has already been done, don't redo it! Often WB projects research new territory or circumstances within your workplace.
- *Have you anticipated the result before carrying out the investigation?*
  A common fault when planning is to anticipate the findings; you cannot be sure what you will find, so leave your options open.

Case Study 12.3   Carrie – prepare for your projects to change and evolve

Carrie was a performer who worked for a small Theatre in Education (TIE) arts production company. Carrie loved her job and had intended to use her work as the basis of a WB project. When government funding cuts meant that the clients of the company she was working for, mainly schools, had to cancel events, the company had to close. This meant that Carrie had to rethink her project. As many other freelance performers were experiencing similar circumstances, she decided instead to look into career transition. Carrie needed a project

Case Study 12.3 (continued)

that would give her the tools to map out what she knew and lead into an alternative career path. As a part of the WB project she interviewed several peer professionals and investigated training to become a freelance voice coach so she could find employment in a vocational performance college setting.

How will you lead and organise the investigation?

Deciding on a research approach is an essential part of planning a WB project; you need to choose a research approach that is most appropriate for the project, rather than opting for the one most familiar to you. Robson (2011) and Denscombe (2014) both provide comprehensive and readable guides to research approaches; your tutor may suggest others, specific to your subject discipline. Costley et al. (2010) offer research methodologies that focus on the work-based learner. You should study some form of research or inquiry methods before starting a large WB project.

Some research approaches, such as case studies, action research and evaluation, lend themselves to the workplace because they are flexible in design and cater for the human element of work research and the individual nature of the projects. Your research question will guide your choice. Research will help you deal with a problem of logic, but not a logistical problem, so combine a project plan with your research approach. As a practitioner researcher researching your own practice, you may find the data-gathering approach you choose often complements existing evidence in your sector or professional field.

TIP **Successful project research**

- *Explore* different research methodologies to make an informed choice.
- *Identify* the methods that will answer your research questions by asking 'how' and 'why' when choosing.
- *Investigate* a variety of research methods to inform data collection and analysis – this will equip you for future projects.
- *Analyse* aspects of change through the research needed for your project – this helps to introduce the project into your organisation.
- *Acquire* skills and strategies that are used elsewhere at work, using your new-found research methods expertise.
- *Reflect* on what you are learning and keep a reflective diary or journal.

Writing your project research proposal

Your project proposal will combine both your project plan and your research approach, and it should clearly communicate what you are proposing to your tutor, your manager and your colleagues. You will be expected to write a plan using a particular referencing style, for example, Harvard (used in this chapter), to standardise the way you refer to evidence-based sources. It is also important that your proposal or plan flows (Forsyth, 2004). You can use appendices to add details of the plan to the report, such as a participant consent form.

TIP **Your WB project proposal might be structured as follows:**

- working title;
- introduction and rationale;
- main aims, key objectives, project context and significance;
- your role as worker/researcher, your relevant expertise and target audience;
- your main research questions;
- your rationale for the chosen research approach;
- your rationale for data collection and analysis and how this will address the research questions, including possible activities, interventions or products to be informed by the research;
- project feasibility, timescale, resources, ethical issues;
- project report and intended outcomes or products;
- strengths and weaknesses of the research proposal, critically reflecting on the planning process;
- references.

Appendix 5 shows an example of a project proposal.

Exercise 12.3   Develop your ideas

As you read through the pointers for writing your proposal, make notes about your own project. These notes can be developed later.

Choosing a title for your project

The project focus should be relevant to your overall academic award. The title should encompass the project as a whole, rather than as a question, for example, '*An Evaluation of Info-Tech services*', rather than, '*What did the clients think of...*'. Keep the title short and focused. Examples of good project titles:

- Investigating Pupil's Progress in Mathematics Using 'Numicon'.
- Developing a Programme of Planned Preventative Maintenance to Increase Service Reliability.
- Developing an IT System to Improve Inter-Departmental Customer Referrals.
- Designing a Patient-Focused Service for the Community.
- Developing an Induction and Training Pack for New Staff.

Planning and organising the project process

The introduction:
- Brief overview of the background and context.
- Explain your rationale: why this project is important and relevant. How will it contribute to the organisation, yourself and the university? Brief reference to publications and policies that set the context and relevance.

Main aims of the project and its significance

- State your chosen research design and justify this with supporting references.
- State the purpose and aims of your project, with brief rationale.
- Include a short critical review of the key literature in terms of themes or issues that are appropriate.
- The target audience – who will your work be relevant to, and why?

The worker/researcher role and relevant expertise

- How might your position of influence/power affect the project? Are there workplace politics to be considered?
- Why are your skills and knowledge particularly suitable?
- Do you have access to necessary data sources? Will permission from others be required? How will your data be kept anonymous and confidential?
- What aspects are directly related to your insider role? How will you approach them?
- Consider your resources – time, finance, equipment, workplace and topic experts, data, and negotiating access to these.

Your main research questions and objectives

- State your research questions. These questions concern the whole project (not details from individual participants).

- State your objectives as the steps of your project, for example: undertaking a literature review; designing a survey; getting permission to access participants and data; gathering data; analysing it; producing a product, and writing the report.

Identify a rationale for research approach, considering and excluding alternative approaches

- Discuss your chosen research method, justifying your choice by using supporting references.
- If it is part of a larger work project already in progress, explain how it fits into the bigger picture.
- Are there any project-related activities, events, interventions or artefacts that will be informed by the research?

State rationale for data collection, analysis of data and how this will address your research questions

- How will you collect and analyse data? If you are using a survey, is it quantitative or qualitative, and why?
- Justify your sampling methodology with a rationale. How many and who will be your participants?
- What about validity and reliability? Will others be able to replicate your project? If not, why?
- Will your data be triangulated (using more than one research method to check results)? How will you collect data that gives different perspectives?
- Do you need help/support/training to analyse data?
- Consider how you should interpret/present your project outcomes for others in your workplace.
- Project feasibility, time scale, resources. Have you considered time constraints, resources and your other work? Be realistic.
- Ethical issues: how will you protect your subjects' confidentiality and do no harm? How will the principles of informed consent be used? Are the subjects capable of giving consent, or will it involve children or vulnerable adults? If you expose sensitive information, how will that be addressed within your organisation? Who should you seek ethical approval from?
- Can your real-time project fit into the academic timetable and your work schedule?
- Try including a Gantt chart or timeline (see Table 12.1).

Table 12.1 Example of a Gantt chart showing timelines

Activity	Wk 1	2	3	4	5	6	7	8	9	10	11	12
Lit search	■	■										
Interview design		■	■	■								
Pilot questions			■									
Start interviews					■							
Finish interviews							■					
Data analysis								■	■			
Draft first 3 chapters			■	■								
Design interventions; create product artefacts				■	■	■	■	■				
Draft ch. 4							■	■				
Draft ch. 5 and 6									■	■		
Submit drafts to tutor					■	■				■	■	
Final writing										■	■	■
Submit												■
Study time needed					■		■	■	■	■	■	■
					2 days		2 days	2 days	2 days	3 days	3 days	1 day

Your project report and your target audience

- How will your findings be used at work? How they will be shared, and who with?

Strengths and weaknesses of your research proposal

- Reflect on the constraints of potential conflicting timetables.
- Are the data-collection methods chosen for expediency or appropriateness?
- Does being work-based mean your project has strengths and/or weaknesses? What are they?
- Will there be value-added outcomes? One example might be capacity building.

References

- All your choices of research design, data collection, analysis, ethical decisions and supporting rationale should be academically referenced using the preferred referencing style of your university; this will be stated in your handbooks. Local policy documents may be used to support your decision of project subject, but also include current research wherever possible.

TIP Further ways to achieve project success

- Outline a structured, linear breakdown of the project's component parts.
- Use a checklist to make sure you remember everything.
- Create a summary sheet to track progress of all components, include responsibilities for each activity if you are relying on others to contribute to your data.
- Identify measurable objectives or milestones
- Be realistic with time:
  - include time for: piloting data collection tools, recruiting participants, gaining approval from ethics and management committees;
  - allow at least 10 working days for tutor response;
  - allow time for a social life – your family and friends still want to see you!
  - include thinking and reading time; the project is located in your work but allow extra time to consolidate it within your HE-level study;
  - allow time for drafting, reworking, printing and handing in – also for contingencies.

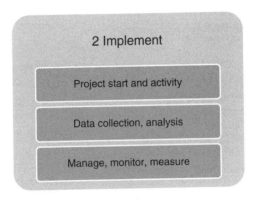

Figure 12.3 Implementing the project process

Implementation: 'Doing' your project, and also 'managing' it

Within WB projects the role of the practitioner/worker/researcher can alter the work dynamics by putting you in a dual role (Workman, 2007: 152). It is positive that you are familiar with the context, the work culture, the subject and the people. However, being a 'worker' and a 'researcher' may cause you to be seen as a 'mole', pursuing your personal agenda by investigating your own organisation. You can access privileged information and insider knowledge to help you to avoid potential difficulties, and also to identify champions to support you. You will find it easier than an outsider to negotiate access to meetings or individuals as well as having the knowledge to fit in with your colleagues' work demands. The project activity includes implementing actions that you need to manage and complete within fixed time limits (Figure 12.3).

Context

Your role and position in the work context will influence how objective or subjective you are (even unconsciously), and it is very difficult to claim that any data is completely bias-free. Acknowledging this means that your perspective is transparent and therefore potential limitations are made explicit. As a practitioner-researcher it is healthy to question accepted practice, so reflect on your position in the organisational context. Consider: your power; connections; networks; level of influence; your existing knowledge; your assumptions – and any other factors that may colour your interpretations and explain your decisions.

Exercise 12.4   Map your position

To get an understanding of those who influence you, and who you influence, draw a mind map (see Figure 12.4) of your position in the organisation and identify those things that affect your role; for example, your job position, gender, level in the organisation, networks, department and so on. Discuss with your tutor or a colleague how this affects your position and how the work context can influence your project.

Being aware of the internal influences on your project is crucial. Your manager may try to direct your project topic, and this could compromise your worker-researcher position. Critical reflection (see Chapter 2) will help you to interrogate your actions and reactions and to interpret situations realistically. Keeping a reflective journal of the project offers an alternative lens through which to interpret your findings. It will help you to juggle organisational, personal, professional and academic contexts and priorities. Ideally the focus of your university study is confidential unless otherwise stated by your company, so clarify this expectation with your manager.

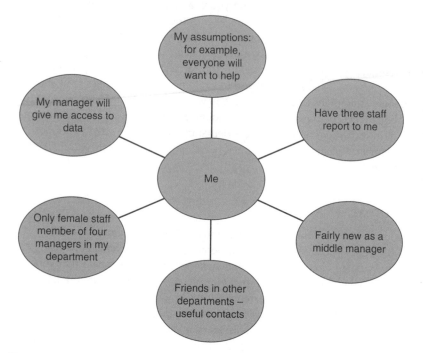

Figure 12.4   An example of a position map

Insider-researcher

Whatever your research approach and position you need to maintain trust and rapport with your colleagues throughout; you still have to work beside them beyond the project, as well as collegiality often being crucial to a WB project's success. Costley et al. (2010) observe that because insider-researchers are invested in their work-based situations, gathering work-based evidence can influence policy and decision-making as well as the individual's practice within the organisation. You may also be required to initiate and manage change as part of your project, thereby becoming a 'change agent'. You may have to acquaint yourself with 'change agency' skills and knowledge to carry out some aspects of your WB project. These may influence your research approach, for example, choosing Action Research (McNiff with Whitehead, 2002) or Appreciative Inquiry (Cooperrider and Whitney, 2005). These methodologies involve others in the project and allow them to contribute to the change process.

TIP **Being a practitioner researcher**

Being a practitioner researcher, you will:

- Develop your leadership and project management skills through monitoring the project's progress against its objectives.
- Involve others, so expect to clearly communicate your progress and expectations.
- Build networking and interpersonal relationships, through negotiating with colleagues.
- Reflect on findings and actions as you record interim stages and final outcomes.
- Navigate the complex activities arising from the project size, outcomes and your role.
- Identify appropriate dissemination activities.
- Identify issues requiring action, and recognise who is responsible for dealing with them. This stage may include follow-up discussions with your manager about the next steps, or finding an internal or external professional, or sector-related, forum to share your findings.

Supervision and other guidance

During the project you will need help from:

- *work colleagues* – they understand your context;
- *friends* – to listen and read drafts;

- *family* – enlist help with domestic responsibilities;
- *university* – access resources and information, for example, your hand-in schedule
- *tutors* – get feedback and guidance, and make sure you follow it up;
- *fellow students* – compare and discuss your ideas and project activities;
- *mentors* – they will encourage and stimulate you;
- *your manager* – negotiate time out for thinking.

Be prepared to be flexible, grateful and to help them in return when they need you to!

Ethical considerations

You should involve your colleagues in your project and gain their informed consent when they contribute data. Access to organisational information must be agreed by your manager, and may raise ethical issues with regard to ownership of intellectual property, or issues of commercial sensitivity or security. The focus on professional values and codes of practice differs from sector to sector, but anyone working with children or vulnerable adults or who is in a position of power over others should gain permission from participants, gatekeepers or ethical committees to ensure that practice is considerate, open and trustworthy. If you have connections with a professional body, then you should be conversant with their ethical guidelines, (for example, http://www.apa.org/ethics/code/index.aspx or https://www.aat.org.uk/about-aat/aat-standards/aat-ethics-and-conduct or http://www.bera.ac.uk). Universities usually have strict codes of conduct regarding research ethics, so you will have to produce evidence that you have followed the requisite procedures.

Exercise 12.5   How ethical are you?

Investigate the ethical issues in your area of work. What are your organisational practices regarding the Data Protection Act, Intellectual Property or informed consent? Do you have a professional ethics code of practice that you have not been aware of? Whose property is the information you deal with on a day-to-day basis? Find out what you can about these and reflect on them. Discuss them with your colleagues or fellow students. How might these issues affect your project? How does this new information impact your practice?

Your research sources should be confidential. This is difficult in a small team, making careful reporting essential. Instead of identifying colleagues by gender, and making the only female manager very conspicuous, you could call them respondent 'A', 'B' or 'C'. It is easy to make your colleagues anonymous for the university, but your own manager may well identify individuals if they have access to the data. Information you uncover might reveal inappropriate practice, hence confronting you with an ethical dilemma about what to do with that information. Your tutor and key colleagues will help you to think through the consequences of your findings, and your reflective diary will help you to analyse the implications. Very occasionally the ethical stance of the company may become completely at odds with your own, and you may have to entirely rethink your job role (Workman, 2007: 154). There are a number of texts available that explore the delicate issues facing the practitioner-researcher, such as Fox et al. (2007).

Case Study 12.4   Susan

Susan is a Teaching Assistant whose project explores how primary children gain reading competences in small groups within the classroom. As an employee of the school she has a Child Protection Bureau certificate for working with children and also ensured that both the Head Teacher and the classroom teacher approved the project. In the planning stage, Susan referred to the British Educational Research Association (BERA) guidelines about research with children and followed her university's procedures for working with minors under 16. Even though the Head Teacher had given permission for Susan to use 'participant observation' in the classroom, Susan also sent an information sheet home to the pupils' parents to let them know that she would be observing their child in their normal classroom activities for her university studies. Susan did a follow-up interview with the main classroom teacher, and asked her to sign a consent form. Within Susan's project the identities of the children were anonymised, and the observations on the children were kept on a private computer that was password-protected and not accessible to the public. As agreed with the Head Teacher, examples of data were sent in with Susan's university studies, but extracts were also used to inform the classroom teacher and Head Teacher of the effectiveness of the group learning for future classroom practice.

Intellectual property

Intellectual property refers to ownership issues around a wide range of products that are the outcomes of new ideas, whether from work activities, inventions, research, literature, performances or copyright of written and artistic works. If you intend to publish outcomes of your project you should record the identities of and gain permission from those participating in the project, as part of their informed consent. Usually research from work becomes the property of the organisation in which it was created, particularly if it has commercial implications, but this may depend on your organisational practices. The government website http://www.ipo.gov.uk offers practical advice about protecting intellectual property. Additionally you should check the terms of the Data Protection Act (1998) to ensure that the data you access and use does not breach the rights of others. If you work in an international context, remember to reference national copyright laws as web-based copyright statements could favour particular national contexts. If in doubt, check out both text and image sources!

Outcomes

This is where it all comes together: the data is collated to inform the final product or activity, and outputs are produced; in many cases new ways of working are created from using the data from the work-based project. The completion of activities and the reports from these activities, along with your learning, are all integral parts of the process. Learning from reflection on the project process is a distinctive attribute of a WB project (Figure 12.5).

Collating the data

At this stage you will be analysing the data to see what your findings are. This may require the use of software tools or processes, typing and reading interviews, highlighting themes, drawing diagrams or even scribbling on Post-its with thoughts. Research texts on analysis will help you organise the data, but you will have to make sense and draw conclusions from it yourself. Talking

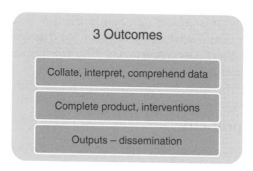

Figure 12.5   Outcomes of the project process

it through with colleagues, and using your tutor or a 'critical friend', will help. Once you have decided on the key findings, decide how these will be represented within your report and in any products or services that you create for your workplace.

Creating the products

Ensure that you plan time in your WB project to complete the product and meet the university report requirements. Common products from WB projects include:

- a written report/feedback/summary specifically for your workplace;
- DVD/USB stick holding videos, pictures or an e-portfolio;
- paper portfolio of written and/or pictorial evidence;
- music or stage production;
- piece of art/sculpture/performance;
- training pack or leaflet;
- written policy or guidance;
- PowerPoint, or some other, presentation.

Evaluation

A common approach in WB projects is to review the impact of the project and reflect on the experience, looking at both the outcomes for the workplace and the personal skills you have developed as part of the learning process. Usually this involves a formal report for the workplace and/or a reflective commentary for the university. These present both your practitioner research and your WB project outcomes to different audiences. A presentation to disseminate the project outcomes may also be expected (Figure 12.6).

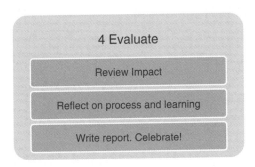

Figure 12.6   Evaluation of the project process

Writing up your WB project

After you have completed your practitioner research and the project work, write up the WB project report to capture the process, outcomes and your learning from the project. This is a formal piece of academic writing that requires explanations of your activities, which are fully referenced in a recognised style, to show how you have theorised your work and used your research to improve practice and deliver work-based outcomes.

You can organise your report in many different ways, but Table 12.2 offers some example headings.

Table 12.2   Key headings for a project report

Section heading	Information to include
Contents page	
Acknowledgements (optional)	
Project summary	
Introduction	Aims and objectives Context Rationale
Project plan	Research questions Literature review Methodology
Project implementation	Activity Findings Analysis
Project outcomes	Products Interventions Dissemination
Project evaluation	Review of impact Critical reflection
Conclusion and recommendations	
References	
Appendices	

An oral presentation for the WB project could be an audio-visual presentation to your colleagues, peers or tutors. Questions from your audience, and discussion of the presentation, will help you to evaluate and summarise your project as well as giving a sense of closure to the learning you have achieved.

Assessment criteria (Chapter 11) are determined by your university in relation to the level of study, the types of evidence and the critical reflection required as evidence in your project report. Supporting evidence may be included in appendices to demonstrate your learning, for example, extracts from your learning diary, or an example of a consent form. As with research methods, advice about 'writing up' can be found in many publications focusing on academic or report writing, some of which are listed in the section on further reading. Learning resources should also be provided by your university.

Remember to celebrate your submission with peers, friends and family!

Summary

1   Stick to the word count – too long or too short and you will be penalised.

2   Make sure you know the hand-in date – and keep to it.

3   Follow instructions with regard to layout and referencing– you will lose marks if you don't.

4   Ensure your report has an introduction, middle and end; does it tell the project story?

5   Acknowledge your sources by using correct academic referencing techniques (check university guidelines) and using anti-plagarism software if available – plagiarism carries heavy penalties.

6   Follow submission guidance whether in hard copy or electronically. If electronic submission is required, practise accessing the site before the deadline.

7   Proofread your project and read it out loud to ensure fluency.

8. Find a buddy to share the learning journey; support each other.

9. Share the project's outcomes with colleagues who helped you; write a report or present at a meeting; thank them for their help.

10. Celebrate your success with all those who have supported you!

References

Armsby, P. and Costley, C. (2000) 'Research Driven Projects'. In D. Portwood and C. Costley (eds), *Work Based Learning and the University: New Perspectives and Practices* (Birmingham: SEDA Publications Paper 109).

Cooperrider, D. L. and Whitney, D. (2005) *Appreciative Inquiry: A Positive Revolution in Change* (San Francisco, CA: Berrett-Koehler Publishers).

Costley, C., Elliot, G. and Gibbs, P. (2010) *Doing Work Based Research Approaches to Enquiry for Insider-Researcher* (London: Sage Publications).

Denscombe, M. (2014) *The Good Research Guide: For Small Scale Research Projects*, 5th edn (Maidenhead: Open University Press and McGraw-Hill).

Eraut, M. (2001) 'The role and use of vocational qualifications', *National Institute Economic Review*, 78, 88–98.

Forsyth, P. (2004) *Powerful Reports and Proposals* (London: Kogan Page).

Fox, M., Martin, P. and Green, G. (2007) *Doing Practitioner Research* (London: Sage Publications).

Garnett, J. (2005) 'University Work Based Learning and the Knowledge Driven Project'. In K. Rounce and B. Workman (eds), *Work Based Learning in Health Care: Applications and Innovations* (Chichester: Kingsham Press), 79–86.

McGregor, S. L. T. and Volckmann, R. (2011) *Transdisciplinarity in Higher Education*, Part 7: *Conclusion*, 1–06–2011.

McNiff, J. with Whitehead, J. (2002) *Action Research: Principles and Practice*, 2nd edn (London: Routledge Falmer).

Raelin, J. A. (2008) *Work-based Learning: Bridging Knowledge and Action in the Workplace*, new and rev. edn (San Francisco, CA: Jossey-Bass).

Robson, C. (2011) *Real World Research: A Resource for Social Scientists and Practitioner Researchers*, 3rd edn (Oxford: Blackwell Publishing).

Workman, B. (2007) 'Casing the joint: explorations by the insider-researcher preparing for work based projects', *Journal of Workplace Learning*, 19 (3), 146–160.

Suggested further reading

American Psychological Association, *Ethical Principles of Psychologists and Code of Conduct 2012*. Available at http://www.apa.org/ethics/code/index.aspx (accessed 18 May 2014).

Association of Accounting Technicians (AAT) (2014) *Code of Professional Ethics*. Available at https://www.aat.org.uk/sites/default/files/assets/AAT_Code_of_Professional_Ethics.pdf (accessed 18 May 2014).

BERA (2014) *Ethical Guidelines for Educational Research*. Available at http://www.bera.ac.uk/researchers-resources/publications/ethical-guidelines-for-educational-research-2011 (accessed 23 May 2014).

Godfrey, J. (2011) *Writing for University* (London: Palgrave Macmillan).

Murray, R. and Moore, S. (2006) *The Handbook for Academic Writing: A Fresh Approach* (Maidenhead: Open University Press and McGraw-Hill).

Reid, M. (2011) *Report Writing* (London: Palgrave Macmillan).

Rowson, R. (2006) *Working Ethics: How to be Fair in a Culturally Complex World* (London: Jessica Kingsley Publishers).

Wisker, G. (2009) *The Undergraduate Research Handbook* (Basingstoke: Palgrave Macmillan).

Work-based learning terminologies

Ruth Helyer and Jenny Fleming

There are wide and overlapping global descriptions and connections around higher-level work-based learning activities. These activities form a sliding scale of emphasis and input from several parties: full- and part-time students; full- and part-time employees; higher education institutes; employers and companies/organisations of all kinds as well as cultural and geographical differences. We have compiled some ideas towards definitions below, which are open to interpretation and reliant on context.

- **Action learning**
  In action learning, through a collaborative approach, participants identify issues, examine them, create an action plan, take action and reflect on that action. However, the nature of action learning varies greatly with the context in which it is applied and the different approaches of those who initiate it. Action learning can be described as a sub-set of action research, although there is a distinction between the two in relation to the use and application of theory. Action learning focuses on learning in context and does not require the sole use of academic theories, but involves application to the practice context and the consequent development of personal or collective new knowledge for practice. Action learning can provide a bridge between individual and organisational learning, and can create change for an organisation as well as personal self-development. Action learning often utilises the formation of a community of practice, of shared work, knowledge and ways of knowing how to enable new social meanings and realities to be collectively constructed. Action learning fits well with the sociocultural theories associated with many models of work-based learning.
- **Cooperative education**
  Cooperative (coop) education, prevalent in the US, Canada, Australia and New Zealand, involves programmes that integrate academic studies with learning through the experience of work; commonly this involves full-time

students spending several days per week working within a company where they have a placement, often with an organisation related to their academic and/or career goals (see Chapter 2). The integration of the learning environments of both the university and the workplace, driven by the university programme, is one of the defining features of cooperative education, in comparison to some other models or frameworks of work-based learning in which the student comes to the university while already an employee. A critical component of cooperative education is that clear learning goals are negotiated and the workplace experience is directly relevant or dovetailed to the student's programme of study. The linkage of academics with business can lead to more opportunities for collaboration between individuals, HEIs and organisations. Cooperative education facilitates the development of a broad range of skills, from generic (problem-solving) to situation and sector-specific (technical skills), as well as workplace know-how (culture, value, attitudes). While the fundamental principles of partnership between students, educational intuitions and employers are common to all cooperative education programmes, there are variances in the structure, length of placement and modes of supervision that are often discipline, institute or country-specific.

Case Study   Cooperative education in sport tertiary education, Auckland University of Technology, New Zealand

In the Bachelor of Sport and Recreation (BSR) cooperative education programme students spend 350 hours of placement with one organisation during the final year of their degree. The placement is generally taken two days per week, and on the other days students attend university classes. An industry supervisor and an academic supervisor from the university provide support for the students. A recent study, exploring student, industry and academics' perceptions of learning through cooperative education in a sport tertiary education programme, found that the coop experience enables BSR students to construct knowledge: about themselves; their placement organisation; and the wider context of the industry:

> '[I learnt], effective team work and communication. Also organisational skills, just those skills that will help you I guess in every day and after. Crucial skills… professionally, I also learnt how to act professionally in an organisation and also communication with speaking and also with things like email writing… I also think being able to apply that theory into practice was really important. Because

---

Case Study (continued)

you learn about it and then you are not quite sure how it is going to apply to what you're doing. So just being able to go out there and actually *do it* was a great benefit.'

Students were able to develop *organisational literacy*, through gaining an understanding of organisational structure, priorities, values and culture. Students also felt that they had developed *career literacy* where they were able to identify, understand and confirm (or in some cases reject) their intended career. The development of *social literacy* was identified by students in their comments that highlighted they had learnt how to work in a team, or to work alongside others. *Profession-specific literacy* was evident as students clearly identified that they had learnt not only discipline-specific skills, but also procedural (the know-how) and dispositional knowledge that are important in the sport and recreation industry. Students acknowledged that at times they were able to apply what they had learnt in the university setting to the context of the workplace, but they also learnt that theory did not always work in practice.

The study concluded that a cooperative education experience included as part of a university degree helps prepare students for their future careers through developing generic *and* specific competencies as well as transferable skills that enhance employability.

Jenny Fleming
Auckland University of Technology, New Zealand
jenny.fleming@aut.ac.nz

- **Continuing professional development (CPD)**
  Many professions have their own associations or professional bodies, which require that their members undertake development activities on an ongoing basis to retain their membership. This often brings with it the right to have certain letters after your name or undertake certain professional duties. The benefits of this tradition is that it instils the ethos of continuing development and lifelong learning into individuals, thereby encouraging self-reflection and the organisation of professional competences, as well as good planning and record-keeping habits (see Chapters 2, 3 and 6). Work-based learning programmes at HE level offer a way in which employees and employers can benefit from undertaking CDP activities without necessitating time away from work.
- **Employability**
  A much-debated term with definitions ranging from good job-seeking skills, such as CV development and interwview techniques, to generic skills, such

as teamwork, communications skills, reflective practice and professional attitudes, through to very specific skills required in such professions as engineering, nursing, graphic design and so on. In the context of the global recession and a highly competitive jobs market there is a growing emphasis on demonstrating additional skills such as adaptability, resilience and flexibility in order to be employable. The graduate employment market is extremely competitive, due in part to recent increases in the annual number of graduates (see Chapter 2).

- **Experiential education**
  This is 'a philosophy that informs many methodologies in which educators purposefully engage with learners in direct experience and focused reflection' (Association of Experiential Education, 2014). It is based on the theories of experiential learning and grounded in the works of John Dewey (1938). The emphasis is on taking students out of the classroom to experience 'real'-life work and community activity, therefore transforming their academic knowledge into knowledge that they can use and build upon.

- **Experiential learning**
  The difference with experiential learning, when compared to experiential education above, is that these learners are usually already out in the 'real' world and community, rather than the university. Experiential learning is the learning gained from experience, from actually 'doing'. Humans learn much of what they know without the involvement of a 'teacher', and do it rather through observation and interaction with others. Opportunities within your own areas of interest offer rich environments for experiential learning. Much has been written about experiential learning, with its major proponents agreeing that in order to progress such learning analytical reflection and experimentation are required. Although experiential learning can be gained in a formal educational setting (as it is knowledge formed through experience) the majority of it has nothing to do with university assignments or assessment; however, HE-level work-based learning programmes are designed to facilitate the transformation of such learning into formats that can be recognised, and even accredited, as higher-level learning (see Chapter 5).

- **Fieldwork education**
  Generally fieldwork is undertaken as short periods of time in the 'field', or 'real world', as opposed to the classroom. Often fieldwork involves observations but may include some participation or project work located in the activities of the organisation. Fieldwork is normally linked with the academic programme in the higher education institution and contributes to coursework requirements. Fieldwork is similar to practicums and placements.

- **Higher Apprenticeships**
  In the UK Apprenticeships study up to level 3, pre-university level, with Higher Apprenticeships studying at university levels 4–7 (see Chapter 11). Apprentices must be employed, and through a recognised programme

of learning will develop the skill, knowledge and competency specified in the standard for their particular occupation. This combination of the practical and theoretical, on-the-job training and closely aligned education, has similarities with the coop model described above. Apprenticeship standards being developed at HE level, include: accountancy, adult social care, construction management, hospitality management, law, journalism, nursing and financial services. Higher Apprenticeship programmes in HE include construction, retail and care management, to name but a few. Employers work with universities to determine how to develop degrees to deliver and assess appropriate components for their Higher Apprenticeship standards, and, where appropriate, with professional bodies to enable an individual to simultaneously achieve professional registration. Degree Apprenticeships are currently under development in the UK.

See University Vocational Awards Council: http://www.uvac.ac.uk/higher-apprenticeship/ or http://www.apprenticeships.org.uk/employers/the-basics/higher-apprenticeships.aspx

- **Industry-based learning**
  Many higher education students benefit from work-based learning by spending part of their study time learning directly in industry, for example, the 'Year in Industry' scheme, http://www.etrust.org.uk/the-year-in-industry

  In the UK some large organisations, for example, construction companies, will sponsor a student through university and offer work experience during vacations, sometimes with possible work opportunities upon graduation.

- **Insight days**
  An insight day is similar to a job-shadowing experience and allows a student to spend a day (or longer) observing in a workplace. The intention is that the student will gain an understanding of what a particular job/career entails. Normally the experience does not contribute to specific academic credit but may constitute part of coursework requirements.

- **Internships**
  Usually the intention of an internship is the development of skills and competencies associated with the discipline or profession, and in these cases the internship is structured and supervised to foster facilitated experiential learning. However, there are different interpretations of the requirements for an experience to be considered an internship, and a lack of formally accepted guidelines. Within HE graduate internships are sometimes undertaken, upon completion of programme of study, while in other programmes an internship is embarked upon by students in the final semester of study (see Chapter 2). Many internship experiences involve an extended work placement of at least one semester. Internships are structured and supervised by experienced practitioners, and students are usually granted academic credit for the workplace experience. In the UK

graduate internships are offered in a range of sectors, particularly charity, politics, arts or media sectors, where jobs are at a premium and are often gained following intern work. Reports suggest that tasks undertaken in internships can vary widely from high-level and appropriate to HE-level learning and future career aspirations to extremely menial.

- **Knowledge Transfer Partnerships (KTPs)**
  KTPs transfer knowledge between a university and a business, they operate as facilitated work-based learning, using an integrated system of people, processes and mechanisms building upon shared reflective learning and organisational development. They are a form of Open Innovation: 'the idea that companies should make greater use of external ideas and technologies in their own business, and allow unused internal ideas to flow out to others for use in their business'; http://www.openinnovation.net/faq/

  Lasting between 6 and 36 months, KTPs involve a HE graduate, placed in the company, a defined project (including implementation and exploitation) and a management process designed to transfer and embed knowledge between a university academic and a business, with business, academic and graduate all benefiting.

  http://www.ncub.co.uk/reports/knowledge-transfer-partnerships-a-best-practice-approach-to-open-innovation.html

- **Negotiated learning**
  This occurs when the framework, or scaffold, of a programme of learning exists but the detailed content of the individual modules making up the eventual award is 'negotiated' between the student, tutor and sometimes also the student's employer. This negotiation of curriculum content really puts the learner in the driving seat, giving them power and flexibility but also responsibility (see Chapters 6 and 11). Sometimes such a degree might state in the award title 'by negotiated learning', but often it will not.

- **Practice placements**
  Unlike general work placements, where students are hoping for transferable work experience, these are career-focused placements, usually found in professional routes relating to science, medicine and nursing. They are often compulsory for the qualification.

- **Professional practicums**
  Practicum is a generic term to describe experiences that provide the opportunity for students to apply theoretical knowledge and/or practical skills learnt in the classroom to authentic 'real-world' settings. Practicum is often used interchangeably with other terms that include experiences that provide opportunities for the practical application of theory to practice, or perfection of practical skills in a safe environment. The purpose of a professional practicum is an induction into the profession. The workplace provides a context for making links between theory and practice, and the development of skills and competencies relevant to the specific

profession. Completion of a specific number of hours is often a requirement for registration in a profession (for example, nursing, engineering). It is common for joint teaching appointments to be made between the workplace (such as a hospital) and the university so that staff can be involved with teaching in both learning environments.

- **Project-based learning**
  Work-based projects are focused on daily work activities and therefore carry the implications of practical experience in the learning process. They are relevant to work practices and update knowledge by solving problems and providing solutions. They transform a workplace activity into deep learning by adding an academic approach to real-time work projects, thereby contributing new knowledge, capability, skills and learning to the workplace. They are usually undertaken by work-based learners with full-time jobs in their own place of work, therefore promoting self-directed learning. Sometimes project-based learning might be utilised by HEIs to integrate academic instruction with practice activity for students who are not participating in actual work environments, as a way to give them some workplace experience; group work and collaboration are often key components to this, and tutors use these kinds of projects (when the student is not employed) to demonstrate the impact of new learning on established practices.

- **Sandwich courses**
  These courses offer a 'sandwich year' as one year of a four-year course where you can either work within your chosen setting or study at another institution (or a mixture of both). In sandwich courses, students normally intercalate ('sandwich') a work placement in between the second and third years of an undergraduate degree programme, making it a four-year degree in total. Many sandwich placements are not assigned credit but are acknowledged on the academic transcript. They may involve additional fees for supervision from the university.

- **Service learning**
  In a service learning programme students engage in activities that benefit the community; this usually involves at least part of the course being carried out in the real world. Service learning programmes integrate work and academic activity and are designed to develop an appreciation of civic and social responsibility and community needs while enabling students to develop skills that will enhance their employability. Service learning normally carries credit within an academic programme.

- **Social learning**
  Social learning is achieved through participation with other people, in a social context. This is relevant for work-based learning as the workplace provides an abundance of social learning opportunities. Social learning rejects the view that knowledge can be delivered from an expert to

someone lacking that information, and instead suggests that learning is constructed with and through people.

- **Vocational education and training**
  Is also called career and technical education (CTE), especially in the USA and Canada, or technical and vocational education and training (TVET), and prepares learners, by developing knowledge, skills and competencies, for specific occupations and employment, often, but not always, based on manual or practical activities. It teaches procedural knowledge and is sometimes referred to as technical education, due to the emphasis on 'techniques'.

- **Work-based learning**
  Work-based learning (WBL) is about learning from the experience of work and work concerns (such as real-time problem-solving and responding to normal work issues). It is learning that occurs where the work activities are happening, or needed, and because of this is associated with situated learning. Learning from doing in this way might be with other colleagues, and result in social learning, or it may be alone or from other life scenarios outside work. Work-based learning is often considered as 'informal', which is true in that it is not bounded by the formality of designated learning spaces – universities, colleges and classrooms – but is instead shaped by experiences (although these could involve more formalised work-based training). However, it is not informal as in casual, easy or inconsequential. Likewise it is often described as 'non-traditional' because it differs from the accepted norms of established education, and again this is true, but it is just different not lesser.

  Work-based learning is widely viewed as encompassing learning about work, at work and through work (Chapter 1). If you are studying at HE level as a work-based learner you could also add that it is for your work. Work-based learning is not usually assessed or accredited, although much has the potential to be (see RPL, Chapter 5) The bulk of work-based learning in UK universities focuses on what students have learned at work, although work-based learning is also viewed as an area of scholarship in itself, which considers how this learning occurs, thus becoming the topic of an altogether more philosophical study. Work-based learning begins with the learner and the workplace; many of the other work-place scenarios described here begin with the educational institution and with existing students.

  Work-based learning can occur via part-time, voluntary and self-employed work, but it is not restricted to those with full-time jobs. Its benefits will also be felt by those who do not have a job but enter the workplace as part of a placement, internship and so on, where what is learned experientially often enables the translation of theory into practice, thereby being transformed through practice assessments or project work into an assessable format. Although frequently unplanned it could also be planned. A large percentage of WBL will not be at HE level, however, and that which becomes involved in HE forms programmes that are flexible and differing; often individually adapted and negotiated, they may include lectures, workshops, tutorials and other more common educational devices; alternatively they may be designed in such a way that the student very rarely, if ever attends the campus. What these programmes have in common is that the learning driving them will have originated from the work situation and remain directly relevant to workers in their work environment, and that student, university and employer will all reciprocally gain learning benefits from the relationship. Tutors and lecturers of work-based learners operate mostly in the capacity of facilitator.

- **Work-based studies**
  Defined courses of study within universities and colleges (especially in the UK) might well be titled 'work-based studies', 'professional practice' or similar; the students on these courses are studying modules and topics that relate to their job or their career aspirations (see Chapter 11). Occasionally such learning pathways will include modules about the workplace, but more commonly they are populated with some generic content (development planning, RPL and so on), but mostly content relating to specific professions, jobs and sectors. For example, the entire cohort might all be health professionals or all from the police force and this sector specialism might be reflected in the award title. Alternatively the major content might focus on a content crossing many sectors, such as 'Leadership and Management'.

- **Work experience**
  A broad term used to describe the activities and experiences undertaken by a student on placement in a workplace environment as part of a course of study. The intention of work experience is often for a student to learn *about work* and to develop some work-appropriate skills.

- **Work integrated Learning (WiL)**
  A term used, especially in the US, Canada, Australia and New Zealand, to describe strategies where academic learning (usually at a higher education institution), is combined with learning in the workplace in an intentional way, and usually planned by the HEI; a collaboration of work and educational experiences. This term can be considered an 'umbrella', encompassing a wide range of models including cooperative education, internships, practicums, fieldwork, sandwich courses and service learning. The integration of theory and practice is central to models of WiL.

- **Work placements**
  Work placements within HE programmes are designed to enable students to develop work-related skills, and an awareness of the culture and structure of a workplace environment. They are part of the philosophy that

integrated academic work and workplace activity produces valuable and authentic learning experiences. Work placements are often undertaken as short, defined blocks within a course of study at a higher education institution, making connections and building on the academic skills the students have learned already. Sometimes they involve assessment and the award of academic credits, but often they do not (see Chapter 2). They are a valuable tool for developing transferable, and specific, work-related skills in a real-work environment scenario.

- **Work shadowing**
  Similar to 'insight days' (above), work shadowing can provide an informal way to raise a student's awareness about different job roles and sectors.
- **Workforce development**
  This term usually refers to training larger cohorts of learners, all from the same company or sector, and has come to be associated with governmental policies (particularly in the UK) around higher-level skills development.
- **Workplace learning**
  Can refer to learning that has arisen from the physical workplace, or has been designed to be delivered in and/or enhance workplace practice. There are obvious overlaps with work-based learning, above.

References

Association for Experiential Education (2014) *What Is Experiential Education?* Retrieved from http://www.aee.org/about/whatIsEE.

Dewey, J. (1938) *Experience and Education* (New York: Touchstone, 1997).

Appendix 1: Extract from a learning CV

Post-secondary

Qualification	Date Achieved
BTEC National Diploma in Business and Finance with Travel and Tourism	2002
Certificate in Education	2013
Studying Media Studies	Due to complete 20-credit university module in April 2015

Employment

Media Company 2 – November 2012 to date – Media ICT Tutor
Achievements to date:

- Developed and delivered training courses to company employees
- including Company Induction, Stress Management and Customer Care
Liaised with all departments to ensure the company maintained Investors in People status
- Developed and delivered training courses to external businesses including Presentation Skills and Train the Trainer

Media Company 1 – February 2011–November 2012 Design and Development Officer
- Designed a range of training courses for UKLG's National Retail Training Team

Travel Agency – November 2008–January 2011 Systems Trainer
- Delivered training in a new computer system as part of the National Training Team

Voluntary work

Assistant Brownie Guide Leader for the past 5 years. Training for holiday licence.

Appendix 2: Extract from a job description

Job Title: **Media/ICT trainer**
Department   **Media Centre**

Main purpose of job:

- To raise the profile of the company to develop long-term readership for children, young people and adults.
- To support the company's lifelong learning initiative through teaching in the Media Centre and in local education establishments.
- Providing innovative teaching materials relating to the newspaper and the Internet.

Personal Qualities

- Self-motivator, flexible, enthusiastic, team player, calm and friendly disposition.
- Fully qualified primary or secondary teacher.
- English/ICT specialist preferred.

Reporting to:
Newspapers in Education manager

- To teach children and adults to use the ICT equipment in the company's Media Centre and encourage them to prepare front page news sheets, school newspapers and meet end of session deadlines.
- To develop teaching programmes, with appropriate lesson plans, to meet the demands of the National Curriculum and other Educational criteria, relating to the use of newspapers and the internet.

Appendix 3: Example of questions asked in training needs analysis

- **Company training needs analysis**

1. What are the key components of the work being performed in your company/department?
2. What skills and knowledge are required to perform the work?
3. What are the measures of successful performance of the work?
4. Are people performing at the levels required?
5. Which roles require specific technical/professional training and what is it?

- **Suitability training needs analysis**

1. In what areas do staff under-perform in your department?
2. Is there under-performance among specific groups of employees?
3. What are the causes of under-performance?
4. What training will help bridge the gap between the standards of performance needed and the actual performance?
5. How does the training the business currently provides meet these requirements (please see attached list)?
   a) Technical training
   b) Business skills training
   c) Other company funded training (state which).
6. What else could be provided?
7. Is anything provided internally which could be improved or deleted?
8. Is under-performance due to any other reason other than a lack of knowledge and skills? If so what?
9. What solutions can be used to remedy under-performance caused by factors other than a lack of knowledge and skills?

Appendix 4: Example of a personal statement

If I were asked to describe myself in a professional capacity, then I would label myself as being hard working, conscientious, flexible, open-minded and patient. Some of these qualities are natural attributes; others have developed over time with experience.

My intention now is to build on these strengths and become a successful primary school teacher. No one is more surprised at that statement than me, as I never thought that I would want a career that involved working with children.

I have always been in occupations that involved working with people and have relished the variety and challenges that this has brought. Six years ago, I made the move into adult training and decided that adult teaching was the direction that I wanted to go in. At this stage, I thought that teaching adults would be more fulfilling, as the subject matter would be at a higher level. I changed my opinion two years ago when I started working at the Media Centre. As a media tutor at the Centre, I teach all age groups including school children and have been surprised by how much more challenging and rewarding I have found this.

Children, particularly at primary school age, are not as conditioned to giving the responses that they think they should. Primary children instantly let you know when they are bored or do not understand something, then it is up to you to turn the teaching session around. Primary children also express their appreciation more readily when they have enjoyed a teaching session and have learnt something. It is a constant challenge to make their lessons interesting and think of new ways to add value to their learning. Each new step taken in this direction is extremely satisfying.

In my spare time, I am also a Brownie leader and have seen firsthand the ways in which a child can develop when they are given the right opportunities. For a child to develop into a well-rounded adult they need more than just academic skills; they also need life and social skills. I am now aiming to become a qualified primary practitioner, but more than that, I want to be able to enrich the lives of the students I teach by ensuring they have a positive and valuable learning experience.

Appendix 5: Example of a project proposal

A. Working title of project

Improving IT Services by Introducing a HelpDesk Strategy for Staff

B. Introduction

In my current role as the Head of Information Technology (IT) for a small Higher Education (HE) institution, I need to streamline services by implementing a new central 'HelpDesk' reporting system for both staff and students. The introduction of HelpDesk technology helps to centralise services, but staff must be retrained to deliver these services. The purchase of the HelpDesk software was approved in the last financial year to implement cost efficiencies.

C. Main aims of the project and its significance

The main aims of the project will be to implement IT change management and improve customer service while thinking about my own role as an effective 'lean' manager (Balzer, 2010) within the HE sector. My experience has mainly been in IT systems management. While no redundancies are anticipated, the change will require staff to diversify and take on new duties. Consequently there will be an emphasis on training. I will introduce new service-level agreements (SLAs) with staff and students to make the changes sustainable and improve the service we provide.

D. The worker/researcher role, and relevant expertise

I have a Higher National Diploma in Computing and Systems Development and have been working in IT for eight years and in my current role for two years. I manage ten members of staff. I am aware of my duty of care to use discretion in the project and develop change management processes that are transparent for both my staff and line manager.

E. Your main research questions and objectives

In the context of this project my questions are:

1. What is the leadership role of the IT manager implementing service change?
2. How can a strategy for staff development improve project outcomes?
3. What effective communication strategies can be implemented to support the project?

My objectives will be to:

- Undertake a literature review.
- Carry out research in the IT sector and professional organisations.
- Interview relevant experts about leadership and change management.
- Develop bids for and purchase HelpDesk software.
- Use existing student surveys data and carry out a staff user survey.
- Attend IT staff and student user group sessions to communicate changes.
- Professionalise HelpDesk staff through staff development.
- Implement the new HelpDesk system.
- Report the outcomes of the project in a report to my line manager and committees; communicate changes to staff and students.
- Write a university report and presentation.

F. Identify a rationale for research approach, considered and excluding alternative approaches

While research in computing is mainly quantitative, for this project I will use a mixed-method approach. Denscombe (2014) says that this strategy uses both quantitative and qualitative methods to develop a single research project while using triangulation to check the impact of particular methods. As an activity for my own staff development I have signed up for a Leadership Foundation course on leading technical teams.

G. State rationale for data collection, analysis of date and how this will address your research questions

The rationale for the data collection will be to better understand how to manage change as well as to find out about customer needs. I plan to conduct interviews with experts in IT leadership, and the Head of Staff

Development. I will interview IT staff to discuss the changes. To establish customer needs I will use questionnaires with staff and existing student data, and attend user groups.

H. Project feasibility, time scale, resources and ethical issues

I can research literature and design my questionnaires and interviews before the study period, but run the project from February to end in early May. Capital funding has been approved but the new software has yet to be purchased. My line manager, the Head of Estates, has given me permission to carry out the research within the institution. Participation will be voluntary and data will be confidential. I will use informed consent with participants and report findings anonymously in my university project report and presentation.

Activity – *start literature earlier*	1	2	3	4	5	6	7	8	9	10	11	12	13
Literature search and review	■	■	■										
Design and pilot data collection instruments	■	■											
Obtain ethics approval	■												
Questionnaires		■	■										
Interviews		■	■	■	■	■							
Data analysis					■	■	■	■					
Produce internal report as product									■	■			
Write final WB project report and presentation											■	■	
Submission date													■

I. Internal project report (product) and target audience

I will produce a report for the Head of Estates as a product that will explain the new HelpDesk service and the new SLAs that were developed as a part of this process. The report will include the financial costs, including efficiency savings and staff redeployment.

J. Strengths and weakness of research proposal

This is a live project so some disruptions or delays might occur with the data collection and implementation.

References

Balzer, W. K. (2010) *Lean Higher Education Increasing the Value and Performance of University Processes* (New York: Productivity Press).

Denscombe, M. (2014) *The Good Research Guide: For Small Scale Research Projects*, 5th edn (Maidenhead: Open University Press and McGraw-Hill).

Index